MARX MEETS
BUDDHA

MARX MEETS BUDDHA

Alienated Society and Alienated Self

Zach Johnson

In memory of my Dad, who never let his religious beliefs get in the way of a reasoned argument, and my Mum, who would have considered an argument an odd way to demonstrate the value of compassion.

CONTENTS

Introduction   1

1. Not Suffering   7

2. Philosophical Economics   17

3. Self Searching   39

4. Visible Hands   57

5. Something Gives   83

6. Capitalist Growths   99

7. Interlude – So Far   127

8. To Be Determined   135

9. Moral Uncertainties   153

10. Awakenings   169

11. Revolutions   193

Conclusion   217

Notes   225

Acknowledgements   233

Index   235

INTRODUCTION

I could, of course, be wrong. Nobody ever knows when they're wrong, do they? Someone can decide they *were* wrong, but by the time they do so, they no longer hold the view they've decided they were wrong about. It would be useful to know you're wrong, at the time that you're wrong, but you can't. I'm right, aren't I?

To make matters worse, there are far more ways to be wrong than ways to be right, although to make matters better, the world provides a wealth of clues which, experience suggests, point mainly in the right direction. Suppose you intend to walk through a doorway. There are any number of directions you could choose that would lead you to walk into a wall, or into a door jamb, or away from the doorway, very few that would lead you *through* the doorway. There is, however, the doorway, right there, providing an almost definitely reliable guide. Phew!

Of course, you're not always facing a doorway. Sometimes you're lost in a desert with nothing to see but sand dunes. What can you do but make a guess, as close as you can manage to educated or inspired, and hope to find your way to more solid ground? I suppose you could refuse to budge, in protest at the unacceptable level of uncertainty. Unfortunately, choosing not to choose also counts as a choice.

If you're worried that you might be wrong, it can be reassuring to notice a significant number of other people who believe the same things as you. It's no guarantee that you're right, but it's definitely reassuring. I believe that Karl Marx and the Buddha both provide meaningful and valuable insights into how people should choose to live their lives today, and that, as a result of commonalities in their approaches to understanding the world, the thoughts of each shed an interesting light on the thoughts of the other. The number of people I've noticed who believe the same things as me is not reassuring.

If I'm wrong, there must be a reason. Maybe I've always suffered from a subconscious urge to find as distinctive a set of ideas as possible that I could believe in. Perhaps, when I was merely a Marxist, a part of me was disappointed by the surprising number of people who agreed with me, and it was only after adding some Buddhist ideas into the mix that I found my intellectual comfy place. It's a theory, but it doesn't fit at all with what I'm fairly sure I know about myself. I find it far easier to think of reasons why I'd be biased *against* being persuaded by Marxist arguments, or Buddhist arguments, let alone both.

I'm an introvert. Big time. I'm the sort of introvert who once read a book about being an introvert and was shocked and bewildered to learn that the supposedly very introverted author voluntarily chose to share their home with a partner! Marxism was not intended for introverts like me. When I was first becoming acquainted with the Marxist frame of mind, I overheard someone use the term 'left-watcher' and I thought, 'Ooh! I like the sound of that.' It turned out, however, to be a term of abuse. Marxists are not supposed to be passive observers. We're supposed to be activists, organisers, instigators. I'm not. An activist me is hard to imagine.

This was in the 1980s, and not long after I became convinced that Marx offered the best way forward, the Soviet Union collapsed. It struck me as a positive development. I assumed that with that painful failure out of the picture, attention would turn to the interesting things Marx had to say about matters closer to home. But I'd got it completely wrong. Strangely, Marxism seemed to interest people even less than it had before. Instead, it was all capitalist triumphalism and people talking – straight-faced – about 'the end of history'.

While Marxism and practical politics worked out whether it was all over between them or merely time for a trial separation, my own intellectual pursuits became increasingly permissive. I swear I didn't go looking for another set of ideas that was widely dismissed due to unfamiliarity or incorrect assumptions, but in no time at all, I found one. On the face of it, you'd expect Buddhism to be a better fit to my personality, and in some ways it was. But in some ways it certainly was not.

For one thing, Buddhists place a lot of importance on the *sangha* or community. But I assumed that was just the extrovert thing – you know how, whenever anything becomes remotely popular, extroverts will present that as though it's a selling point? 'The great thing about going on a meditation retreat is being with lots of other people, while you sit in silence, with your eyes closed, focusing on your breath.' Extroverts will make that sort of claim about *anything*.

But even with the sangha put to one side, there was a more significant problem. While Buddhism is fundamentally an exploration of some of the ways human beings cause themselves unnecessary suffering, there's no escaping the fact that, historically, this endeavour has been bound up with beliefs and practices that many of us in the modern world find difficult to take seriously. Learning about Buddhism is rather like being given a guided tour of the Large Hadron Collider at CERN, and the guide explaining to you:

> We use different types of magnet to control the particle beam. These quadrupole magnets serve to focus the beam, while these dipole magnets bend the beam to direct it around the collider. We also pass the beam through this bank of Tibetan Prayer Wheels, which increases the strangeness of each particle by between 13.4 and 13.8 per cent, after which...

It can be disconcerting. But if it seemed strange to be taking an ancient religion seriously, matters were about to become a whole lot stranger. The more I learned about Buddhism, the more I was struck by the conviction that its underlying philosophical approach to the world had so much in common with the one underlying Marxism, that I had to describe them as similar, and I struggled to find a justification for not describing them as the same. If you're not sceptical about this, then I'd strongly urge you to work on developing a healthier level of scepticism. I'm convinced it's true, but even I find it bizarre.

I don't share my thoughts with people all that often, but when I do, I like to be taken seriously, and I couldn't help suspecting that the direction my thoughts were taking me was not going to help with that. For a long time, it hardly seemed to matter. Marxists were struggling to find any way forward, and as for Buddhism, even those who valued the sangha seemed more interested in sitting in silence than in trying to convince others to join them. So I was content to keep my ideas to myself.

With the arrival and developments of a new century, however, history began to make it increasingly clear that it had only been pretending to have ended in order to tempt the more gullible into making fools of themselves. I was presented with more and more reasons to feel that I really ought to say something about something, and not just to myself, maybe even do something about something, and with somebody else. In 2008, capitalism crashed so badly that even the wealthiest must have had momentary doubts about the wisdom of trusting the market. Interesting political movements developed, though nothing that tempted me into anything more than passive approval. But then, in 2015, the Labour Party started shaking up the political world with its radical proposals for capitalism with less brutality, and I felt I had to contribute something to this shift of politics in the right direction.

The new 'social media' option looked inviting, the possibility of being politically engaged without actually having to meet anyone. It became clear, however, that I have the same problem on social media as I do when discussing something in a group of people in real life. It's not that I have nothing to say. It's just that everyone else seems so much more keen to be heard, and almost anything that strikes me as worth saying, somebody else will probably want to say, so why not leave it to them? It would appear this is not the ideal attitude with which to gain influence on social media.

After much delay and procrastination, I went out with my local constituency Labour Party, delivering leaflets and even canvassing – talking about politics with complete strangers – which impressed me, although I'm not sure it made much impression on anyone else. Even as I was doing so, however, I couldn't help wondering if I could be doing something else. Was there anything I had to contribute that other people couldn't do just as well or better? And there the answer was, tapping me on the shoulder, coughing politely next to my ear, that rare insight into the fascinating conversation that Marx and the Buddha might have had. But what was I supposed to do with it? Fashion it into a motion that could be considered, with bemusement, by my local Labour Party branch? Make a, surely doomed, attempt to interest somebody in it on social media? And more importantly, what if I was wrong?

I'd been sure I was right for years, but that didn't prove anything; there are plenty of people who seem to me to offer clear evidence that being sure you're right is perfectly compatible with being wrong. But then, when such people have presented their ideas clearly, I've sometimes found that useful in clarifying my own ideas. So, if I were to explain my own ideas clearly then, worst-case scenario, I might become *usefully* wrong. Alternatively, I might be completely ignored, leaving me able to sink back into comfortable obscurity with the feeling that at least I made the attempt. Either of these possibilities seemed like a change for the better. And then, of course, I could be right, and people might notice. Given this situation, one conclusion that occurred to me was that I should write a book. It seemed unlikely that I would complete such a project, but I decided to give it a try.

1. NOT SUFFERING

This Dhamma that I have attained is deep, hard to see, hard to realize, peaceful, refined, beyond the scope of conjecture, subtle, to-be-experienced by the observant. But this generation delights in attachment ... For a generation delighting in attachment ... this conditionality and dependent co-arising are hard to see ... And if I were to teach the Dhamma and if others would not understand me, that would be tiresome for me, troublesome for me.

– The Ayacana Sutta[1]

The story of Buddhism truly began when the Buddha became the Buddha, when Siddhattha Gotama became 'the awakened one'. After he had relinquished his wealth and position, leaving behind his family to join the forest-dwelling seekers of wisdom, after moving from one teacher to another, mastering one set of teachings and then another but never feeling he had found the answer he was looking for, after joining others in ascetic practices but deciding that this too did not offer any answer, after taking his seat beneath the Bodhi tree and resolving to meditate until he had found the truth, finally, he opened his eyes and saw the world anew. According to the earliest Buddhist texts, not long after this profound and world-changing event, the Buddha thought the thoughts expressed in the words given in the quotation above. Is it just me, or are they not quite what you'd expect?

For those who have some familiarity with Buddhism, I imagine the words most likely to surprise are the final ones: 'that would be tiresome for me, troublesome for me'. Coming from someone who's supposed to be the embodiment of compassion, it's difficult not to detect a tad too much self-concern there, isn't it? He did, of course, change his mind. (Clearly, a willingness to change your mind is one of the characteristics of an awakened being.) Depending on the account of Buddhism you accept, either the deity Brahma Sahampati presented him with a different point of view or, alternatively, he just had a bit of a rethink. Either way, he decided to test his ability to teach. He sought out the five former companions who had abandoned him, after he had abandoned the ascetic practices they had been engaging in together over the previous years. After initial doubts, they listened, and their response proved him wrong to have doubted and right to have changed his mind. He spent the rest of his life finding ways to teach others.

For those not familiar with Buddhism, the most surprising words are surely 'conditionality and dependent co-arising'. They don't exactly have the ring of 'Major World Religion' about them, do they? They could not easily be inserted into *The Sermon on the Mount*. Perhaps they're not typical of the most popular Buddhist scriptures, but they're far from untypical of Buddhist teachings as a whole.

I suspect one reason the Buddha changed his mind and decided teaching might not, after all, be so tiresome, was that he started thinking about the challenge of how to most effectively communicate his message: how could he find ways of teaching that would be as accessible as possible for as many people as possible, but also deep enough for those who wished to gain a greater understanding? How could he explain 'conditionality and dependent co-arising' to those who wanted an explanation, while also offering useful guidance to people who had no interest in complicated concepts and might be put off by them? It's one of the characteristics of the Buddha's teaching that he always tried to adapt to his audience, to what he believed would be most beneficial to them. He provided a wide variety of teachings, from allegorical stories to reflections on the nature of the self, from lessons on different forms of meditation, to considerations on the nature of perception.

In this chapter I'll discuss the most popular presentations of the Buddhist *Dhamma*[2] (most often translated as 'teachings' although in the quote above I think 'understanding' or 'insight' might be more suitable).

In Chapter 2 I'll describe how Marx's ideas developed. Subsequent chapters will expand on the ideas of Buddhism and Marxism and explore the relationship between them.

One reason I like that passage from the *Ayacana Sutta* is that it makes clear that all Buddhist teachings, from whatever tradition of Buddhism, should be understood as attempts to find a way of conveying something that the Buddha wasn't sure it would be worth even trying to teach. I think it's useful to bear this in mind while learning about Buddhism.

At the same time, I feel a little uncomfortable saying this, because one reason religious people are potentially annoying is thanks to that 'get out of jail free card' they all have up their sleeves. If they ever find themselves without a sensible response to criticism, they always have the option of smiling, indulgently, and explaining that, however logical your argument might appear, there's no way you'll be able to appreciate the truth until you're willing to take that all-important leap of faith. As I suggest that the Buddha's message is intrinsically difficult to explain, the more suspicious reader might wonder if I'm slipping a Buddhist version of that card up my sleeve, that anyone unconvinced can just be told they've failed to grasp the subtle, complicated message the Buddha is trying to convey.

So to be clear: I'm not doing that. There are reasons the Buddhist view of the world can be difficult to make sense of, but make sense it does. It aims to offer a convincing account of the real world and of people's experience of life. Its account of the world can be judged according to its internal consistency and whether it fits with your own experience.

If you look for an account of Buddhist beliefs that you can judge the truth of, what you're most likely to find are the 'four noble truths'. There are various ways in which these are presented, but I think this simple version is a reasonable starting point:

1. There is suffering.
2. The cause of suffering is desire.
3. To be free from suffering, let go of desire.
4. To let go of desire, follow the eightfold path.

One thing I like about the four noble truths is how clearly unsuited they are to being described as 'four noble truths'. What we have here are not some proclamations of truth handed down from on high. What we have here, surely, is an argument, and a counter-intuitive argument at that,[3] which – given how influential it's been despite being counter-intuitive – suggests there's something interesting going on.

As it stands, it's unclear exactly what's being argued. Are we supposed to believe toothache is caused by the desire not to have a toothache? Are we supposed to let go of the desire for other people to be happy? Or for ourselves to be awakened? It also raises some obvious objections: is desire really such a bad thing? Can't it be quite enjoyable? Aren't there some things we *should* desire?

If we want to develop a better understanding, the first problem we have to recognise is that the translation into English is awful. I don't mean this translation in particular – all translations are problematic. Some translations are certainly worse than others. A surprising number of people, including some apparently serious Buddhists, seem happy to translate the first truth as 'Life is suffering', which would mean that either the third truth must be false, or that the eightfold path must include the recommendation that you should end your life. (It doesn't.)

Even the best translations, however, cannot escape the problem that the two concepts around which the truths are centred are difficult to translate into English. The biggest problem is *dukkha*, most commonly translated as 'suffering'. Any discussion of the four truths will point out the problem with this – and struggle to offer a clarification. Alternative translations include 'unsatisfactoriness', 'stress', 'pain', 'angst', 'anguish', and 'unease'. The word apparently derives from a term referring to a badly fitting axle or 'a wheel out of kilter', suggesting a continual feeling of life not proceeding in the way it's supposed to.

The lesser problem is *tanha*, which I've translated as 'desire'. Other translations include 'thirst', 'craving', 'longing', 'clinging', 'grasping' and 'greed'. It's difficult to judge, but I get the impression the most favoured translation may be shifting from 'desire' to 'craving'. I don't object to either as an attempt at the least inappropriate translation, but the problem I see with this shift is that it suggests the way to narrow down the correct sort of 'desire' is in terms of how strong the emotion is. It seems to me that what's really needed, is to see how this idea fits into Buddhist understanding as a whole.

To explain why this is the case requires going into the details of that Buddhist understanding, as I shall do in later chapters. While I don't think it's possible to fully understand the intention of the four truths without that deeper understanding, fortunately I *do* think it's possible to understand them in a way that is at least persuasive, and that suggests they're deserving of further investigation.

To do this, I suggest viewing dukkha as that peculiarly human form of suffering that stems from the desire for the present moment to be something other than it is. Some might object that this isn't a uniquely human form of desire. Maybe not. Perhaps when a dog looks at an empty bowl, it conjures up an alternative reality in which the bowl is full of food, and wonders, in a doggy way, why it can't be there instead of here. I have no idea. But what we can all, surely, agree, is that no other species can begin to compete with human beings when it comes to the harshness with which we can judge the present moment.

We're all familiar with the proofs of this, running around our heads every time the present isn't quite the way we feel it should be: *This is so unfair, I don't deserve this, it's not my fault, it wasn't supposed to be like this, why me, if only I'd made a different choice, why now, why do these things happen to me, why do I even bother trying...?* The continual turning of a mind out of kilter, constantly at odds with the undeniable fact that the present moment can't be anything other than it is. If we could let go of such thoughts, would that not be letting go of unnecessary suffering?

One criticism made of the four truths – and of Buddhism as a whole – is that it suggests giving up on a better future, that to let go of desire is to accept things the way they are. In terms of the definition I'm suggesting: if you're not critical of the present, then you can't be hoping for, or trying to bring about, a future that improves on it.

The first point to make about this is that many of the ways we judge the present are nothing to do with wanting a better future. They're about comparing the actual present with a possible – or rather an *impossible* – alternative present, a present we wish could be, even while we know it can't. Or, if not making comparisons, then making vague, harsh judgements built on top of an unspecified 'something better than this' – which equally serves no purpose. So, at the very least, there's a whole host of pointless desires for the impossible that, if they could be let go of, might result in less suffering.

But even if we consider thoughts that *are* about wanting a better future, there's no reason such thoughts would be incompatible with accepting the way things are. Suggesting otherwise seems to me to confuse two different ways of relating to the future: the future as a fantasy alternative to the present and the future as a realistic choice or plan. The criticism assumes that we relate to the future as just another alternative to the present, somewhere you would rather be, only at a different time instead of as an alternative now.

If, however, you're thinking seriously about the future as something you hope will come about, then it can only be reached by starting from the present as it actually is. Instead of wasting time thinking about how you wish the present was different, it would make more sense to try to understand the present as clearly as possible, so as to work out how it could develop into the future you would most want to see.

It could be argued, I suppose, that it's impossible to want a better future without in some sense *desiring* to be there and judging the present as lacking by comparison. I don't believe that has to be the case. It depends on the way you experience the relationship between yourself, the present moment, the future, and the process of change – all questions that are relevant to the Buddhist understanding of the world, and which we'll return to in later chapters.

The fourth truth (the least truth-like of them all) suggests that to let go of desire you should follow the 'eightfold path'. This refers to a path, each part of which is traditionally qualified by the interestingly vague yet precise-sounding adjective 'right'. Namely: right view, right intention, right speech, right action, right livelihood, right effort, right mindfulness and right concentration. There are, of course, alternative translations for some of these phrases and different understandings of what, exactly, they mean. The eight are sometimes helpfully divided into three groups: the first two categorised as wisdom, the next three as morality or ethics, and the final three as meditation.

Out of all the teachings and practices Buddhism has to offer, it's meditation that people seem to have found most appealing. So much so that 'Buddhist meditation' is sometimes presented as though it can be conveniently plucked out of its surroundings, and taught and practised as a self-contained route to calm, happiness and freedom from stress.

Actually, it can! Or at least it seems to work, to some degree, for some people. But those who present or teach such practices are rather inconsistent about whether, or how, they should associate it with Buddhism. If practices that have been associated with Buddhism can be used to help people with their health or wellbeing, that's fine. When, however, such practices are presented as though they're what 'Buddhist practice' consists of, then some who practise them might reasonably expect such practice to lead to something more meaningful, and to wonder if it's in fact doing so.

Some meditation teachers, in such circumstances, will offer reassurance that patient practice will be worth it: the meditator is sure to eventually crest that hill, experience the change that will leave them knowing what it was all for. Others might claim that, if the meditator simply lets go of the idea that there's any goal to achieve, then they'll realise they're already everything they need to be, and that, if they have any doubts or confusion, the appropriate response is to let go of the idea that there's anything to doubt or to be confused about. Any meditator who has such doubts, however, might also find it worthwhile to learn about other aspects of the Buddhist path.

If you want a better understanding of what Buddhist meditation is supposed to be all about, or if you're not interested in meditation so much as in alternative ways of understanding the world, the wisdom aspects of the path are the obvious place to look. And there's much of interest to be found there, reflections, for example, on the nature of the self, or a curious conception of 'emptiness' and of the forms that emptiness can take – ideas that are even more interestingly counter-intuitive than the idea that suffering is caused by desire.

The more fully you come to an intellectual understanding of Buddhism, however, the more you come to understand that a purely intellectual understanding of Buddhism is not what Buddhism is all about. One of its central insights is that insights worth having need to be grasped experientially, to be integrated into one's habitual way of relating to the world. And to do that, a practice of mindfulness and concentration, of meditation, is the recommended way.

In some traditional approaches to Buddhist practice, it's the ethical parts of the path that are given priority – priority, at least, in terms of being the first part of the path to practise. The original order in which the parts are presented is changed, and the path is seen as following a sequence. As Leigh Brasington puts it:

> The Buddha's teachings can be divided into three parts: sila, samadhi and panna: ethical conduct, concentration, and wisdom. Or to put it into the vernacular: clean up your act, concentrate your mind, and use your concentrated mind to investigate reality.[4]

According to this approach, to see the Buddhist insights most clearly you need a concentrated mind, and to develop a concentrated mind you need a clear conscience, you need to be at peace with yourself and the world, so – first things first – follow the ethical teachings of the Buddha. But for someone who's wondering whether Buddhist practice is for them, it seems unlikely that the Buddhist approach to ethics would have a particular appeal, unless they'd already developed an interest in Buddhist meditation or in other aspects of Buddhism.

One of the interesting aspects of Buddhism is, in fact, how all the different aspects fit together, reinforcing and reflecting each other. Your understanding or experience of each is enhanced by a deeper appreciation of the others.

If someone learns enough about Buddhism to become convinced that it's worth learning more – if they become curious enough about what exactly Buddhist wisdom has to offer, or wonder if Buddhist meditation might be worth a closer encounter – the suspicion might occur to them that those nice, simple-sounding, 'four noble truths' that appeared to promise a neat summary of what Buddhism was all about were actually just a way of drawing them into something that is not, in fact, remotely simple. I'm inclined to describe this suspicion as a 'truth', one that, in my experience, is very effective, and one that I intend to run with, by promising to return, in later chapters, to some of the more interesting aspects of the eight paths of the fourth truth, and the other three truths that the fourth allegedly follows from. Before we move on, however, I'd like to return to a theme that isn't going to go away: the problem of translation.

I mentioned earlier that 'suffering' is a bad translation of dukkha. To be honest, I have no idea if that's true. I'd be very surprised if it isn't, given the number of Buddhists who say it is. But I can't read Pali, and I'm guessing most accounts of Buddhism that I've read were written by people whose understanding of it is also limited or non-existent. So it's not out of the question that 'suffering' is the most perfect translation of dukkha you could possibly wish for.

What I am sure of, is that the biggest translation challenge for Buddhists is not translating from Pali – or Sanskrit, or Tibetan, or Mandarin, or whatever – into English or any other language. The biggest challenge is translating from lived experience into words. When the Buddha tried to work out how best to explain what he had to teach, I can see no reason to assume that he thought, 'Ooh, *dukkha* – that's the perfect word for what I want to say.' Like everyone else, he had to work with what was available.

The limitation of language, of course, can hardly be claimed as a revelation. It has affected every sensitive soul. It's why people write poetry. It's why some people can find more beauty in the precision of a mathematical theorem than in even the most well-sculpted sonnet, and why others can't begin to comprehend how anyone can associate mathematics with beauty. It's part of the reason why silence is so often golden, and why 'silence is golden' is such an inadequate description of any, let alone all, of the manifold experiences of silence.

It's a common problem. But I think Buddhism has reason to see it as particularly problematic. For all their limitations, languages developed to describe the world as we commonly experience it. But a fundamental argument of Buddhism is that, in important ways, the way we experience the world is misleading. The Buddha wanted to explain the way he'd come to understand the world, but he had to contend with the way that the concepts available for explaining his insights could themselves lead to misunderstandings, and the language available for expressing those concepts could distort the understanding it was trying to describe. The same, I think, was true for Marx, to a lesser extent, but for the same reason.

2. PHILOSOPHICAL ECONOMICS

At the time Marx was trying to make sense of what would become known as capitalism, you would have searched in vain for discussions of 'economics'. Those who made a particular study of the role of economic activity in society were said to be studying 'political economy'. The world we're familiar with, with its excess supply of economists expounding on the subject of economics, only developed in the late nineteenth century, at a time when increasingly powerful trade unions and political parties were trying to influence economic decisions in favour of the working class, and after Marx had published the first volume of *Capital* (the subtitle of which was *A Critique of Political Economy*). Theorists such as Alfred Marshall, William Stanley Jevons, Leon Walras and others, wanted to establish 'economics' as a rigorous, objective science, like physics or chemistry, and they certainly didn't want it too closely associated with something so open to dispute as politics.

There is, inevitably, a significant overlap between the subject matter of economics and political economy, and significant variation within each. But as a generalisation, I think you could see those who study economics as being like people who've inherited an airline and are trying to work out how to make it run as smoothly as possible and, in particular, how to minimise the number and severity of crashes. The political economists who preceded them, on the other hand, were more like people who were going about their business when, one day, they looked up, saw a winged metal tube with people inside it, flying through the air, and asked themselves, 'What the hell is going on here?'

Capitalism crept up on people. Nobody saw it coming. Nobody planned it out in advance. Those whose actions contributed to creating it acted out of short-term motivations, with no real conception of the way their actions would contribute to the transformation of their society and of the world. By the time people began to realise they were dealing with something new and started trying to work out how best to take advantage of it, it became clear to them that they didn't really understand how it worked.

One of the reasons capitalism could creep up on people was because, for a long time, the way it developed was through the gradual expansion and transformation of something that had been around for as long as anyone could remember, and which had never been seen as problematic or difficult to understand: the market.

Markets had existed since the earliest civilisations. Indeed, they had played an important part in the way those civilisations had developed. In addition to the exchange of goods, they were the sites where different cultures met and enriched each other, exchanging knowledge and ideas. Prior to capitalism, however, they had always been marginal to the main economic activities people engaged in, growing crops and creating homes and belongings – either for themselves, or for other members of their community, or for those who had political power over them. Most of the goods traded in markets were either the excess that communities didn't need, or unusual items that couldn't be found or created locally.

As capitalism developed, markets became ever more central to economic activity, until, under mature capitalism, the only production that counts is production for the market. Today, any economic activity which is not for the market – domestic work, voluntary work, people working on their allotments or doing DIY – is hardly seen as a proper part of the economy at all. The market is no longer a welcome option for when you can afford to use it – it's inescapable.

One way you might imagine the change from a pre-capitalist world to a capitalist world is as the change from a world where, if you mentioned 'the market', you might get a response such as, 'Should've gone yesterday, now we'll have to wait another week', or perhaps, 'What, the one in Brick Lane?' to a world where, if you refer to 'the market', you're more likely to be understood as referring to that amorphous national or global entity around which every important economic decision revolves and toward which politicians pay obeisance like courtiers to a king.

Human beings have always tried to find new and better ways to obtain what they need to live, or what they want to make life more enjoyable. They have never simply accepted the limitations they were faced with, but rather investigated ways of overcoming those limitations, looking for new opportunities to take advantage of.

Through most of human history, from the earliest human societies, right through to the emergence of capitalism, the understanding that people had to develop could be divided into two kinds. On the one hand they had to gain a deeper understanding of nature. For example, working out how better to hunt and gather, how to stay safe and warm, how to domesticate animals, or to develop agriculture. On the other hand, they had to understand themselves and each other – to develop ways of working together effectively, cooperating, dividing tasks between different people, and so on.

Once their understanding had allowed them to move on from simply struggling to survive, and they began to produce a surplus beyond what they needed, the attention of some turned from how they could exploit the opportunities offered by nature to how they could exploit each other. One expression of this was the division of society into classes. Whether it was slavery, serfdom, the caste system, or in some other form, some people gained enough power to live wealthier and more leisured lifestyles while others had to work not only to provide for themselves but also for those who had power over them.

As capitalism developed, the way different classes related to each other became more confusing, and the nature of the opportunities the market offered to people were difficult to make sense of. The market was clearly not a part of nature, and yet the more it became central to how society was organised, the more impossible it was to understand simply in terms of people's conscious choices. Trying to make sense of it seemed to have more in common with trying to make sense of nature than dealing with how people chose to behave. Why was one commodity more profitable than another? Would governments be better off imposing tariffs on imported goods, or promoting free trade? The operation of the market seemed to create its own rules. The opportunities it offered were difficult to understand. And capitalism wasn't only affecting economic developments – it was bringing about changes in demographics, in class structure, in politics, in the way people thought about themselves and society.

This is why people like Adam Smith, John Stuart Mill[1] and Karl Marx, who were attracted first of all to philosophy, ended up devoting so much of their time to studying political economy. Because they were trying to make sense of what it means to be a human being at a time when human beings were beginning to relate to their own economic activity, and therefore to each other, in a fundamentally new way.

Adam Smith is best known as the author of the first great work of political economy, *An Inquiry into the Nature and Causes of the Wealth of Nations*, but he was at least as proud of his earlier work *The Theory of Moral Sentiments*, which he published in 1759 when he was Professor of Moral Philosophy at the University of Glasgow. In writing this earlier work, Smith was reacting to the negative portrayal of human nature offered by a number of philosophers preceding him, most notably Thomas Hobbes. Hobbes argued that, if left to their own devices, people would live in a state of 'a war of all against all' and that the only way to create a civilised society was for people to hand ultimate authority to a powerful sovereign.

Smith had an altogether more upbeat assessment of his fellow humans, as he made clear in the opening of the book:

> How selfish soever man may be supposed, there are evidently some principles in his nature, which interest him in the fortune of others, and render their happiness necessary to him, though he derives nothing from it except the pleasure of seeing it. Of this kind is pity or compassion...[2]

Smith rejected the idea that the inclination to be selfish undermined the possibility of virtuous behaviour. Although people pursued their own self-interest, there were aspects of human nature that meant this pursuit led them to behave in social and moral ways. People used imagination and reason to understand each other. To understand others, people imagined themselves in the position of other people, and could take pleasure from other people's pleasure. And in trying to understand and judge themselves, they imagined how other people saw them and so naturally wanted other people's approval. This meant that pursuing their own self-interest often coincided with seeking what was good for others.

Smith had doubts, however, about how far this would extend to strangers. Inevitably, people would care more about those close to them. Fortunately, as he considered the society he was living in, he found something that he believed would lead self-interest to work in favour of everyone: the extension and transformation of the market, and the changes to the economy that this made possible.

Turning his attention to economic developments, Smith saw the market and the division of labour as providing another way that people's self-interest could work for the good of society. As he studied the factories and workplaces that were becoming an increasingly prominent part of the economic landscape, it was clear to him that the labour employed there was far more productive than under the feudal setup. By focusing on a single product, workers could develop skills specialised to particular tasks and make use of machinery that would have been impractical in smaller-scale production.

The produce of these enterprises could then be sold, and because the labour had been used more productively, enough money could be earned to make a profit at the same time as paying the workers. The workers could then buy the things they needed from the market. Such enterprises were set up in the self-interest of the investors, just as the workers worked for their wages out of self-interest, but the result was that society as a whole became more productive and created more wealth.

In addition, competition between firms to sell their goods meant that those enterprises that were most efficient, or that produced the goods for which there was most demand, were more successful, while less efficient companies, producing goods that people were not willing to pay for, went out of business. So money naturally flowed to those businesses that had the most to offer, and businesses had an interest in producing new and more desirable products as efficiently as possible.

Some have argued that Smith's account of human behaviour in *The Wealth of Nations* contradicts the one in *The Theory of Moral Sentiments*. But in both works, Smith took it for granted that people were first of all focused on their self-interest, and he tried to show how this could nonetheless lead to people behaving in ways that were good for each other. In his arguments about morality, what modified people's self-interest were other human feelings and motivations. But in his political economy, self-interest was mitigated by something outside of the conscious decisions of human beings: the operation of the market. And as the market became increasingly important, its imperatives would take precedence over the human, moral ways that people would consciously choose to relate to each other.

In a sense, one of the most impressive aspects of *The Wealth of Nations* is that it was published in 1776: while capitalism had been developing gradually for centuries, it was only just becoming clear how radically it would transform the world.

The period between the book's publication and when Marx read it in the 1840s saw two very different but related revolutions. The industrial revolution transformed the economy and society of Britain and went on to spread capitalism around the world. The French revolution swept away the feudal order and promoted political ideas that would form the basis for later socialist and communist movements.

In 1844 Friedrich Engels published *The Condition of the Working Class in England* which described the capitalism that he and Marx were faced with, a capitalism very different from the one Smith had described. This capitalism found its starkest expression in Manchester, where a hundred or more cotton mills churned out products, profits and pollution, and where the men, women and children who worked in those mills spent what little free time they had in the surrounding slums, struggling to survive poverty, overcrowding and disease.

At the time *The Wealth of Nations* was published, there were no cotton mills in Manchester. The textile industry was a small-scale domestic activity built around the 'putting-out' system, where merchants left materials to be worked up in weavers' cottages. Early cotton mills were reliant on water power. It was the developments in steam power taking place as Smith went to press that would make possible the industrialisation that transformed centres like Manchester, other towns in the north of England, and later the world.

In the 1830s Marx studied law and philosophy at the University of Berlin, and whilst there became involved with the Young Hegelians, a group of radical thinkers who were inspired by, but also critical of, the philosopher Georg Wilhelm Friedrich Hegel. What inspired them was Hegel's conception of the world as constantly changing and interconnected, each moment containing within it the change to follow. As Engels described it:

> ...for the first time the whole world, natural, historical, intellectual, is represented as a process, i.e., as in constant motion, change, transformation, development; and the attempt is made to trace out the internal connection that makes a continuous whole of all this movement and development.[3]

The most obvious problem that the Young Hegelians had with Hegel was his conservatism. Although his philosophy seemed to be all about change and progress – and he himself had found the French Revolution inspiring in his youth – as he got older, Hegel came to accept the status quo and to see the existing Prussian state as an expression of the 'Absolute Spirit' that his philosophy aimed towards. For the Young Hegelians, however, the ideals and aims of the French Revolution were not over. Germany needed its own transformation and the creation of a republic.

What was even more consequential for Marx, however, was the criticism of Hegel's philosophical idealism – his focus on the development of ideas. Marx's rejection of philosophical idealism in favour of materialism was central to his understanding of how history developed. In addition, the route by which the critique of Hegel's idealism was replaced with materialism reflected a changed understanding of the concept of alienation, one that would be central to Marx's thought.

I should probably admit that I'm not sure I really understand philosophical idealism, let alone the 'absolute idealism' of Hegel. Whenever I try to imagine an idealist world, where everything is dependent on the development of minds and ideas, I find myself stuck on the same (possibly irrelevant) question: supposing, in such a world, some especially impressive scientific minds take it upon themselves to study the parts of the apparent world that their apparent bodies appear to be interacting with, and they conclude that the stuff they've studied can be conceptualised as consisting of different elements that interact with each other in ways that depend on their atomic structure. Are we supposed to believe that the stuff they studied was not the same sort of stuff until their impressive minds conceptualised it in the particular way they did? And if so, how did they come to conceptualise it in this strangely complicated yet wonderfully useful way, rather than in some other way? Or was the stuff they studied the same sort of stuff even before they studied it, in which case, did the sort of stuff that it was not in some way determine the sort of conceptual sense their minds would make of it? Perhaps I'm completely missing the point. More than likely.

As though the idealism wasn't confusing enough, it's not the only reason Hegel's philosophy is difficult to understand. Of all the philosophers who've lived, he's widely considered to be one of the most difficult to make sense of – which is saying quite something. Plenty of people far cleverer than me, have spent far longer than I have trying to understand him, and they all seem to have come to slightly different conclusions about what, exactly, he was arguing.

But for the sake of having a starting point for understanding what Marx made of him, let's take Hegel as thinking something roughly along these lines: history consists of the unfolding of the Absolute Idea or Absolute Spirit, which is identical to God. In the course of this development, individuals come to conceive of parts of this Absolute, including themselves, as separate from Absolute Spirit, alienated from Absolute

Spirit – to see Spirit as something separate from them, as an object *for* them rather than inseparable *from* them. The task of history and of philosophy is to clarify how everything that appears alienated is in fact part of the unfolding Absolute, and can be logically reintegrated with the Absolute and so re-establish the perfection of God. Or something like that.

It's sometimes said that Marx stood Hegel on his head. It might be more accurate, however, to say that Marx's fellow Young Hegelian, Ludwig Feuerbach, stood Hegel on his head and Marx then taught the inverted Hegelianism how to walk on its hands. In *The Essence of Christianity*, Feuerbach argues that Hegel's idealism was itself an act of alienation. Instead of material reality being the alienated form of Absolute Spirit, the reality was that actual, material, human beings, such as Hegel, created the ideas of religion and God and Absolute Spirit and saw them as something that created the material world. The ideas of Christianity were an alienated expression of human reality: these ideas had been created by human beings, but were viewed by them as something separate from them, which had created *them* and which they were subservient to. The task of philosophy was to clarify how everything, including religion, was created through the development of material reality.

The young Marx was fully on board with this account and reflected it in his own writing:

> Religion is the sigh of the oppressed creature, the heart of a heartless world and the soul of soulless conditions. It is the *opium* of the people.
>
> The abolition of religion as the *illusory* happiness of the people is the demand for their *real* happiness. To call on them to give up their illusions about their condition is to *call on them to give up a condition that requires illusions*.[4]

Like the other Young Hegelians, the young Marx believed that in order to bring about progressive change, it was important to subject the politics and ideas of existing society to a relentless critique. In 1843, after the Prussian censorship closed down the newspaper Marx had been editing in Cologne, he and another Young Hegelian, Arnold Ruge, moved to Paris with plans to co-edit a new journal. Marx wrote to Ruge describing his plans for the journal:

> The reform of consciousness consists *entirely* in making the world aware of its own consciousness, in arousing it from its dream of itself, in *explaining* its own actions to it. Like Feuerbach's critique of religion, our whole aim can only be to translate religious and political problems into their self-conscious human form.
>
> Our programme must be: the reform of consciousness not through dogmas but by analysing mystical consciousness obscure to itself, whether it appears in religious or political form. It will then become plain that the world has long since dreamed of something of which it needs only to become conscious for it to possess it in reality.[5]

As Marx's thought developed, however, he came to see that this approach to 'the reform of consciousness' did not properly move on from idealism. The Young Hegelians had rejected Hegel's idealist approach to reality, but they were still engaging with society purely in terms of ideas. If the ideas current in society were bound up with the social and material reality, then the consistent approach would be to ask what it was about that material reality that influenced people's ideas, and to work out how that material reality itself could be changed. It was this that led Marx to a deeper study of political economy.

Marx's engagement with political economy, along with his increasing contact with socialists and anarchists in Paris, and his growing familiarity with the actual conditions of working people, led him to an increasing recognition that the alienation which is most fundamental to most people's experience stems not from religion or ideas, but from their lived experience in their working lives. At this stage in his thinking, Marx's writings make clear the comparison between alienation in economic activity and in religious belief:

The more the worker exerts himself in his work, the more powerful the alien, objective world becomes which he brings into being over against himself, the poorer he and his inner world become, and the less they belong to him. It is the same in religion. The more man puts into God, the less he retains within himself.[6]

But as his thinking developed, Marx came to see economic change, rather than changing people's ideas about religion, as the most effective way to overcome alienation:

Religious estrangement as such takes place only in the sphere of *consciousness*, of man's inner life, but economic estrangement is that of *real* life – its supersession therefore embraces both aspects.[7]

Marx began to move on from the Young Hegelians and develop a more meaningfully materialist approach to understanding society. Sidney Hook describes the changes, whilst also making clear the extent to which Hegel's approach to understanding history continued to influence Marx. For Hegel:

Nothing was independent of anything else. A meaning could only be grasped in relation to some meaning (or system of meanings) which it implied and which implied it. In effect, if not in intent, what Hegel did was to dissolve all things into their relations, construe these relations as logical categories and present the inter-relationships of the logical categories as a process. The order of the logical development of ideas in this realm of abstraction was the same as the order of the succession of events in history.[8]

Whereas for Marx:

...as a result of his attempt to understand the nature of the *historical* process Marx was compelled to abandon his idealism, he still retained his belief in the underivable character of activity. But it was now a *natural* activity, not a logical activity. It was the activity of matter, not of spirit. Every existing thing had a place in a material continuum of directed movement. The logic of Hegel received a naturalistic foundation. Nothing could exist outside of this continuum of directed movement. Nothing could be understood except in terms of the logical relations of this continuum.[9]

By the late 1840s, the fundamentals of Marx's understanding of history and capitalism were in place. This coincided with an upsurge in social and political conflict that culminated in revolutions across Europe in 1848. As a contribution to these developments, Marx and Engels published an agitational pamphlet called *The Communist Manifesto*, which incorporated a concise account of their ideas. The revolutions, however, failed to bring about the changes that had been hoped for, and the manifesto was not widely read. As capitalism stabilised, it became clear that real social change would be a very long-term affair.

Over the following twenty years, Marx would lead an interesting life, although for most of it he engaged in little political activity. It wasn't until the 1860s that Marx became involved with – and the most prominent representative of – the International Working Men's Association, also known as the First International. It was in this role that he would gain notoriety as a defender of the 1871 Paris Commune.

In the intervening years, having been expelled from Prussia, then France, then Belgium, Marx arrived in London, along with his wife Jenny and their three children. They would go on to have seven children in all, but only three survived into adulthood (along with one child Marx had outside of marriage). During these years, Marx was constantly promising – and failing to deliver – new literary works. Efforts were delayed by excessive perfectionism, but also by incessant poverty. Despite financial support from Engels and others, and from occasional writing work, the family would make regular trips to the pawnshop. And matters were not helped by Marx's continual health issues, from problems with his liver to repeated attacks of carbuncles and boils.

There are, of course, many other details of this period of Marx's life which, like these, would be categorised as 'human interest' aspects of his life. But Marx also spent a great deal of this time in the British Museum Reading Room, reading government reports, thinking, studying different accounts of political economy, thinking some more, deepening his understanding of capitalism, walking up and down in his room (I'd assume) thinking, sitting in an armchair (surely) thinking, writing reams of disorganised notes, thinking some more, and, in between times, doing a lot more thinking. And needless to say, it was this latter part of his life that was, in fact, by far the most deserving of 'human interest'. Indications of this appeared in numerous articles and a few short books or pamphlets, but the clearest evidence arrived in 1867 when the long-promised first volume of *Capital* was finally published.

Marx's *Capital* is a very long and often boring book that contains, dispersed throughout it – sometimes in strikingly clear passages, sometimes hidden within tedious descriptions and calculations – important insights into the workings of the capitalist economy and capitalist society. Part of the reason *Capital* can be challenging, but also rewarding, is because Marx is trying to do two things at once. On the one hand, he wants to engage with political economy on its own terms and demonstrate that, if capitalism is understood correctly in those terms, it will be seen to involve exploitation and to contain contradictions that lead to repeated crises.

At the same time, however, he also wants to make it clear that the way political economy presents the economic system reflects and reinforces the alienated nature of the capitalist economy. The categories and concepts of political economy are abstractions from, and objectifications of, the actual social connections between human beings. The very use of the concepts and terms of political economy reinforce the misleading sense that they refer to an economy that functions separately from human decisions.

Marx begins *Capital* by considering the fundamental building block on which the capitalist edifice is built, the commodity. A commodity is something that contains two kinds of value: use-value and exchange-value. Everything human beings create has a use-value, which is the value that arises (as you may have guessed) from its use. If it wasn't seen as in some way useful, why create it? The creator of a *commodity*, however, does not make use of that use-value themselves. Instead, they sell it on the market, where it has a quite different kind of value, its exchange-value, a value that determines how much it can be exchanged for in terms of other commodities – expressed most usefully in terms of the commodity that provides a 'universal equivalent': money.

This was a distinction Adam Smith had made, but Smith was considering markets in general. He saw the expansion of the market under capitalism as a natural and inevitable development of people doing, more effectively, what they'd always tended to do. In the course of trying to work out what determined the value of commodities in the market, he mentions the difference between what he calls 'value in use' and 'value in exchange', pointing out that the latter could not be based on the former, since something extremely useful, like water, has very little value in the market, whereas diamonds, which are rather less useful, can be exchanged for far more.[10]

The reason Marx was particularly interested in the nature of the commodity was because of the way in which its dual or contradictory nature is reflected in capitalist society as a whole. A capitalist society is organised around 'generalised commodity production', so everything tends to become commodified, and everything tends to be seen less in terms of how useful it is for society and more in terms of how much money it's worth.

In the context of capitalism, even 'use-value' doesn't have the same significance as it did in previous economic systems. Throughout all previous history, the vast majority of the things people produced were produced for the specific use they offered. Under capitalism, while it's important that commodities have a use-value, the producer doesn't care what that use-value is. They might produce items of furniture they'd quite like to own themselves, clothes they wouldn't be seen dead in, electronic components they don't understand, or copies of books advocating the overthrow of capitalism. All that matters is that somebody out there considers them useful and is willing to pay for them. All that matters is that they can sell what they produce on the market so as to realise the exchange-value.

So far, so vaguely interesting, you might reasonably think, but this examination of commodities as a whole merely laid the groundwork for a much more significant insight. It was through considering the nature of the commodity, thinking about use-values and exchange-values and their relationship to the capitalist mode of production, that Marx noticed, in amongst all the mass of commodities capitalism brought to market, a very curious commodity indeed, a commodity like no other. Marx considered the recognition and understanding of this commodity to be one of his most important insights – the key to explaining the whole secret of how capitalism worked. That commodity was labour-power.

Okay, on the face of it, not the most exciting of commodities, hardly the sort of high-tech wonder you might have hoped for from the much-vaunted capitalist drive to innovation. Something, in fact, that we all already have, that everyone always has had. But what Marx was interested in wasn't the general activity of 'labour', which could be done just as well by a serf, a slave or even a conscientious capitalist. He was interested in the specific way that labour ends up being performed in the context of a capitalist enterprise, where the employer purchases a commodity from the worker. To make this distinction clear, Marx referred to the commodity that workers sell as 'labour-power': the use-value that this commodity provides to the employer is the ability to carry out the labour of producing other commodities, and its exchange-value is the wage that the worker is paid.

The fact that everybody has labour-power that they can sell is one way in which the commodity is distinctive. For workers, it's the commodity they *have* to sell in order to be able to buy all those commodities they consume so they can continue living their lives and have more labour-power to sell the next day.

Another odd quality of the commodity labour-power is easy enough to see – unlike most commodities, after the contract has been signed and the labour-power sold, the seller does not get to say 'thank you for your custom' and go off to spend their well-gotten gains. For whatever quantity of labour-power they've sold, the seller has to turn up at the buyer's place of business to do the buyer's bidding, minute by minute, hour by hour. It's almost as though what they've sold is not just their labour-power, but a part of their actual life.

But that's from the point of view of the worker. In capitalism, the viewpoint of the capitalist is more important. Although even here the secret of labour-power is not obvious. From the viewpoint of the individual capitalist, labour-power is just one of the commodities that capital has to buy – along with raw materials, non-living varieties of machinery and tools, premises, and so on – so they can engage in the business of creating and selling other commodities.

Since this is capitalism, where the functioning of the economy is alienated from society and does not follow directly from the conscious decisions of human beings, if we want to see the significance of the commodity labour-power, we need to stand back from the way it appears to those buying and selling it, and think about it in terms of the economic system as a whole. For Marx, the distinguishing feature of labour-power, the feature that made it the key to understanding capitalism, was that it was the *only* commodity capable of creating more exchange-value than it cost. If that sounds confusing, it's because it is! If it was easy, it wouldn't have taken so long before somebody worked it out.

To make sense of this, let's set capitalism to one side for a while and matters will become more straightforward. Imagine instead a nice, simple, abstract society. The details of how it's organised aren't important. As in any society, people produce things and consume things. Let's suppose the members of this society have decided, for some reason, that each year they'll only do the work required to produce the exact equivalent of what they consume. As a result, at the end of the year, the society will have exactly the same amount of wealth with which it started.

Imagining this is made more complicated by the fact that not everything that's produced will be consumed entirely in the space of a year. But for the sake of argument, let's assume exact equivalents can be worked out. So, for example, the exact proportion of a pair of trousers that are consumed during the year can somehow be measured, and the equivalent amount of trouser can be produced, so that a new pair will be ready to replace them when the old ones fall apart or are thrown away because they went out of fashion.

Now suppose, one year, the people change their minds and decide to work a little longer or harder than is needed to replace what they consume. They do some additional work and produce more than they consume. At the end of the year, the society will be wealthier than it was at the beginning.

Of course, the society might find ways to produce more wealth without increasing the amount of work done. Perhaps they dig a well to save people fetching water from the river, or they invent electricity and make good use of it. The society will then be able to produce more without putting in more work. But the basic situation described above won't have changed. It only means less work would be required before everything they've consumed has been replaced and they can begin, if they so choose, to increase their wealth.

In a capitalist society, the same situation described for the society above applies to each individual capitalist company. But since this is capitalism, everything works in terms of exchange-values rather than use-values. Over the course of a year, a company spends a certain amount of exchange-value on raw materials, labour-power, machinery (or accounting for depreciation on machinery) and so on. It uses these to produce commodities, which it sells for a certain amount of exchange-value. If the exchange-value earned from the sale of commodities is exactly equal to the amount spent to create the commodities, the company will break even. But if, for the same cost, the labour-power that was purchased works harder, or longer, and produces more commodities, then the company earns more exchange-value than it invested, what Marx calls surplus-value, which in this context we could also call profit. For the company, that surplus-value, or profit, is the whole point.

As with the society above, the company might find ways to produce more commodities without the workers having to do more work. It might find a source of cheaper raw materials, or invest in machinery that makes the labour-power more productive. But the basic situation would not have changed. It would just reduce the amount of labour-power needed to produce commodities with the equivalent value of everything the company invested, and after which the labour-power begins to create surplus-value.

There are some important differences between the society described above and a capitalist company, differences that follow from the difference between use-values and exchange-values. For one thing, the description of the society said nothing about who ended up getting any surplus that was produced. That would depend on the politics of the society concerned. In the case of the capitalist company, on the other hand, the surplus-value obviously goes to the capitalists, the company's owners or shareholders, the people who paid for the labour-power that created it.

Also, if the society increases its wealth, producing a surplus of use-values, it's difficult to see why *somebody* in the society wouldn't use them. They're useful, after all. But for the company, it isn't enough just to produce a surplus of commodities. They have to be sold on the market so the exchange-value can be realised. If they can't be sold – because there's no demand, or because a competing company with better or cheaper commodities fulfils the demand – then the commodities turn out to be useless. They may have perfectly good use-value, but from the point of view of the company, and of capitalism, if the exchange-value can't be realised on the market, producing the commodities was pointless. I'll come back to some consequences of this in Chapter 6.

If Marx had pointed out that, under feudalism or slavery, the subordinate class had to carry out surplus-labour beyond what was needed to produce for its own needs, and what this surplus-labour produced was appropriated by the dominant class, nobody would have been particularly impressed or surprised. But capitalism isn't supposed to work like that. Everybody is supposed to be equal. In fact, in capitalist terms, everyone *is* equal. Everyone meets in the marketplace and exchanges their commodities at mutually agreed prices. The exploitation is hidden by the fact that, for the majority of people, the only commodity they have for sale – and that they *have* to sell in order to live – is their labour-power, whereas a small number of people are in a position to purchase that labour-power, and to keep the surplus-value it produces.

Capitalists would, no doubt, object that those with nothing but their labour-power could never produce commodities if it wasn't for capitalists providing the raw materials, machinery, organisation and so on. Although, presumably, slave owners and feudal lords could have made a similar argument.

Using the terminology of political economy, Marx was presenting an explanation of how the rate of exploitation could be represented by a formula: it was the ratio of the surplus-value earned to the labour-power purchased. In broader terms, Marx was making the point that the capitalist mode of production was one in which an adequate understanding of the economy had to include a formula for the 'rate of exploitation'; it was an exploitative society, a class society, in which the interests of different classes were fundamentally opposed, and where the working class had reason to want to replace it with a way of organising society that did not require exploitation.

It's worth being clear that the exploitation described here is not the responsibility of individual capitalists setting out to exploit anyone. It's the result of the capitalist economic system. The capitalist, indeed, has no choice but to exploit labour, otherwise they could not stay in business. Nobody has to *decide* to exploit anyone. Rather, *because* the economy has become alienated from the direct, conscious decisions of human beings, because the operation of the market determines so much of how the economy operates, it has become possible for exploitation to occur without it being at all obvious to capitalists, or to workers, or to economists.

For the capitalist or the economist, there's no reason to see labour-power as different to any other commodity: it's just one of the costs of production. For workers, many may feel exploited in the sense that they're not being paid enough. But there's no reason why they'd recognise that, even if they were paid an amount that seemed reasonable, they are still being exploited. But this must be the case because, unless they're successfully exploited, the employer can't make a profit and will have no reason to employ them.

None of this is to deny that, in many ways, capitalism is an advance over previous ways of organising society. The way capitalism became established involved a lot of force and violence, but established capitalism can afford to be more civilised. For one thing, the way capitalists come by their position is different to the way people became feudal lords. It may still be the case that the main way in which people become owners of capital is through inheritance, but there are also possibilities for social mobility. Not so many possibilities that there's any danger of the majority of the population ceasing to be available for continued exploitation, but enough so the idea we live in a meritocracy does not seem entirely absurd.

Even for the majority who remain in the working class, the championing of freedom and equality that came with the move out of feudalism was far from meaningless. Outside of the time they're at work, people are relatively free to live as they want. If they can find more than one employer willing to hire them, they're free to decide who to work for. As free owners of their labour-power, they can negotiate their contracts, and if they can form trade unions, such negotiations can become less one-sided.

When the social power of the working class has become strong enough, they've managed to bring enough pressure to bear to gain a part in the democratic process, giving them more say in who gets to run capitalism. During periods when trade unions and the labour movement have been relatively powerful, they've managed to ensure that increases in productivity lead to increased wages or more free time, and not only to increased profits.

Workers have also benefitted from what capitalism does most effectively – producing more things more efficiently. The increase in availability of cheaper consumer goods, including labour-saving devices for the home, along with new technologies, medicines, modes of travel and communication and so on, has allowed people to live richer lives. The increasing complexity of society has provided more varieties of work and leisure. In addition, increasing numbers have benefited from the opportunity of improved education.

There are, in short, many positive developments that capitalism has made possible. The more these positive aspects of capitalism have developed, however, the more difficult it has become to see why it would not be possible to retain them, and indeed extend them, whilst organising society in a way that does not involve privately owned companies, inequality, alienation and exploitation.

Thinkers and writers don't always recognise which of their ideas – or which ways of expressing their ideas – will be most useful. Adam Smith, for example, only used the phrase 'the invisible hand' three times, and each time in a specific context. It would be hard to find any recent account of his economic theories, however, that does not make use of this metaphor to describe how 'the invisible hand of the market' guides the self-interested actions of individuals in a way that is beneficial for society as a whole.

By contrast, nobody should be asked to count the number of times Marx used the term 'alienation'. And, contrary to what some have suggested, he never stopped using it. This use did decline, however, as he developed his analysis of capitalism. To an extent, he replaced it with the concept of 'commodity fetishism'.

I'm pretty sure I'm in the majority amongst modern-day Marxists in taking the view that alienation is a more useful concept than the mature Marx gave it credit for (and I'm no big fan of 'commodity fetishism'). To be fair to Marx, at the time he was writing, the most obvious association of 'fetishism' was with religious fetishes – objects that were created by human beings but then seen as possessing supernatural powers – nothing to do with kinky sex! He was pointing out how, in a similar way, people produce commodities but then allow the demands of commodity production to dictate how they live.

What Marx describes with the concept of commodity fetishism aims to explain the specific form of alienation that results from capitalist social relations. But, unless they're engaging with Marxist ideas, people are unlikely to understand this. For most people the term 'alienation' is just as meaningful and may be easier to relate to.

You could argue, in fact, that the imprecision of the term 'alienation' is appropriate, and a good thing, because the alienation described by commodity fetishism is experienced in complicated ways by each individual in how they relate to the people they work with, or work for, and in their sense of disconnection from the society they are part of. Marxism can engage with those feelings of alienation, and explain how, in important ways, they relate to capitalism.

The kind of alienation that Marx was concerned with, as with Hegel, relates to a conception of the world as being one unified, changing whole in which each part relates to everything else. Alienation refers to the way that a part of this whole appears to exist as something separate. If alienation is viewed in this way, then there's another form of alienation which is fundamental to human existence – capitalist or otherwise – and to which Marx paid little attention. This form of alienation, however, had been investigated in great depth two and a half thousand years earlier.

3. SELF SEARCHING

One of the core teachings of Buddhism is the 'three marks of existence' (also known as the 'three characteristics of conditioned phenomena'). These are: *anicca*, which, thankfully, has the uncontroversial translation 'impermanence'; *anatta*, which is variously translated as 'no-self', 'not-self' or 'non-self'; and *dukkha*, which, for want of something better, I'll generally translate as 'suffering'.

To be honest, I find the listing of these three, in this way, to be confusing. It's not as though they're three independent building blocks; there's a clear relationship between them. You could make the case – as others have, and I will shortly – that no-self is the most significant example, or implication, of impermanence. And the Buddhist teachings make clear that suffering can be caused by the failure to relate appropriately to impermanence and no-self.

It's probably worth mentioning that the Buddha's teachings were handed down orally for several centuries before being written down. The Buddha had to work out all this stuff in his head, and find ways of explaining it that would be memorable. Hence all the numbered lists. In addition, there were different schools that interpreted the teachings slightly differently, many of the details of which no longer exist, and what was finally written down was agreed on by a 'council'. All things considered, what we've ended up with is an impressively coherent explanation of something inherently complicated. But it isn't always easy to make sense of.

By the time all the agreed-upon teachings had been written down, of those schools that had debated the meanings of the teachings, only the

Theravada remained. But, as befits a religion that puts so much stress on impermanence, Buddhist thought did not stand still. The most significant development was known as the Mahayana. Beginning amongst Theravada monks, Mahayana would later form into separate schools of Buddhism.

The Mahayana thinkers did not see themselves as innovators, but rather as providing a restatement of what the Buddha taught. Mahayana is, to put it mildly, complicated, but it's probably fair to say it involved two main developments. Firstly, it argued that earlier Buddhism was too focused on the achievement of awakening for the practitioner. Its ideal was the *bodhisattva*, an enlightened person who is motivated by compassion to bring awakening to all sentient beings. Secondly, it gave more importance to the concept of 'emptiness' (*sunyata*), a concept we'll return to shortly.

When Buddhism spread to the wider world, it did not usually arrive, as some religions have tended to do, declaring, 'Cease your heathen ways, accept our gift of Truth!' It tended more towards an approach of asking, 'Do you see how this way of understanding the world and yourself deepens the way you've been looking at things?' As a result, it often mixed with and became influenced by existing cultures and religions, rather than replacing them.

In Tibet it mixed with shamanist traditions and developed alongside the Bon religion, exchanging ideas, adopting esoteric teachings, developing rites and rituals, searching for reincarnate lamas. In China, the Buddhist path merged with the Taoist way of simplicity and spontaneity and arrived at Chan. And when Chan moved to Japan, the great Chan masters and classic Chan stories became great Zen masters and classic Zen stories, as the translation into Japanese extended beyond the language. Similar processes took place with Korean Seon and Vietnamese Thien.

When it spread to the West, Buddhism came under some generally positive influences, such as new developments in science and psychology, and more questionable influences, like hippies and profit-making opportunities. Indeed, the biases of the Western world have probably resulted in our gaining a distorted image of Buddhism. Whilst some

Westerners may be attracted to the exoticism that can be found in Buddhism, probably the majority – and in particular those likely to write books about it – are more likely to be refugees from religions like Christianity, attracted by a religion they can take seriously without being required to believe in the supernatural.

As a result, the schools that have received the most attention have been those that speak most effectively to such an audience: Theravada, Zen and (despite all the superstitious parts) Tibetan Buddhism. Other schools, such as Pure Land, Nichiren and many others, have received less attention. And even within the schools we're most familiar with, the focus has been on those aspects that Western converts find most amenable.

Given how Buddhism has developed over the centuries, I think it's fair to say that the account I present in this book is fairly typical of the accounts found elsewhere – in the sense that it's wholly inadequate, horribly biased, and many Buddhists would object that it misrepresents some aspects of Buddhism while not paying sufficient attention to others that are essential. Fortunately, if I understand Buddhism correctly, the most appropriate way for other Buddhists to react to any perceived inadequacies in my understanding or presentation, will not be with annoyance and ill-will, but with acceptance and compassion.

Despite the variety that exists within Buddhism, I can't imagine many Buddhists would object to the idea that impermanence is the most fundamental of the 'three marks'. According to Buddhism, no physical or mental object is permanent. Everything is a formation or fabrication (*sankhara*) – everything has a dependent origination, comes into being, changes and ceases to be.

This impermanence is part of why desire causes suffering: the things we want to get, or to keep, are all unstable, unreliable, impermanent. In some ways, of course, we want change. We want to gain things that we lack, to become something we're not, to escape aspects of the present that we dislike. We want the present moment to be other than it is. But then, when we've got the change we want, we want the change to stop. We don't want to lose what we have. We are always dissatisfied.

I don't think this aspect of impermanence is difficult to appreciate, but matters become a lot more complicated when we turn to the impermanence that was most significant for the Buddha. This is an impermanence which is more difficult to understand and, to the extent you understand it, to accept – that we have no permanent or persisting 'self'; there is no part of us that is continuing to be us, or that we are continuing to be, even as everything else changes.

One of the most significant moments in Western philosophy arrived when Descartes was paying close attention to the nature of experience, much as the Buddha had before him. While the Buddha's focus had been on understanding the nature of suffering, Descartes' was on the question of what, if anything, he could truly know with confidence. His conclusion was one of the most famous statements in philosophy: cogito, ergo sum – I think, therefore I am. While he couldn't be sure about the relation of his thoughts to any external reality, he could at least be sure that he was a thinking thing.

Like Descartes, the Buddha had paid close attention to his experience – but doing so led him to the opposite conclusion. As he watched his experience unfold, he could see nothing that could be considered a self. There was no thing that continued to be him from moment to moment, only a process of change. There were thoughts, but no thinker.

I suspect most people are likely to have more sympathy with Descartes' point of view than the Buddha's. We all have a sense that we have a core self that holds steady through life, that we are continuing to exist from moment to moment, that there's something thinking our thoughts, experiencing our experiences. After all, when I said about the Buddha, that 'he could see no self', what was that 'he' that I was referring to? Was that not 'him', the thinker who thought he had no self?

From the Buddhist point of view, 'he', like everyone else, was a particular person. But each person consists of different parts, all of which are changing, none of which can be seen as a persistent self. Buddhism views sentient beings as consisting of five *skandhas*, or groupings, namely: form (*rupa*), sensations or feelings (*vedana*), perceptions (*sanna*), mental formations (*sankhara*), and consciousness (*vinnana*). Some accounts of Buddhism devote a lot of explanation to how each of these should be understood. Needless to say, the original meanings don't translate simply into English. I'm not convinced that the details are what matter. The choice of how to divide up the person, or even how many divisions to include, no doubt reflects the understanding that existed at the time. You could make an argument for choosing differently. What matters is that, however you divide a person up, you can find no part that can be considered a separate, distinct persisting self.

So where does a continuous sense of self come from? For a Buddhist, a person remains the same person due to the processes of cause and effect in which these different parts interact and develop. We have a sense of self because of the way in which our experience of the present moment is created by the moment just gone and, in turn, gives rise to the next moment. Walpola Rahula provides a useful description of this – clarifying, as he does so, how it's possible for a Buddhist to believe in rebirth despite there being no self to be reborn:

> As there is no permanent, unchanging substance, nothing passes from one moment to the next. So quite obviously, nothing permanent or unchanging can pass or transmigrate from one life to the next. It is a series that continues unbroken, but changes every moment. The series is, really speaking, nothing but movement. It is like a flame that burns through the night: it is not the same flame nor is it another. A child grows up to be a man of sixty. Certainly the man of sixty is not the same as the child of sixty years ago, nor is he another person. Similarly, a person who dies here and is reborn elsewhere is neither the same person, nor another ... It is the continuity of the same series. The difference between death and birth is only a thought-moment: the last thought-moment in this life conditions the first thought-moment in the so-called next life, which, in fact, is the continuity of the same series. During this life itself, too, one thought-moment conditions the next thought-moment.[1]

The most fundamental reason we suffer from feelings of dissatisfaction is not because the things we desire are impermanent, but because we have no persistent self that can gain or become or lose anything. Since we think of ourselves as remaining the same self, there always seems to be the possibility of being something better, of having something more. There's always something to desire and never a point to be reached where you have everything you could want or are everything you could be. If we accept there is no persistent self, we can experience the changing world with no sense of attachment to what's impermanent, no desire that it should be something other than it is.

In describing no-self, early Buddhist texts sometimes refer to the skandhas that make up a person as being 'empty' of a self. The Mahayana schools of Buddhism generalised this way of seeing things, applying it to the impermanence of all parts of the world. The concept of emptiness is seen as the fundamental reality of existence. Understanding anything – whether a person or any other part of the world – means recognising that it is not a single, separate thing, it has no essence or self, it consists of different parts that are changing and interacting.

Emptiness is an odd term and, like so much of Buddhism, sounds regrettably negative. It isn't meant to imply that 'there is nothing there'. Rather, things that appear self-evident or self-contained, actually can't be understood in isolation. Nothing can exist as a separate 'thing in itself'; this is the sense in which it's empty. But this doesn't mean that there is less there than at first appeared, but rather that there's more to it – to understand any part of the world, you have to understand its relation to everything else.

Emptiness is seen as relating to 'dependent origination' – everything exists dependent on other things. If we understand emptiness, then we can see that every 'thing', every distinct conception, is a kind of illusion. In other words, the sense that it is something separate is an illusion: everything is in fact a part of an unfolding process, inseparable from its context and all the other apparently separate 'things' with which it interacts, which it is a part of, or which are part of it.

The concept of emptiness serves a useful purpose in bringing together no-self and impermanence so that they can be seen as a way of looking at everything. This does carry the potential danger, however, of obscuring why earlier Buddhist teachings focused on the emptiness of the self. They did so because the illusion of having a persistent self is far more significant than the illusion of persistence in other objects. It's one thing to see that a house or a tree is empty, impermanent, made up of parts and without an intrinsic nature or essence. But seeing the emptiness of your self is far more consequential.

One possible way to clarify both the idea of emptiness and why its application to the sense of self is particularly important is to consider this seemingly simple assertion: it's logically impossible for anything to simultaneously change and remain the same. If something changes, then it does not remain the same; if something remains the same, then it does not change.

While these claims may not seem controversial, we constantly describe the world in ways that contradict them. Suppose, for example, I describe how Mount Lamington in Papua New Guinea stood for centuries, covered in dense vegetation and forming a familiar part of the landscape. And then, in 1951, it unexpectedly became the site of a major volcanic eruption. That description is all about the same thing – Mount Lamington – and yet, the whole point is to describe an event which most people would recognise involved that same thing changing rather significantly. Or suppose I tell you that yesterday my printer was working fine, but now it's broken. Again – same thing, the printer, but regrettably not the same. Or if I point out that the guy in the flat above mine is not as annoying as he used to be – same guy, but changed for the better. You get the idea.

The reason we're continually making statements like these, that refer to how the 'same thing' is not the same as it was, and why it's perfectly reasonable and meaningful to do so, is because all the 'things' we talk about are in fact processes. Or rather, sub-processes – parts of the process of the changing world.

In attempting to simplify, or make practical, our interaction with, and thinking about, the world, we divide it up into neatly distinguished 'things' and see change as the interaction between them, when in reality they're all part of the same changing process.

Another way of saying this is that we try to work out the best way to conceptualise changing reality. We abstract those processes that seem most distinct and meaningful, and conceptualise them as separate things. Where we go wrong is not in using concepts, but in mistakenly seeing what they refer to as being distinct and separate, not recognising that they are, in the Buddhist sense, empty. Bertell Ollman makes the same point, with reference to Marx:

> All thought and study of the whole (Marxism included) begins by breaking it down into manageable parts. Marx's criticism, therefore, is not based on the fact of abstraction, but on the character of the parts abstracted and, more especially, on the view of them as absolute, natural and finished, rather than – as in the case of Marx's abstractions – relative, historically specific and incomplete.[2]

When applied to mountains, or printers, this might not seem a big problem, and the guy upstairs would probably be fine with the idea that he's changed for the better. But when we apply it to that sense we have that there's a core part of us which remains who we really are, then the situation becomes more confusing. If we have such a self, it can't both change and remain the same. Perhaps, unlike everything else in the world, it really does remain unchanged. Perhaps we are all blessed with a unique, unchanging, eternal self or soul. If this is the case, however, then it's surely worth asking a question that people who believe this, oddly, don't tend to ask: why would such an unchanging self or soul be seen as a valuable thing to have?

Presumably, it would have come into being, or been put into place, at birth, or conception, or some time in between. It would then remain exactly what it was on arrival, while you transition into a walking, talking, fully participating member of society. It would be untroubled by your adolescent angst, unruffled by your entry into adult life. It would remain oblivious to your mid-life crisis, unconcerned by your descent into senility. And then, after you died, if you'd been a good girl or boy, it would get to go to heaven, or be reborn in a happier or better person, where it would remain completely unaffected by its new situation. Well, whoop-de-doo!

Excuse me if I can't quite see why I'd be particularly thrilled to be in possession of such an unchanging self or soul. Why would I see it as any more worth treasuring than my appendix or my tonsils, or the fillings in my teeth? Actually, that's not fair to the fillings in my teeth – if you've ever lost a filling, you'll know how annoying that can be.

The point is, if a 'self' is worth having, it must be affected by the events of your life. But if it's affected, then it changes, and if it changes, then how can it be the thing that you remain, that you continue to be from birth to death? How could you say, 'Well, admittedly, my body has completely changed, and it's true that my thinking has developed, but I remain the same person because of this self, which has also gone through quite a few changes?' Does the self have its own unchanging mini-self that marks it out as the same self? You can't be simultaneously a thing going through changes (which is to say, a process of change) and, at the same time, a thing separate from that process that is experiencing the change.

The whole reason we value having a self makes no sense. If a self is something unchanging, then it's totally uninteresting. Why would you want to have it? Why would you want to be it? If it does change, then it's not remaining the same thing, not providing any basis to view it as the core of what makes you who you are. We value it because we instinctively think of it as both changing and remaining the same. But if it existed, it could not do both.

This is why no-self and emptiness are not realisations of something lacking, but of something liberating. It's only because things have no permanent existence that the possibility of change exists. We and the 'things' around us are not static, not disconnected. We are constantly changing possibilities.

Developments in philosophy and science over recent centuries have led many people to adopt something similar to the Buddhist understanding of no-self. In the eighteenth century, David Hume argued for a 'bundle theory' of the self, which has much in common with the Buddhist description of skandhas. Today, the majority of philosophers subscribe to some understanding that questions the idea of a persistent self.

The most notable difference between modern philosophers and the Buddha is not so much in the details of how they understand the self, but in the conclusions drawn – or not drawn – about the implications for people's lives. Some philosophers suggest that rejecting the idea of a self will affect how you experience your life and your relationship to the world, but their arguments are presented only as an intellectual case, and one that few people are even likely to encounter. For the Buddha, the aim, one might say, was not only to interpret the way we relate to our sense of self in different ways, but to change it.

Among scientists who study the brain and how it relates to experience and behaviour, the consensus opinion also rejects any idea of the self having a distinct, continuing existence. A deeper understanding of the brain, however, although it has provided valuable information, has not necessarily led to a deeper understanding than that developed by Buddhism. A good demonstration of this is the book *No Self, No Problem: How Neuropsychology is Catching Up to Buddhism* by Chris Niebauer, who is himself a neuropsychologist who, I'd suggest, has failed to fully catch up to Buddhism.

Niebauer's focus is on the way the left brain is constantly seeing patterns and creating narratives – and sometimes getting things wrong. The sense of having a persistent self is one of those mistakes. All such mistakes lead him to the same conclusion: 'Simply by becoming aware of the left brain's propensity to see patterns, we can begin to take them less seriously.'[3] Anything that strikes us as 'a problem' can just be shrugged off as something that isn't real, as being no more than a construct of the brain. It seems to me that in saying this, Niebauer is making his own mistake and failing to appreciate what the Buddha was arguing. The account of dependent origination given by Guy Newland (using the alternative translation 'dependent arising') makes the mistake clear:

> Dependent arising means that things come into being in dependence upon causes and conditions. Understanding dependent arising correctly refutes the idea that things exist in and of themselves

– because they must depend on other things. In the same moment, it also refutes the nihilist extreme – because it shows that things do arise, they do come into existence, and they affect one another. Thus, Tsong-kha-pa advises that if you think that you may have found the profound view of emptiness, you should check to see if you have negated too much.[4]

Niebauer, surely, has negated too much. The story we tell ourselves about who we are may not be a perfect reflection of reality. It may include significant illusions of a kind, but it's an attempt to conceptualise something real. The pattern we're trying to conceptualise really exists. We're attempting to understand the changing person that we are. The ideas that you, I and Niebauer have about ourselves and each other may be, to varying degrees, inadequate, but they're ideas about real people whose actions and thoughts have consequences and can't be shrugged off as nothing but the left brain telling itself stories. Just because a person has no self does not mean they're not consequential, nor that they have 'no problems', only that any problems they have can be either dealt with or accepted, without needing to cause dukkha.

Philosophers, neuropsychologists, and many people who've been exposed to their ideas, as well as countless people who've been exposed to Buddhist ideas in the past, have accepted that there is no self. Frankly, there's something strange about how easily some people are persuaded. You'd think people would be more resistant to the idea, even distressed by it. Much of the discussion of the idea fails to acknowledge just what a profoundly significant realisation the non-existence of a self really is.

A comparison might help to clarify how odd this is. Suppose somebody, ever since they were old enough to understand the idea, has believed in God. The way they relate to the world, the way they find meaning in it, is intimately bound up with this belief. If they somehow became convinced, by an argument, or in some other way, that their belief in God had always been an illusion, everyone would expect this to be a significant event in their lives, wouldn't they? We'd be unlikely to casually assert, 'No God, no need to worry about damnation'. We might want to argue it, but with some sensitivity. By contrast, it's striking how many Buddhists and others present the non-existence of the self as though it's nothing but getting rid of a burden, with no sense that we might feel we're losing something that seems important to us.

Hopefully, most people who lose their belief in God come to feel that it's not so great a loss as it might at first seem. Hopefully, they come to view their previous belief in an illusion as being less desirable than a more realistic engagement with the world as they now understand it, and to realise that their lives can be just as, or more, meaningful without that belief. However the realisation affected them, you wouldn't expect the change to take place as though it were nothing more than losing a philosophical argument.

But why is our belief in a persistent self seen as less significant than a belief in an external God? If you've assumed, all of your life, that you have a self and that it's an important part of how you relate to the world, and you realise it is in fact an illusion, surely this should provoke at least as much – for want of a better term – soul-searching. Perhaps part of the difference is that the belief in God, however early it's adopted, however much its truth is taken for granted, is an explicit idea that has to be learned. The significance of ceasing to believe it is therefore obvious. In contrast, the sense of self is so unconscious that it's hard to grasp what it means to have it and what it would really mean to lose it.

Part of the problem in addressing this subject is the ambiguity of the word 'self'. I keep referring to the 'persistent self', because the way we use the word 'self' is inconsistent. It's often used in the same sense as 'identity' or 'person'.

Developments in the social sciences have included many discussions of the self – the socially constructed self, how the self changes over time, the way we have a different sense of self in different social situations, and so on. If they followed the logic of their own arguments, then these accounts would reject the sense of a self in the same way that Buddhism does. Indeed, it's easy to make the mistake of thinking they're saying the same thing. But it's really not the case. They describe how the 'self' changes, while continuing to imply that there's somehow a persistent 'self' that's experiencing the change.

People write or read about the changing self, with a sense that they have a self that starts the writing or reading, and that then explains or learns about how the self changes, and after having learned more about the nature of itself, that same self now understands itself better – it has changed, but it's still the same self!

In a sense, it's unreasonable to criticise, because you and I are doing much the same thing. If you accept that there is no persistent self, can you honestly claim that you have no sense that it is the same 'you' that now understands the nature of what you are in a different way to how 'you' used to? Has the way of experiencing the self that you've taken for granted your whole life really been replaced with a sense of yourself as an unfolding process?

It seems to me that the best we can claim is that we know there's an illusory sense of self we're failing to let go of. I don't know how to let go of the sense that there's a persistent me, inside here, being critical of these writers who talk about the changing self while implying that the self that's changing is somehow the same persistent self. It's a habit that the constantly changing process of me seems unable to let go of. How about you?

One approach to dealing with this problem has been formalised in Buddhism, especially Mahayana Buddhism, as the 'two truths doctrine'. This suggests that reality has to be understood both at the conventional or provisional level, in which we talk about objects and everyday inter-actions, and at the ultimate level, in which everything is empty. Person-ally, I'd suggest that 'two truths' is an unfortunate way of describing this, because it's really one truth understood in two ways or on two levels, but you can see how the distinction is worth making.

The Buddha was faced with the problem that he had to try to do two things at once. He wanted to teach people that they lacked any persistent self, but the people he wanted to teach would inevitably be interpreting what he said from the perspective of their own sense that they had a self. Inevitably, much of what he taught could be interpreted in a way that ignored the 'ultimate truth'; it was expressed with words and concepts that could reinforce the very illusions he wanted to undermine. It's an

unavoidable result of the need to use concepts and language. Every
noun summons up a conception of a separate thing. Every pronoun
conjures up a persistent self. This is true for 'me' and it's true for 'you'.
Even when you're told that you have no self, the very words seem to
imply otherwise.

It's useful to compare the illusion of a self with two other aspects of the
world that are more 'empty' than they appear. In these cases, as with the
illusion of the self, the reality is counter-intuitive, and we gain from
seeing reality more clearly. There are, however, significant differences. It
would seem appropriate to start with a comparison to those most 'solid'
of 'objects' – solid objects! Those things that you pick up or put down
or throw around or trip over or interact with in other ways that would
suggest their solidity is undeniable.

They appear solid, but in reality they're mostly empty. Not only in
the Buddhist sense, but in the hard science sense. Anyone who isn't
strangely sceptical or ignorant of science will know that solid objects are
made up of atoms. Many will also be familiar with one of those meta-
phors that tries to make the strange reality of atoms more conceivable.
For example, if you were to expand an atom to the size of a football field,
it would consist of a nucleus about the size of a golf ball in the centre,
and a few electrons circling around it, out to the edge of the field. Everything else is empty space (or, possibly, not exactly empty space, but
energy waves, or probabilities or something equally not solid).

All those seemingly solid things – your body, the book (or digital device) you're reading, your clothes, the floor beneath you, the bricks and
mortar around you – are all primarily nothing. There are subatomic particles that can pass through all that stuff like it wasn't there. It's valuable
to see past the surface appearance to that deeper reality. If scientists had
not done so, then much of the technology we enjoy today could not have
been created. But for most of us – and indeed for those scientists themselves – in everyday life, the 'illusion' of solidity is a perfectly adequate
way to perceive things.

It could reasonably be questioned whether this example of 'emptiness' can usefully be described as an illusion at all. There is a deeper

reality, but in our everyday lives, the solid objects around us behave just as you'd expect them to. You could see their solidity and their emptiness as perfectly compatible. There's a good reason why we perceive them as solid, and it's a good thing that we do. If we could see the deeper reality, we'd see nothing but a sea of particles flowing through time, which could hardly be described, or experienced, as 'seeing more clearly'.

When somebody learns that solid objects are almost entirely empty, nobody expects them to react by walking on tiptoe, or lying down spreadeagled, or engaging in whatever other behaviour seems least nonsensical as a way to minimise the likelihood of falling through the floor. By contrast, when Buddhists explain the almost equally counter-intuitive reality that people have no self, they absolutely expect people to adjust their way of relating to the world to take this realisation into account. How realistic is this? Nobody suggests it's easy, but the whole Buddhist path is about working out how best to relate to the world given this counter-intuitive realisation.

Some might argue that it's reasonable to treat the illusion of having a self in the same way that we do the solidity of physical objects. It's an interesting insight, and worth thinking about – not just for a few specialists like scientists, but for everyone thinking about how it makes sense to relate to the world. But just as physical objects are generally best treated as solid, perhaps, in our everyday lives, it's sensible to treat our 'selves' as though they persisted.

The sense of a self came into being for a reason. An important part of becoming a human being is distinguishing between yourself and the rest of the world. Somewhere between being a baby that realises those two things with the five sticky-out things waving around in front of its face can be made to move just by wanting them to, whereas all those other objects out there don't respond in the same way, and being a toddler who knows the right kind of sad face that will get Mum to tell one more bedtime story, the illusion of a self gets mixed up with the important understanding of how to relate to the rest of the world.

The sense of having a self would seem to lie somewhere between experiencing solid objects as solid and learning to believe in God. It developed as we began to interact with the world, but it's possible to imagine being without it. So it should be more realistic to lose one's sense of having a self than it is to expect to walk through walls. On the other hand, the sense of having a self continues even if you've intellectually rejected the idea, in a way that would not be the case (or at least not to the same extent) with something like a belief in God. So the question would seem to be whether, given the difficulty, it's worth trying to lose that sense of self?

We have some evidence available to us that earlier Buddhists lacked, but what it tells us is contradictory. People with some kinds of brain damage or who've undergone brain surgery have, in some sense, lost their sense of self. But far from being a positive development, it seems to be experienced as distressing. It makes it more difficult for them to relate to the world. Some might see this as demonstrating that Buddhism's aim of letting go of the illusion of self is misguided. But that would be to ignore the fact that the Buddha, and many Buddhists since, have experienced something they saw as losing the self, and clearly experienced it as liberation. Perhaps what this implies is that the sense of self is more complicated than early Buddhists had any reason to recognise. But even if this is the case, the Buddhist view is surely valuable and worth investigating.

Another example of something that appears to have a more independent existence than is actually the case is, of course, the capitalist market. It's nothing other than people relating to each other in a particular way, yet it appears as something beyond people's control that determines how they have to relate to each other. Like the solidity of objects and the persistence of self, the capitalist market came into existence for good reasons. It served a useful function. It provided a way for economic production and distribution to become more socially integrated.

I suggested at the end of the previous chapter that both the market and the self are examples of alienation. I think this is reasonable, since they both involve a part of our interconnected, changing reality appearing as though it's something separate. There are, however, big differences. The market appears as something alienated from us. So overcoming that alienation, and taking more conscious control of the economy, implies regaining something. The self, on the other hand, we don't experience as something alienated *from* us, but as *what we feel we actually are!*

Because we experience ourselves as being that core, unchanging self, everything we actually are – experiences, actions, thoughts, feelings – seem accidental, arbitrary. We can imagine our self existing in completely different circumstances, being a better or happier person, having more possessions, doing more enjoyable things. The reality of what we actually are can seem lacking by comparison. In a sense, it's everything we actually are that is experienced as alienated from the 'self' that we think we are – as actions the self does while imagining doing something else, experiences it has while imagining it could be having different experiences.

The changes that would be needed to overcome these two forms of alienation are also completely different. Buddhism suggests that the intellectual understanding of no-self needs to be deepened by practices such as meditation and mindfulness, by changing our habitual way of thinking and feeling, so that the illusions that cause attachment and discontent can be overcome. But no amount of meditation is going to overcome the alienation of capitalism.

In one sense, the market has more in common with solid objects than with the self – it really exists separately from the experience of individual people. Objects appear solid because of the nature of material reality. The market appears out of our control because it's a social reality created by society as a whole, separate from each individual. The only way it's possible to truly escape the alienated nature of capitalist society is if enough people come to understand the nature of capitalism and work together to change the way society is organised.

Neither form of alienation would be easy to overcome, but the Buddhist challenge is surely greater. Buddhism suggests that it's possible to become completely 'awakened' and let go of the illusion of self. It's difficult to judge how realistic this is – whether it would be possible for anyone, let alone you or me, to go through life with no sense at all of a persistent self. There's no question, however, that it's possible for society to do without capitalism. Society existed without it for most of human history. Even in the last century, there were nations that managed to develop their economies without it for decades.

Critics of Marxism would point out, of course, that all those economies ended up failing (or surviving in a state that it would be difficult to describe as success). They'd argue that, whilst simpler societies may have managed without capitalism, it's the only way for a complex economy to work. Anyone suggesting that it's possible to replace capitalism will be told that the attempt to do so has already been tried and it failed.

Generally speaking, when people try to do something but fail, the most common response is to suggest they should learn from experience, if possible, and then try again. If, for example, someone tries to run a marathon, or to run for public office, or to run a profitable company, but they fail, if they try but fail to cure cancer, or to throw a crumpled up piece of paper into a waste paper basket, to form a logical argument or a successful drum and base combo, to remain consistent or sober, that sort of thing, I think most people would agree - that's the kind of advice they're likely to receive.

In the case of trying but failing to replace capitalism with something better, the consensus seems to be that the most appropriate response is to conclude it's impossible. It's a point of view. As you may have suspected, I incline more toward the approach of 'learn from experience and then try again.' If my reasons for doing so aren't clear enough, hopefully they'll become clearer in future chapters.

4. VISIBLE HANDS

Imagine you're lucky enough to have had a secure permanent job for years, and every year there's been a friendly meeting with your boss where your work progress has been reviewed and you've been given the details of your latest pay rise. This year, you attend the meeting, as per usual. You avail yourself of the cup of tea and the chocolate hobnob. You go through the ritual of mock-humility, as your boss heaps praise on the sterling work that you and your team have been doing. But then, your boss leans back, with a heavy sigh, comments on how, sadly, things are not all they might be in the wider world, and goes on to explain how the company's accountants have done the required accounting, and economic consultants have been suitably consulted, and the regrettable but unavoidable conclusion has been drawn: there will be no pay rise this year.

Most people in such a situation would, I imagine, feel somewhat conflicted. The lack of a pay rise can't be literally unavoidable, can it? There must be some leeway, some wiggle room. You could point out why you deserve that pay rise, but your boss has already conceded as much. If you were to question the conclusions of the accountants and economic consultants that the company has so conscientiously employed, would your boss not be justified in feeling you'd strayed beyond your own area of expertise?

This is much the same situation that's faced by any left-wing person who has somehow failed to equip themselves with a thorough grounding in economic theory, and yet dares to suggest that perhaps society could be a little fairer, only to have someone respond with all the assurance of a kindergarten teacher, that the economy doesn't work like that; redistribution is a lovely idea, but the economy simply won't weather it. The measures would backfire. The market would react badly. It can't be done. It would not be sensible.

This is the great achievement of those who managed to convince the world that economics is an objective science, like physics or chemistry, that can judge claims about economic possibilities as being unambiguously right or wrong. In a sense, we all know it's not true. Come election time, politicians don't generally spend a lot of time debating the boiling point of water or how, exactly, photosynthesis works. They do argue about economic policy – a lot. Because we all know there are choices to be made. And yet, the idea that there are definitively correct answers to economic questions persists, having its effects on how people talk about and understand what's possible.

It's striking how even some of the most well-informed people seem to accept this idea. Noah Harari, for example, in his bestselling book *Sapiens: A Brief History of Humanity* casually comments that, 'Unlike physics or economics, history is not a means for making accurate predictions.'[1] You'd think an Oxford educated historian might recognise that the subject matter of economics is not quite the same sort of thing as the subject matter of physics, wouldn't you?

Actually, there is some indication that he does. In the following chapter, he refers a few times to how science is shaped by 'political, economic and religious interests'.[2] So on the one hand, he thinks economics has more in common with physics than with history, yet, at the same time, he thinks the way it relates to science is similar to religion and politics? Is Harari confused, or does this reflect something intrinsically confusing about economics? Or both? If Harari is confused, how is the average voter supposed to make sense of it?

It's true that there are limits to what's economically possible. Nature imposes some and, in a market economy, the market adds some more. But economists and politicians are adept at presenting the fact that there are limits as though it's the same thing as saying we have no choice at all. Time and again, discussions that reflect opposing values and priorities end up morphing relentlessly into arguments about who has the 'correct' understanding of how the economy works, between the person who understands the demands of the market and the person who's in denial about it, between the hard-headed realist and the fool who thinks you can make the world a fairer place.

If you're a left-wing politician in this situation, hoping to convince an audience of your case, it's tempting to argue on the terms presented – to insist that your opponent is wrong about how to run the economy and that your approach is the right one. You could point out how austerity makes no economic sense because if everybody 'tightened their belts' so much that nobody buys anything, then nobody could sell anything either and the economy would grind to a halt. Or you could point out that greater redistribution of wealth is good for the economy because the lowest earners are more likely to spend their money, which will create more demand.

These are good arguments. Unfortunately, that doesn't necessarily mean people will be persuaded by them, especially after your opponent shakes their head at your foolishness, and presents their own argument couched in confusing economic jargon, insisting that policies like yours in the past have led to disaster. To which you respond by pointing out that, no, that was due to wider economic events in the global economy and besides, your opponent's policies haven't been working because look at these growth figures. To which they respond by saying, no, the figures would be even worse under your policies because consider these figures, backed up by this authoritative sounding economic body. And anyone still listening will likely be struggling to work out how to judge who is presenting the most objectively accurate analysis.

You could, instead, challenge the framing that there's only one correct answer on how the economy should be run. Admit that, yes, your opponent's proposals are one way to run capitalism, and your proposals are another. The question is – who is it going to work for? But it's understandable if you're reluctant to concede that your opponents might know what they're doing, in a context where everyone is insisting there's only one correct way to run the economy, and that it isn't your way.

There is an alternative approach to thinking about all this, although, if you're planning to stand for election, or hoping to be invited by a respectable broadcaster to take part in a discussion about economics, you might want to steer well clear of it. It involves considering a non-market economy. I don't mean advocating for one – we'll get round to that later – but rather, using the idea of a non-market economy as a thought experiment, a point of comparison, which, as it turns out, can help to reveal how the market serves to obscure the underlying economic reality.

Let's revive that imaginary society from Chapter 2, with its use-values that get consumed and its optional production of additional wealth, and let's flesh it out a little. For the sake of simplicity, we'll make it fairly small, say a few thousand people. And let's isolate it from any wider economy; perhaps it's located in a remote valley or on a rogue moon. The economy might be organised through some sort of communal or democratic mechanism, or maybe by a benevolent or despotic dictator, or a supercomputer. Whatever the details, the requirements are basically the same.

Whoever (or whatever) is organising the economy needs first of all to take stock of the resources that are available. The society we're considering has its fair share of resources. There are natural resources like farmland, water, mineral resources and so on. There's the labour-power of the people, with their knowledge and skills and ability to learn or develop those skills. There are houses and workplaces. There are tools and machinery and the ability to mend them or create more. There are various other things.

What's required is to work out how to use and organise these resources so as to provide everything the people need, and also a reasonable amount that they don't *need* but that could make their lives more enjoyable and fulfilling. Then all the things that are produced, and the services that are provided, have to be shared out in a way everybody is happy with or, failing that, in a way everybody is willing to accept. Finally, all this has to be done in a way that is sustainable over the long term. Small-scale communities have done this sort of thing throughout history. The same essential requirements apply to the economy of any society.

Now, let's return to the capitalist economy in which you're actually living, and suppose that some politician or social movement advocates for a change: the provision of childcare, freely available, on demand, to anyone who wants it, twenty-four hours a day, every day of the year. I don't have to tell you what the reaction would be. Every politician and economist, indeed every reasonable, right-thinking person would agree, 'We can't afford it.' Even those more in favour of the proposal would try to sound realistic, and ask, 'How could we afford it?'

If you consider the proposal in terms of the simple economy we just described, however, it's clear that the idea that 'we can't afford it' is utter hogwash. We know it's hogwash, because it's already the case (or you'd certainly hope it is) that every child who needs it has an adult responsible for them twenty-four hours a day, every day of the year. The resources are already being allocated to provide the equivalent of what is being proposed. It's just that, for the most part, they're being allocated through families, which probably means, in particular, by mothers, but also by fathers, grandparents, siblings, friends, and so on.

What's being proposed is not the allocation of resources to something that wasn't being provided before (the most obvious implication of 'we can't afford it'), but the reorganisation of something that's already being provided. And far from being a less efficient way to provide it (the other possible implication of 'we can't afford it'), it's difficult to see how the suggested reorganisation could fail to be *more* efficient. By taking advantage of the division of labour, more children would be looked after in larger groups for more of the time, so the total amount of labour required would be less.

The benefits are easy enough to see. Parents who wished to do so could more easily take part in education or develop their careers, and contribute to society in a way other than looking after their children. Other parents could have a night out or a weekend away, without having to work out how to handle the childcare. Any parent who needed a break to recover their mental or physical wellbeing could do so. No child would be stuck being looked after by a parent who's at the end of their tether. People would have more freedom and choices, and less work would be required. Everyone would win! Why would a society not do this?

In theory, there's no reason this could not be done in a capitalist society. After all, capitalist societies already provide free schooling. In fact, some of the more reasonable of the more successful capitalist nations do provide free or subsidised childcare – to some people, some of the time. But any move to introduce or extend such schemes will be resisted by capitalists, not because there's something intrinsically problematic about free childcare, but because capitalists themselves indirectly benefit from the free childcare that's provided by their employees or relatives of their employees, and by other workers, outside of the hours for which those workers are paid.

From the economic point of view, the task of feeding, looking after and raising the next generation, until they're ready to sell their labour-power, is a necessity. But these activities are also an expression of personal relationships of love and caring. So capitalists can rely on workers to carry out the necessary labour without being paid.

Let's consider another proposal: a fully funded, comprehensive public health service. If none exists, create one. If one already exists, fix all those holes that have either always been there or that have crept in over the years of funding cuts. Include dentistry, social care, mental health, opticians. Provide free prescriptions, glasses (with a decent choice of frames), free parking at hospitals – or free transport to and from hospital. All the things you'd need to be able to say that everyone has equal access to the sort of healthcare everyone should have a right to. Waiting lists no longer than administratively unavoidable. Decent pay for all health workers. You get the idea.

Unlike the childcare example, this would involve devoting more of society's resources to implementing the proposal. Actually, some of this would just be reorganisation, as with childcare, but for the sake of simplicity, let's ignore that and focus on the fact that the allocation of some additional resources would be required. Again, the claim would be made that 'we can't afford it'. But again, the claim would be hogwash, although in this case, slightly diluted hogwash.

The reality is that anything a society is capable of doing, it can literally 'afford to do' – it has the resources. There are only two questions. Not, 'can we afford it?', but, firstly, 'do we want to do it?' – do we want to devote resources to this rather than to something else? And secondly, 'can we organise the resources in such a way as to achieve what we want?'

The first question is perfectly reasonable, and it would absolutely be worth having such debates, perhaps followed by some sort of democratic decision about what members of society would like resources to go towards. And perhaps, if such debates took place, someone might put forward a perfectly good argument explaining why some people should have to wait months for their hip operation, or have to choose between getting a dental check-up and buying shoes for their kids, so that someone else can buy a holiday home in the Algarve or a yacht. It's impossible to know, because any such discussions are shut down before they begin, as economists and politicians declare 'we can't afford it', and their assertion is accepted as though it's an entirely adequate response.

If capitalism worked the way its advocates say it should, then one of the functions of money should be to direct the actual resources of society wherever is most useful or socially desirable. Consumers should be earning money, which they spend on the things they need or want, and in so doing direct that money to the companies that most efficiently produce the most necessary or desirable things. If this isn't happening, that's a reason to intervene in how the system is working, or to consider if there might be a better system.

Can we intervene to make it work better? To a significant degree, clearly we can: in many ways we already do. Only a truly fanatical market fundamentalist would suggest that all schooling should be private or all roads should be toll roads. Capitalism is clearly adaptable. It's capable of providing a free health service. It was capable of providing free university education until politicians managed to convince people that, despite economic growth, it couldn't afford that after all. It can afford a standing army and to build expensive items like nuclear submarines even when the market for them isn't exactly booming.

But governments in a capitalist society will always be influenced by the fact that they're running an economic system that relies on companies making profits. And the taxation required for any sort of public provision will be objected to as undermining the competitiveness of the nation's businesses – or subtracting from the money consumers might have spent on the commodities that capitalists are trying to sell. So, if there isn't sufficient political pressure to do otherwise, governments will spend as little on public services as they can, which means that the public services are likely to struggle, which will be presented as proof that public provision doesn't work and that public industries should be privatised so that everyone can benefit from the positive effects of the market.

There are many other examples we might give of how suggestions that clearly make sense from a human perspective come into conflict with what allegedly makes 'economic sense'. For example, it might seem obvious that we should invest in solar or wind energy rather than increase the number of oil wells or coal mines, but if you want to convince the people who matter, you better be able to make the case that doing so could also be more profitable.

This approach of standing back from the existing reality of capitalism, and considering society in a more abstract way, can raise other questions about aspects of the economy that are taken for granted. For example, why do we need landlords? We need land, housing and so on, but what purpose does it serve for some people to own property and to be given a share of resources simply as a reward for that ownership? This isn't a particularly radical or socialist question. Adam Smith talked about how landlords 'love to reap where they never sowed'.[3] John Maynard Keynes looked forward to 'the euthanasia of the rentier'[4] and the creation of an economy where resources weren't siphoned off by people who made no economic contribution.

By 'rentier' Keynes wasn't referring specifically to landlords – although they're the most obvious example – but to all those who derive income purely as a reward for ownership. It's widely recognised that this aspect of capitalism has grown significantly over the past few decades.[5]

Far from carrying out the 'euthanasia of the rentier', government policy has operated more like a rentier recruitment scheme.

Keynes would not have considered those who invest in businesses that engage in useful production as rentiers. But how are such people any more necessary than landlords? If you consider a large manufacturing company for example. Clearly you need the factory, offices, workers, raw materials and so on. But what purpose do the owners or shareholders serve? Everything the company offers to society could be done without them. The only reason they exist is because of the way in which capitalism has developed, and because society has not taken the decision to reorganise in a way that replaces them.

Of course, pointing out problems with capitalism is all very well, but its defenders will point out that no complex economic system is perfect, and despite its problems, capitalism has shown itself capable of producing and distributing the things people need. By contrast, the attempts that have been made to replace capitalism have failed. This is undeniably true, but just as there are many ways to run a capitalist economy, the same is true – arguably even more so, given the lack of market constraints – for a non-capitalist economy. So let's consider one of the attempts that failed: the Soviet Union.

Whilst the failure of the attempt to create a viable communist economy is obviously what's most significant now, it's worth pointing out that, for a long time, matters looked very different. The Soviet Union may have spectacularly failed, but only after it had spectacularly grown in economic and political significance. In 1917, Russia was one of the least economically developed nations in Europe, yet in the space of decades it managed to transform itself into a nation capable of taking on and beating the industrial and military might of Nazi Germany, and then going on to be one of the two 'superpowers' of the Cold War.

During the 1930s, while the leading capitalist economies were mired in economic depression and trying to recover from the crash of 1929, the Soviet Union's rate of growth outpaced anything to be found in the West. This is not to deny that – hidden from the world – there were terrible things happening in the Soviet Union at the time, from purges and gulags to famines. We'll consider the relevance of this shortly. But it doesn't change the significance of the economic advance. Many believers in the idea that capitalism is the epitome of efficiency, and that getting rid of it would result in the economy grinding to a halt, would have been left scratching their heads in confusion.

And this growth continued after the war. Even into the late fifties, many in the Soviet Union were hoping, and many analysts in the West were fearing, that the Soviet Union might overtake the West economically. But it clearly didn't happen. Just when the Soviet Union seemed to be catching up, it began struggling to organise its economy effectively. It could achieve great things where it focused its resources, allowing it, for example, to beat the United States into space, but it struggled to compete on the broader and, for most people, more important task of providing basic consumer goods, let alone developing new ones. So what went wrong?

There's a story about the Soviet Union which I believe is set in the 1960s. It tells how the central planners ascertained that a serious shortage of kettles was likely to develop across the whole of the Soviet Union. Their next five-year plan therefore included requirements for the state manufacturer of kettles to increase production by so many metric tonnes. The state manufacturer of kettles duly swung into action and delivered the requested increase, on time and in full – by changing the manufacturing process so that each kettle weighed slightly more!

The story may be apocryphal, but it does say something meaningful about the nature of the Soviet economy. On the one hand, they had freed themselves from the limitations imposed by the market. They could organise production without having to worry about whether what they were producing would be able to make a profit if it was sold on the market. This was particularly useful during the process of industrialisation and in the creation of the sort of infrastructure and major industries that were needed for a modern economy.

But they'd also lost the mechanisms by which the market enforced efficiency and ensured that products provided their users with something they valued. They'd done away with the incentives and constraints that the market had provided. So the producers didn't have to worry about bankruptcy, and the workers didn't have to worry about unemployment. They'd failed to effectively replace the market incentives and constraints with anything else.

It wasn't just the threats of bankruptcy or unemployment that were missing. In capitalist democracies, people with original and challenging ideas had economic motivation for promoting and pursuing them, and no political reasons not to. By contrast, in the Soviet Union, there was no economic motivation to stand out, and the political system often gave people reason to keep their heads down and try not to be noticed. Gaining attention might mean having more demands put on you without getting any reward. Or worse, if your suggestions were taken as criticisms of the way things were currently being done, you might be seen as a troublemaker and be made to regret it.

The idea of communism is to free society from the dictates of the market mechanism, so that people will have a sense that they're creating their own society, that they're cooperating together to produce a better society for everyone. But this was not the experience of the people of the Soviet Union. They were at least as alienated as people in a liberal democracy. The economy was not their economy; it was a set of instructions handed down from a central apparatus over which they had no control. They weren't working to produce their own world. They were doing what was required to get by.

One conclusion you could draw from all this is that one of the requirements for a functioning post-capitalist economy is meaningful democracy. This is not, I admit, the most obvious conclusion. That award, apparently, goes to 'capitalism is the only economic system that could ever possibly work'. But if we were to accept *that* conclusion, there wouldn't be anything more to say, so let's explore the 'democracy required' conclusion, which is much more interesting.

The reason this conclusion might make sense, is that the politics of a non-capitalist society – including its level of democracy – are relevant to how the economy works in a way that simply isn't the case for a capitalist economy. The whole point of capitalism is that the operation of the economy is to a large extent taken care of by the market. Capitalism doesn't care about the political context in which this happens. Democracy is optional. You'd be forgiven for thinking otherwise, however, because capitalists have done an impressive job of promoting the idea that capitalism somehow encourages or requires democracy.

The very term 'liberal democracy' has somehow become a way of referring to capitalism without mentioning capitalism, and yet implying that capitalism is inevitably democratic (and, as a bonus, 'liberal', which you can take to mean classically liberal, socially liberal or neoliberal according to taste).

It's true that early capitalists demanded more democratic government and an end to aristocratic privilege. But the democracy they were demanding was really only democracy for themselves. It wasn't until there was enough pressure from those excluded from being able to vote, that anything like a universal franchise was put into place. And the contradictory histories of the first capitalist nations – and the capitalist nations that came into being later even more so – clearly show that, when it comes to democracy, capitalism can take it or leave it.

Capitalism worked fine in nations that proudly boasted of their democratic credentials, like Britain or France, but it also worked in nations that were prevented from being democratic, such as the colonies of Britain or France. Capitalism continued to do its thing in Germany while democracy was extended, then destroyed, and then re-instated. It didn't have a problem with South African apartheid. Franco's dictatorship in Spain caused it no apparent problems, and it was only mildly put out by social democratic interventions in Sweden. According to neoliberals, capitalism gained significantly from the overthrow of democracy in Chile and was somewhat improved by the overthrow of tyranny in Iraq. It's now cohabiting happily with the so-called Communist Party of China. In short, the invisible hand has shown itself happy to entwine its fingers with those of any political suitor that comes a-calling, so long as they offer as dowry the legal and infrastructural requirements of capitalism.

If you get rid of the market, however, political choices suddenly become a lot more important. With the invisible hand gone, someone has to get their hands dirty organising the economy in its place. For Marx, this wasn't an unfortunate complication. It was the whole point. Getting rid of the market was a way to make people's political and social choices matter. So the question of how democratic the society is, becomes far more directly relevant to whether the economy will work.

This doesn't mean, of course, that if a post-capitalist society was democratic, then its economy would inevitably work well. There's no proof of this. But neither is there any proof that it wouldn't. The 'communist failures' sadly did not provide us with evidence one way or the other. They only demonstrated something that would not work, something that most of us wouldn't want anyway.

For critics of communism, there are two separate criticisms to be made of the communist nations that have existed: that they were authoritarian, and that their economies failed. But perhaps their economies failed *because* they were authoritarian. The question would then become, was the authoritarianism inevitable? Why or how did it come about?

If capitalists have been surprisingly successful at convincing people that capitalism is democratic, they've been even more successful at convincing people that communism is authoritarian, although in this case they've had a lot of help – from communists.

One contribution some Marxists have made to creating this impression has come from their strange enthusiasm for the phrase 'the dictatorship of the proletariat'. Perhaps in the nineteenth century 'dictatorship' had a different ring to it, but it couldn't have been *that* different, could it? I mean, 'dictator', 'dictate' – you know? I struggle to see why anyone with Marx's aims and values would think it a good slogan around which to organise.

Even if you recognise that the proletariat is supposed to be the majority (which it wasn't in any of the countries that had communist revolutions in the twentieth century), and even if you understand that the 'dictatorship' is supposed to describe a temporary situation until communism is no longer threatened by counter-revolution, it's still difficult to see why anyone would proclaim it as though it were a description of something desirable or something to celebrate, rather than something that might, regrettably, be necessary. To see why it's so inappropriate, you only have to compare it with the sort of political organisation that Marx actually thought desirable.

The best indication of this can be found in *The Civil War in France*, in which Marx defends the Paris Commune of 1871. Marx describes the Commune as, 'the political form at last discovered under which to work out the economic emancipation of labour.'[6] And what Marx found so inspiring is one of the most radical experiments in democracy there's ever been.

The Commune elected councillors by universal suffrage, revocable at short term. And it did the same for all public servants, from magistrates and judges to administrative and educational staff. Furthermore, they were all paid the same wages as other workers. Educational institutions were opened to everyone and freed of interference from church or state. Factories were handed over to their employees to be run as cooperatives.

And yet, in 1891, when *The Civil War in France* was republished for a twentieth-anniversary edition, Engels chose to end his introduction with these words: '...do you want to know what the dictatorship looks like? Look at the Paris Commune. That was the Dictatorship of the Proletariat.'[7] Seriously, 'dictatorship'? Did it not occur to anyone that there might be a more appealing and appropriate word?

Perhaps I'm giving too much importance to the phrase 'the dictatorship of the proletariat'. Whatever its significance, there's certainly a far more obvious reason why people might have come to associate communism with authoritarianism. Namely, that every state that was seen as communist in the twentieth century could be described, not unreasonably, as authoritarian!

Any Marxist would feel a little discomfort at using the word 'communist' to describe these nations, given how little they had in common with the sort of society nineteenth-century communists hoped to see. But given that it's the way they're generally referred to, and that they undeniably have a historical connection with the actual development of communism, I'll continue to use this term.

Given the history of those communist nations, the association of communism and authoritarianism is understandable. Indeed, the critics of communism who are easiest to sympathise with are those who've been genuinely horrified by some of the activities of those authoritarian regimes. What's less easy to understand is the assumption that any future attempt to replace capitalism would take the same political form.

Looking at the authoritarian communist nations of the twentieth century and concluding that if a society decided to replace the market as a way of organising the economy, then it would inevitably be inclined to reject democracy in favour of authoritarianism, makes as much sense as looking at people taking part in a Mexican wave and concluding that, if you sit somebody in a sports stadium, they'll have an irresistible urge to stand up, raise their hands in the air, and sit back down again. Those communist states came into existence in a particular context, and they were connected by particular historical events.

There were two main ways in which communist states came into existence after the Second World War. The countries of Eastern Europe, from which the Soviet Union had recently driven the Nazis back to Germany, found themselves on the communist side of the Iron Curtain. This is not to say that communism was just imposed on them. They all had their own communist movements, of varying strengths and in varying political contexts, and the reputation of those movements – along with that of the Soviet Union – had been enhanced by the part they played in the fight against fascism. But it's hardly a surprise that the political parties that had been aligned with the Soviet Union were the ones that ended up in charge.

The second group of countries joined the communist side in the context of the Cold War. Many of them did so in the context of political struggles for independence from colonial powers. As relatively weak countries, politically and economically, they naturally sought the support of one of the two superpowers. Despite its own history, the United States showed little sympathy for popular movements trying to fight for independence from powerful imperialist nations. The Soviet Union, on the other hand, was happy to support their struggle against powerful capitalist countries. As a result, movements for national independence overlapped with movements for communism. The balance and relationship between the two types of movement varied in different countries, but once such countries gained independence, the Soviet Union had a lot of influence on their political and economic choices. It was not a good influence.

The most significant nation that does not fit neatly into these two groups is China. Although China, too, was strongly influenced by the Soviet Union, there's another important factor that connects China in 1949 with Russia in 1917 – both were relatively undeveloped economies, where peasants still made up the mass of the population. To see why this is important, it's time to look at the communist revolution that you really have to go back to if you want evidence of communism leading to authoritarianism. And it is, indeed, when we look at Russia in 1917 that we find evidence of Marxists having got things seriously wrong, starting with Marx.

Marx saw communism as only being possible because of developments that would already have taken place under capitalism. Capitalism would develop the technology and social organisation that would make it possible to move beyond the market and create a more directly social way of organising the economy. Capitalism would also create a proletariat that would make up the majority of society, a proletariat that would go through the process of uniting and organising in order to advance their collective interests, and in so doing, they would develop a political awareness of the sort of society they wanted to create. When communist revolutions took place, therefore, he assumed they'd happen in the most economically advanced capitalist nations.

Marx was wrong. He wasn't completely wrong. It was in such nations, towards the end of the nineteenth century, that Marxist ideas began to have influence in major political parties. The most significant example was the Social Democratic Party of Germany (SPD), which, in addition to organising politically and in the trade unions, also became a vital part of working-class culture, running its own libraries, newspapers and stores, organising lectures, theatre and music, and setting up social clubs.

The SPD became the largest socialist party in the world, with over a million members, and by 1912 it was the largest party in the German Reichstag.

In reality, the politics of parties like the SPD had been gradually changing, as they played an increasing part in the democratic system within wealthy nations. Party members began to see their role as more about working within capitalism than against it. For a long time, the extent to which this was the case was not clear, but it became so in the most dramatic way with the outbreak of the First World War. The SPD and other socialist and labour parties had organised together in the Second International, and jointly pledged to stand against any war, by uniting the working class of all nations against their national governments. But when war broke out, fearful of losing the position it had gained within Germany, the SPD voted in favour of war credits, effectively siding with its own nation rather than the international working class. Most other members of the Second International followed suit.

After the war, and the collapse of the Second International, 'social democracy' would come to refer to those parties that had rejected the aim of communist revolution in favour of working towards progressive reform within capitalism. It was these reformist social democratic parties that would end up being the main voice for the working class in the major capitalist economies, while the more revolutionary or communist parties became marginalised. There were to be no successful revolutions in the most advanced capitalist nations. The only countries where revolutions were successful were the less developed nations that Marx would have seen as not ready for communism. In a sense, you could argue that Marx was right – the attempt to successfully move beyond capitalism in such countries ended up failing.

In 1898, Russian Marxists founded their own Social Democratic Party. They hoped it would someday be as significant as Germany's. But whilst Germany was one of the most advanced economies in Europe, Russia was one of the least developed. The proletariat made up only a small fraction of the population and was massively outnumbered by the peasantry. So Russia's Social Democratic Party was inevitably far smaller and less influential. It was also illegal and, after 1903, it was split – between the Bolsheviks and the Mensheviks.

Although plenty of people had been talking about the prospects for revolution in Russia, the February revolution – the first of the two revolutions of 1917 – took everyone by surprise. None of the Marxists in Russia, whether Bolshevik or Menshevik, expected the revolution to lead to communism. Rather, they welcomed it as the belated arrival of the sort of bourgeois revolution that had happened decades earlier in more advanced capitalist nations. Their aim was to support and encourage the establishment of a bourgeois democracy, and to build the workers' movement while capitalism developed, creating the conditions where a communist revolution would be possible.

What changed was the arrival back from exile of Lenin, the Bolshevik leader, who had come to the conclusion that the increasingly international nature of capitalism and the specific events of the First World War had changed the situation for Russian Marxists. Lenin believed that the overthrow of capitalism in a country like Russia would serve as the trigger needed to create revolutions in more economically advanced countries like Germany. These countries would then come to the aid of less developed countries, allowing them to overcome the challenges of their economic development.

The political developments over the following months are too complicated to detail here, but as events and arguments unfolded, the majority of Bolsheviks came to agree with Lenin, and in October they led a revolution to establish communist rule. A communist party had taken control in Russia, despite not believing that the country was ready to move beyond capitalism on its own. They focused their efforts on retaining power in Russia and encouraging developments elsewhere. As part of these efforts they brought communist parties together to form a replacement for the collapsed Second International. The Communist International was founded in Moscow in 1919. Its official language, however, was not Russian but German. The expectation was that its headquarters would move to Berlin after the imminent revolution.

Lenin was wrong. He wasn't completely wrong. There were attempted revolutions in Germany[8] and in Hungary.[9] There were uprisings in a number of other European nations.[10] But none succeeded. Within a few years, the Bolsheviks were faced with a task none of them had believed would be possible – to carry through a communist revolution in a nation where the proletariat made up a small percentage of the population, and without the support of other nations.

In their attempts to hold on to power, the Bolsheviks undoubtedly behaved in an authoritarian way. They cancelled planned elections. They acted against striking workers. They even militarily crushed the rebellion of sailors in the port of Kronstadt, who had played an important role in the October revolution and who were demanding many of the same things they had been fighting for then, and which the Bolsheviks were failing to deliver.

Marxists disagree about how to view these events. Some argue that the context in which the Bolsheviks were acting justified their actions. They were in the middle of a civil war, fighting against the 'White Russians' – an alliance of anti-communist forces supported by Britain, France, the United States, and other capitalist nations. Failure would have meant devastation for everyone they aimed to represent. Even the most democratic of nations don't generally go in for elections and toleration of dissent when they're in the middle of a war.

Others argue that some of the Bolsheviks' actions were excessive and only undermined what they claimed to believe in. Even at the time, there were prominent Marxists critical of the Bolsheviks' tactics, many of them struggling to find the right balance between being supportive of the revolution and criticising some of its actions. Rosa Luxemburg, for example, wrote in 1918:

> Socialism in life demands a complete spiritual transformation in the masses ... Social instincts in place of egotistical ones, mass initiative in place of inertia, idealism which conquers all suffering ... No one knows this better, describes it more penetratingly, repeats it more stubbornly than Lenin. But he is completely mistaken in the means he employs. Decree, dictatorial force of the factory overseer, draconic penalties, rule by terror – all these things are but palliatives. The only way to a rebirth is

the school of public life itself, the most unlimited, the broadest democracy...[11]

What is surely undeniable is that the measures taken by the Bolsheviks in this period created the mechanisms and policies that enabled Stalin, after Lenin's death, to develop an ever-increasing level of authoritarianism, pushing through the forced collectivisation of agriculture, increasing purges of those who had played a central role in 1917, and other measures that undermined all the promises that had been made at the time of the revolution.

As politics became increasingly centralised, so the only economic options were to either allow the market to reassert its influence, or to develop a centrally controlled economic system that enforced decisions wherever necessary. So for both political and economic reasons, there was a continuous increase in the size of the state bureaucracy and the Communist Party. Before long, the majority of Communist Party members had not joined a party that was struggling against authoritarian capitalism, but one that was imposing authoritarian communism, and they were less influenced by knowledge of Marxism than by the patronage of Stalin. Being a party member, or part of the bureaucracy, gave people more power in society and more opportunities to exploit that power to their own material advantage, creating new forms of social division.

As I pointed out earlier, there's nothing about capitalism that inevitably leads to democracy. Capitalism does, however, relate to democracy in a unique way. It makes it possible for democracy to play a role in society that would be impossible in a non-capitalist system. It makes it possible to have a meaningful level of democracy without the democratic process being a threat to the power of the most wealthy.

The economy is primarily controlled by the invisible hand of the market. So you can have a multi-party democracy, and so long as all the parties that are electable accept that capitalism is how the economy works, the people with the most wealth can be sure that their wealth – and the power that goes with it – will not be taken away from them. The worst they might have to put up with is having to pay slightly higher taxes or accept a few more trade union rights. It's a price they may be happy to pay in exchange for reinforcing the legitimacy of a system that works so well for them.

The situation in the Soviet Union was very different. Once significant disparities in power and wealth had become established, there was no way they could allow any meaningful democracy. If they had, then an election might have led to those with the most privileges losing the source of their wealth and power, and being reduced to the level of a mere average citizen.

This relationship between the market and democracy reflects the relationship between the market and ideology. The ideology that claims people under capitalism are free and equal is persuasive because it's true! People really do meet as equals in the marketplace, mutually agreeing on terms of exchange for the commodities they're selling. Nobody forces anyone to work for them. It's the operation of the market that ensures people have to work for others. Even the idea of meritocracy has some truth to it. From the point of view of any particular individual, there's nothing technically preventing them from improving their position in society if they have enough skill, talent and luck.

The Soviet Union took its best shot at promoting its own ideology. It told people they were living in a workers' state where everyone was free, and equality had been achieved. Those attempting to sell this message had certain advantages – control over the media, the history of a revolution against autocracy, the 'Great Patriotic War' against fascism. But what they lacked was that magic key that capitalism has – an economic system backing up their claims, disguising the reality of social relations. Workers could see perfectly well that it was not a workers' state, and that they had no say in decisions that affected their lives.

When people feel alienated under capitalism, it isn't clear who or what to blame. They may have a sense of disconnection from society, but the operation of the market seems almost like a natural phenomenon. It's beyond anyone's direct control. The government's role in determining their lives is limited. Their circumstances are the result of 'the way the world works'. Or worse, it's their own fault – they had the same chance as everyone else but failed. They didn't do well enough in school. They failed to market themselves successfully to potential employers.

Alienation for workers in the Soviet Union was different. There was nothing confusing about it. Decisions about their lives were out of their control, and it was clear who actually had the control. The power lay with the same people who were telling them lies about how free and equal they were. No wonder they envied those living under capitalism, where people could choose who to work for without dealing with an oppressive bureaucracy, and where they could choose what to buy from shops that were full of consumer goods.

Before we leave behind the subject of authoritarianism, it's worth considering an expression of it that doesn't attract much attention, let alone condemnation – the authoritarianism of the workplace. Whilst nobody should minimise how bad authoritarian government is, workers in capitalist enterprises – regardless of the form of government they are living under – experience a form of authoritarianism every time they turn up for work.

It's understandable if many people doubt whether the concept of authoritarianism is applicable to the workplace. Under capitalism, economic relations – including the relationship between workers and employers – are not seen as places where concepts like democracy or authoritarianism apply. We're not dealing with an autocratic leader, merely the purchasing power of capital.

Every buyer wants to get as much value for money as possible from what they buy. And the employer has bought the worker's labour-power. For the capitalist, furthermore, it's essential to make as much profit as possible. They're competing with others to see who can stay in business. The employer not only feels entitled to, but is obliged to, exercise close control over the way the labour-power they've purchased is used. They not only decide exactly when work should start and stop, they dictate, as much as they can, exactly what work is done, at what pace – and in some cases, even how much time is spent on toilet breaks. Your average feudal serf would have been open-mouthed in disbelief if a feudal lord had taken an interest in such things!

Just as the employer relates to the employee as the seller of a commodity, the employee relates to their own labour-power as something they have to sell in order to live. So long as they receive appropriate wages, it can seem reasonable that the boss gets to decide how their labour-power is used. Most employees carry out their assigned tasks in the knowledge that, if they don't, they risk losing their livelihood and possibly having their lives turned upside down.

Work is merely a way of earning money. Money is what really matters to people, because it's what enables them to live the lives that really matter to them – outside of work. The life that matters to people, the life that belongs to them, is the one that starts after they leave the authoritarianism of the workplace, and are able to live their lives freely, limited only by their ability to pay for the things they need or want.

Does the above description sound like your own experience of work? For all too many, I imagine, it's all too close. But for others, I'm sure, it's nothing of the kind. However much the market may want to treat everything as a commodity, work can never shed its reality as an expression of human life. There are plenty of jobs that can provide a sense of satisfaction, an enjoyable experience of cooperating to do something worthwhile. For many people, their work is an important part of their identity. Some people even get on reasonably well with their boss!

This is one of the ways in which capitalist alienation is manifested. The dual nature of commodities as both use-values and exchange-values can take some strange forms, but nowhere more so than in the case of labour-power, which can be simultaneously a source of satisfaction and a process of exploitation involving an authoritarian relationship between the buyer and seller.

One of the ironies of capitalism is that, objectively, it creates a far more socially integrated world, but it does so via the actions of private companies and individuals, relating via the market. Because all capitalist production is for exchange, all production is intrinsically social; people produce things for others, not for themselves. But far from creating a sense of unity, of working together for the betterment of everyone, capitalism divides people and leaves many feeling isolated and alienated. Even for those lucky enough to find satisfying work, their connection to the wider world is partly mediated through the market.

Many of those involved in creating the communist nations of the twentieth century were hoping to move beyond this situation and create a society more focused on human needs, a society where people's social connections were more conscious and direct, providing a feeling of solidarity and a sense that they were working together for the common good. But those attempts failed, and the mass of people remained alienated from society, not through the operation of capitalism, but because the political and economic decisions that affected their lives were being made by governments and bureaucracies over which they had no control.

Those critics of Marxism who say we should look at the communist regimes of the twentieth century and swear to ensure no such thing ever happens again are absolutely right. We need to learn the lessons of those failures.

One obvious lesson, although perhaps not the most relevant, is that anyone who thinks a successful communist society can be introduced in an isolated and underdeveloped country, is fooling themselves. More generally, it's likely that *any* nation that implements significant change will depend on support and solidarity from workers in other nations.

The experience of the Soviet Union also suggests that it's foolish to throw away an economic setup that works, however imperfectly and unfairly, on the assumption that a better replacement can be relied on. It would be better to introduce changes gradually. There are plenty of changes that would create a fairer society, give more power to workers and lay the basis for further change. Workers and consumers could be given more power, private ownership could be replaced with cooperatives or nationalisation, and there are plenty of other, more significant changes that could be introduced over time. It would certainly be good to implement the euthanasia of the rentier (although we should probably avoid Keynes' terminology, which is liable to be misinterpreted if it's suggested by a Marxist rather than a liberal).

There's one lesson, however, that is clearer than any other. If there's one concern that Marxist politics should be focused on, it's protecting the democracy we have from any threat, making it more meaningful and extending it to every sphere of life. The whole point of replacing capitalism is to escape alienation and give everyone a sense that they have a say in creating and changing their society. Only through a deepening of democracy could communism become meaningful, successful or worthwhile.

5. SOMETHING GIVES

There is a Zen story that tells of a monk who is travelling along a hot and dusty path when he comes across an old well. Looking down into the well, all he can see is darkness and shadow. He imagines still water. He fears dry earth. Finding a pebble at his feet, he drops it into the well, watches it disappear into the darkness, and then hears the unmistakable sound as it splashes into water.

It occurs to him that the certainty he now has that there is water in the well is like the certainty he has that there is a state of awakening in which he would be freed from illusion and suffering. But equally, he knows that this certainty is not the same as the experience of awakening, any more than hearing the pebble splash into the water is the same as the feeling of water splashed onto his face and sliding down his throat.

*

There are many stories like this in Buddhism. Many Buddhist teachings stress the importance of the difference between appreciating something at an intellectual level, and the direct experience of it – the insight becoming a part of how you experience the world. This is particularly the case in Zen (or Chan), which developed partly in reaction to a Buddhism that was seen as over-systematised and academic. Bodhidharma, who is supposed to have transmitted Buddhism from India to China in the fifth century, is said to have described Zen like this:

A special transmission outside the scriptures
No dependence upon words or letters

Direct pointing to the human heart
Seeing into one's own nature.

This attitude is not, however, unique to Zen. The distinction is there in all Buddhist traditions. Although I'm in no position to judge the value or the practicality of profound experiences of awakening, I do think it's important to remember that the aim of Buddhist practice is to change our habitual, everyday way of experiencing the world. However, I also think there's the danger that this stress can lead to the value of intellectual understanding being downplayed, or even dismissed. It can make Buddhist practice seem more mystical or beyond explanation than is justified.

There's also a danger of giving the impression that intellectual understanding on the one hand, and emotional or experiential awareness on the other, are more distinct or disconnected than is really the case. In practice, every intellectual insight is accompanied by an emotional reaction, and our experiences can become more meaningful to us if we can find ways to make sense of them and communicate them, however inadequately, in words. Hearing the pebble hit the water may not be like feeling the water splash onto your face, but it does provide an insight worth having.

When I was first trying to decide whether, or to what extent, Buddhism made sense to me, there were two related intellectual problems that had me particularly stumped. Firstly, there was the question of how a Buddhist is supposed to make any sort of positive choice about the future. There are some things Buddhist teachings make clear you should do – meditate, be mindful and so on. And there are moral precepts affecting some decisions. But there's a whole world of decisions out there not covered by any of that. Faced with multiple choices, why do one thing rather than another? Isn't any choice an implicit expression of concern for your future self, an expression of desire, a failure to simply accept things as they are?

The second problem concerned one possible, at least partial, answer to the first – the importance that Buddhism gives to compassion. The problem I had with this was that I couldn't find any explanation of why compassion would logically follow from the Buddhist understanding of the nature of reality, of impermanence and no-self. There's no question that compassion does play a major part in Buddhist teachings. Take, for example, this from the Dalai Lama:

> ...as we deepen our conviction that every sentient being has the potential to be free from suffering, then of course our compassion toward other sentient beings will increase.
>
> ... So if your understanding of emptiness does not contribute positively in any way toward this goal, there is no worth in it at all. What is there to be admired about a realization of emptiness that does not lead to greater compassion?[1]

And later in the same book:

> These three factors – bodhichitta, great compassion, and the wisdom of emptiness – constitute the essence of the path to full enlightenment ... We could say that these three aspects of the path are the necessary and sufficient conditions for attaining buddhahood.[2]

As though the direct reference to compassion wasn't enough, *bodhichitta* refers to 'a spontaneous wish to attain enlightenment motivated by great compassion for all sentient beings'.

Not much doubt then, that compassion is central to the Buddhist path. But why? I could find many assertions or descriptions of it being so, but no explanations. It's not that I didn't accept that compassion is a good thing, it's just that it wasn't clear to me why or how it fitted into the Buddhist understanding of the world.

The most obvious explanation I could see appeared to be a confusion between two senses of selflessness. In its common usage, it's a synonym for altruism, for putting others before yourself, but the Buddhist meaning is about the absence of a persistent self, for you and for others, and it was unclear to me why this would imply anything about compassion.

I did wonder, for a while, whether the importance given to compassion was a later development and not something in the Buddha's original teachings. And in fact, the stress on compassion in particular is, to a degree, a development of Mahayana Buddhism. But not only does compassion also appear in the earliest texts but to make things more interesting – or more confusing depending on how you look at it – it appears as one of the four *Brahmaviharas*, literally the 'abodes of brahma', also known as the 'four immeasurables'. These are: loving-kindness or benevolence (*metta*), compassion (*karuna*), empathetic joy (*mudita*) and equanimity (*upekkha*).

One account of these suggests that loving-kindness is the most fundamental attitude, with compassion being the expression of loving-kindness when it encounters suffering, and empathetic joy the expression of it when it encounters happiness. This would seem to be confirmed by the fact that the early texts also describe a form of meditation called 'loving-kindness meditation' in which the meditator directs feelings of loving-kindness, first to themselves, then to someone they care about, then to a stranger, and so on, until (ideally) they're feeling loving-kindness toward all sentient beings.

When the weather's fine, I like to spend time sitting on park benches. At the time that I was trying to puzzle out this 'Buddhist compassion conundrum', as an experiment, I'd spend some of that time engaging in something akin to loving-kindness meditation, directing positive thoughts and emotions toward the other people in the park: 'May you be happy. May you be free from suffering. May you find your place in the world and be content.' That sort of thing. Then I'd spend time relating to them in a way that seemed to me equally consistent with Buddhist teachings, wishing neither anything positive nor negative, simply accepting whatever would be with equanimity, free from any attachment to any particular wish for their future. The former way of feeling and thinking was undoubtedly a more positive experience. It's interesting – you should try it.

Some might conclude that this is all you need to know. Clearly, the Buddhist teachings on loving-kindness and compassion are right – just go with it. Which is fair enough. For some of us, however, one attraction of Buddhism is that it makes sense. There are explanations for why trying to understand its teachings, and following its practices, might be worthwhile. But when it came to practising compassion, I could find no explanation. If the cause of suffering is desire, and this is based on a mistaken belief that people have a continuing self, then why seek anything in particular for yourself or for others?

The closest I could find to an explanation was this sort of thing from Rob Burbea:

> ...it could be said then that these factors – craving, identification, and *avijja* – are 'builders of the self and the world'. In contrast, *metta*, compassion, *samadhi*, equanimity, and even generosity, build less self and less world.
>
> Thus it is not just because they bring clarity, steadiness of attention, and a sense of well-being that these beautiful qualities are so valuable on the path. They also contribute significantly to a deeper understanding of dependent origination. And this understanding is indispensable for the liberation of awakening.[3]

I think this is true, although I'm not sure I would have been convinced if I hadn't arrived at a similar conclusion myself, through a very circuitous route. I'd like to describe that route now, because I think it's thought-provoking and useful. But first it's worth making clear that the argument I'm going to present – if indeed it's deserving of the name 'argument' – has some particular limitations. The way that I want to clarify the place of compassion in Buddhist practice involves imagining four scenarios and comparing the emotional reactions that each provoke.

My conclusions follow from my own emotional reactions, so for someone else to consider my conclusions valid, they would have to have the same, or similar, reactions. It has crossed my mind that I may not be an entirely typical representative of the human race. I'm reasonably confident that my own emotional reactions are unlikely to be too *untypical*, but you never know, do you? And I suppose it can't be entirely ruled out that you, dear reader, could be even less typical than me! Whatever the case, I'd encourage you to take the time to imagine the scenarios, and to consider your own emotional reactions. If they don't match mine, I suspect you'll nonetheless find it interesting.

So, to proceed: the first two scenarios both involve giving some sort of gift to someone you care about. Let's call them scenarios 1a and 1b. Pick an appropriate person. Imagine it's their birthday in a week or two, or some other kind of anniversary. Think of a gift you're sure they'll like. Feel free to be extravagant.

In scenario 1a, you imagine presenting them with the gift. You watch their reaction as it becomes clear that they like it every bit as much as you'd hoped. Take some time to note how imagining this makes you feel, before you continue with the next scenario.

Scenario 1b is essentially the same but, unfortunately, it turns out you can't be there when they open the gift – a prior engagement. Such is life! But you imagine them receiving the gift, loving it just as before, and knowing it's from you. Again, take some time to imagine this, and note your emotional reaction. The question to then consider is: how much difference does it make that you can't be there? How much does it affect how you feel when you imagine them enjoying your gift?

My assumption here is that, however much you may regret that you couldn't be there, the pleasure at the thought of them opening the gift is not greatly reduced. After all, the main source of your pleasure is the thought of their happiness, isn't it? What do you think? How much difference is there?

If you've finished thinking about that, let's move on to the next scenario. This involves giving some sort of gift to yourself. Perhaps there's something you've been thinking of buying, or regretting was beyond your means. Imagine you've found a way to order it nonetheless. Or maybe there's some activity you've always wanted to try or some event you'd like to attend. Book yourself an imaginary place.

Spoilt for choice, I know, but settle on something and imagine how, on the day, the package arrives, or you attend the event, or engage in the activity. It's every bit as good as you'd hoped. Try to make a mental note of the emotional experience of imagining this. Feel free to take your time

– remember you're not indulging in an enjoyable fantasy; you're engaging in an important and worthwhile investigation into the way in which you relate to the world!

Are we ready to move on? Okay, let's call that scenario 2a and now consider how it compares with scenario 2b. Scenario 2b is the same as scenario 2a, but bearing in mind that you can't be there. There is no persistent self. There is no thing being you, here, now, looking forward to that future, that could also be you, there, then, experiencing the future you're looking forward to.

Did you forget that was the case? Or did I – despite my best efforts in Chapter 3 – fail to convey what having no persistent self means? I rather assumed that one, or both, of these would be the case. I could, after all, have specified, when describing scenario 2a, that you should imagine you were suffering from the illusion of a persistent self. But given that this is the way almost all of us exist almost all of the time, I assumed it would be superfluous. (If I was wrong, and I underestimated you, then I apologise, and may I say – I am mightily impressed!) Go ahead and try to imagine scenario 2b and consider how your emotional response to it compares with scenario 2a.

For most people, I imagine, the thought that you can't be there, in the future that you're looking forward to, will make a significant difference. To put it mildly. Far more so than not being able to be there in scenario 1b. If I'm right, then I'd suggest part of the reason for this is likely to be that you've failed to grasp what it means to have no self. This probably sounds surprising. After all, if you failed completely to imagine it, then scenarios 2a and 2b would be identical.

But could it be that the suggestion there could be no 'you', there, in the future, experiencing what you were looking forward to, rather distracted you from the equally significant assertion that there is no thing being you in the here and now? Are you now feeling that there is something being you, here and now, that used to think it could be you there and then, in the future, and now feels that it will never get to experience that future after all? The reality is, there is no self in the here and now either! Feel free to spend some time trying to get your head round that one. See if you can grasp it sufficiently to see if it makes a difference to your experience of imagining scenario 2b. I don't mind waiting – you may be some time.

I'd assume (to continue my long list of possibly mistaken assumptions) that any attempt to make scenario 2b more appealing, or less problematic, by letting go of the sense of self in the present would not be likely to go well. What you'd likely be left with is the sense of a self (don't ask me where) which once thought it had a self in the present that would also be there in the future, but then realised that the self it thought it had in the present couldn't be there in the future after all, and now realises that it doesn't *even* have a self in the present – but is somehow failing to grasp that 'it' doesn't exist either!

If, contrary to my scepticism, you have completely succeeded in letting go of any sense of a persistent self, then you must be feeling just fine with scenario 2b. After all, if you have no self in the present, then what could feel any sense of loss at realising it couldn't be there in the future?

Let's set aside all this confusing emotional messiness for a while and engage in the far more enjoyable activity of intellectual analysis! The only reality that makes sense, so far as I can see, is that scenario 1a, 1b and 2b are all describing essentially the same thing – the experience of pleasure in this moment, derived from the thought of happiness being experienced in the future, despite there being no expectation of directly experiencing that future happiness. Scenario 2a, on the other hand, is the illusion around which we build much of our lives.

If this is correct, then the most interesting question about the scenarios is surely this: why would you not be able to derive *at least* as much pleasure from scenario 2b as from scenario 1b? The only difference, after all, is that in scenario 1b, the person whose future happiness you're imagining is somebody else. I can think of no good reason why this difference should lead to such a result. There is, however, a very significant bad reason: a lifetime of assuming that, in order to be able to look forward to the future, to take pleasure in the prospect of the future, you need to have a self that is here now, and will be there then.

It simply isn't true. The human mind is not so narrow that it has to limit itself to the direct experiences of life in order to find any source of happiness. There are all sorts of ways we enjoy the world that can't be related to the supposed importance of having a self directly experiencing it. For example, when we imagine ourselves doing things we know we'll never do, or remember experiences we can never go back to and live again, or when we take pleasure in fictions, or in other people's anecdotes, or learning about other people's lives, in imagined future or alternative worlds, or in thoughts of other people receiving gifts.

And, yes, we take pleasure in thinking about our own future – the future of this person. But we don't need a self in order to do so. The reality is that everything that was worth looking forward to in scenario 2a is equally worth looking forward to in scenario 2b. It's just that instead of seeing it as something you can't have yet, it's an experience of the present (as all experience, in fact, is). The only reason scenario 2b seems problematic is because the idea of having a self is so deeply ingrained in our assumptions about what has to be the case.

We don't have the same problem with scenario 1b, because the idea of taking pleasure in someone else's happiness strikes us as entirely unproblematic. It's the most natural thing in the world for a human being to take pleasure in somebody else's happiness, especially if it's someone they care about, and even more so if they feel they've contributed to that happiness. It would take a peculiarly selfish person to feel such an experience was undermined by the desire to take the place of that other person. And yet, it's the equivalent of that which gets in the way of enjoying scenario 2b.

When looking forward to your own future happiness, that natural empathetic joy can be undermined by desire, by the wish to be that person, experiencing that pleasure, and comparing that desirable future situation with your current situation, feeling as though there's something lacking in the present that you hope to have later. The desire to be there in that future can get in the way of your being able to enjoy the thought of your own future happiness with the same sense of kindness, with the same lack of desire or craving, that's possible in the case of someone else's future happiness. (This is even more likely to be the case if the 'gift' you plan for the future is not something positive but the end of something negative – having the mortgage paid off or receiving a medical all-clear.)

This is all the result of the illusion of having a self. If you could let go of that illusion, you could enjoy the thought of your own future happiness without desire, and without the kind of suffering that I think the Buddha means by 'dukkha'.

If you want to avoid all this confusion about what it means to take pleasure in thoughts about the future, you might think a good way to do so is to follow an approach to living which is often advocated by Buddhists – and, indeed, by many non-Buddhists – to 'live in the moment'. It's easy to see how this would make sense from a Buddhist perspective. If you have no self that can be there in the future, then focus on the here and now. There is, however, something distinctly odd about the concept of living in the moment.

When someone suggests you live in the moment, I don't think they mean you should just live in the moment for *this* moment, then go back to the way you were living before, or proceed in some other way. They must, at least, be implying that you should also live in the moment in the *next* moment, and surely also the one after that, and ideally quite a few more moments after that as well, all the way into what comes dangerously close to being 'the future'. Obviously, they can't say that, because it would rather undermine the idea of 'living in the moment'.

The problem is, the very concept of 'the present', and the experience of it, is meaningless without the context of the past that created it and the futures that could follow from it. What would the experience of living in the moment even be if it had no connection to the past or the future? Just a momentary burst of sense data with no connection to anything else?

Perhaps the reason living in the moment sounds attractive, in a way that scenario 2b doesn't, is because it's expressed in terms of grasping what is, rather than letting go of what can't be. Scenario 2b, especially when compared to scenario 2a, might make someone feel that, if they have no future self, they have 'nothing to look forward to'. But, so far as I can tell, nobody responds to the suggestion of living in the moment in the same way, even though, logically, there's more reason to do so – the concept implies ignoring the future in a way that scenario 2b doesn't.

In a sense, saying 'live in the moment' is really just a simpler way of saying 'let go of desire' – don't think about what you want in the future, or how the present could be different from what it is. Living in the moment, in a way, implies not having any sense of a persistent self – if there were such a self, living in the moment, it wouldn't have enough time to persist.

Maybe what people really mean when they recommend you live in the moment is a combination of the experience of focusing on the present moment and trying to avoid distraction, but also engaging, in some sense, in an example of scenario 2b. In this scenario, the gift you plan for the person you're becoming, is to continue doing what people really mean when they recommend you live in the moment!

I can't point to any particular Buddhist text to back me up on this, but the best sense I can make of the Buddha's teachings is that what he was trying to lead people towards was not exactly 'compassion' or 'loving-kindness' – concepts which, like so many of the concepts available to us, are caught up in a web of meaning that revolves around the sense of a self, and of separate others.

What he was trying to guide people towards was the way of emotionally relating to the world that would make most sense – that would follow most naturally from – an understanding and experience of the world in which there is no self, in which there is as little difference as possible between the way of emotionally relating to scenario 1b and scenario 2b.

Such experience would include being mindful of the present moment, but with no sense of a self that is 'having' that experience, and that could have different experiences, but rather, simply the experience of the present moment happening – an acceptance, a recognition, that the present moment could be nothing other than it is.

But also, as part of this, there would be an awareness that this moment only has any meaning, can only be experienced, as part of an unfolding reality with a particular past and possible futures. And following from this, there would be an inevitable preference, an intention, that this moment, and the next moment, be part of an unfolding reality that leads to a future in which there is less illusion, less suffering, a more awakened world.

If this interpretation is correct, then it surely explains the initial reaction of the Buddha, after his awakening – the doubts about whether he could convey what he'd come to realise. Imagine if he had put all his efforts into trying to directly explain to people this way of relating to the world. You have to wonder whether he would have persuaded many people at all, let alone founded a religion that would survive for millennia.

Instead, he tried to give people reasons to cultivate the kinds of emotions that were closest to the way of emotionally relating to the world that he wanted to guide them towards: loving-kindness, compassion, empathetic joy and equanimity – and to let go of emotions like hatred, craving, greed and attachment, which only make sense in the context of a self.

For those who were sufficiently interested, he also offered deeper teachings about the nature of the self and the world. And he encouraged everyone to engage in practices like meditation and mindfulness that might lead them to change in worthwhile ways, and hopefully someday to have the experience of the world that he had arrived at himself.

One problem with presentations of Buddhism that put so much emphasis on letting go of desire is that it's easy to interpret this as not caring, as being indifferent. It's a particular problem, because this type of presentation is likely to be encountered before the more complex and confusing idea of no-self. When somebody encounters the four noble truths for the first time, it's easy to assume that the Buddha wants them to free their self from desire. But from the point of view of a self, letting go of desire and attachment can mean letting go of attachments to the world, and being left with an unattached self that is uncaring, indifferent.

There are, in fact, many ways in which Buddhist teachings don't fit with this rejection of desire. You're supposed to want to follow where the eightfold path leads. 'Letting go of desire' is itself something you should presumably desire to achieve. Practising compassion implies the desire for others to be free from suffering. This can seem like an inconsistency, but it reflects the problem of having to find a way to teach the Buddha's insights to people who inevitably still think in terms of that persistent self.

It seems to me that, the more you develop an understanding of Buddhism, the clearer it becomes that the Buddha wasn't against desire in the broadest sense of the term. He doesn't so much want to free the self from desire, as he wants to free desire (in the sense of wanting there to be a better future) from the distortions of being bound up with the illusion of a self, from the illusion that taking pleasure in the idea of that better future requires you to have a self that will be there. It is not wanting good things for the future that causes suffering; it's wanting to be there, wanting to be – and believing you could be – somewhere other than here, now.

If you free desire from the illusion of self, what you end up with is something that might be referred to – for want of better words – as compassion, loving-kindness or empathetic joy. If there is no reason to see the future experience of this person as separate from, or more important than, the future of everything else, then there is good reason to want all future experience to be as positive as possible.

This way of looking at the relation between self and desire also provides a way of thinking about another problem that can arise as we learn about Buddhism – a problem which, far from being solved by the concept of no-self, is actually caused by it. Namely, as you develop a clearer idea of what letting go of your sense of having a self is like, it may strike you as anything but liberating. It may seem more like losing something.

It doesn't help that so many Buddhist concepts, such as no-self and emptiness, sound negative. It's easy to end up thinking that, if there is no self, then you have no future, that you have nothing – emptiness in the most negative sense. But if you could truly let go of any sense of self, what would remain would not be nothing, what would remain would be everything – everything seen from the point of view of this particular, constantly changing, person, interpreted based on the past experience of this person, but with no reason to divide up 'everything' in such a way that more importance is given to the experience of this person, as opposed to the experience of anyone else, now, or in the future.

What would be left would be the experience of life happening, moment to moment, with no part separable from any other. You can't 'lose' anything real by seeing things more clearly. Everything that you were, you still are. Everything that was worth looking forward to is still worth looking forward to. Everything is the same, but you relate to it differently. Nothing changes – but everything changes.

This seems to fit with the way that experiences of awakening are often described. For example, as Peter Harvey describes it:

> The attainment of such a breakthrough is known in Chinese as *wu*, 'realisation' and in Japanese as *satori*, 'catching on', or *kensho*, 'seeing one's nature' ... It is a blissful realization where a person's inner nature, the originally pure mind, is directly known in a sudden reordering of his or her perception of the world. All appears vividly; each thing retaining its individuality, yet empty of separateness, so being unified with all else, including the meditator. There is just an indescribable thusness, beyond the duality of subject and object; a thusness which is dynamic and immanent in the world.[4]

This account of the aim of Buddhist practice makes sense to me. Hopefully, it helps to make clear why losing the sense of a self would be a good thing, but also how much of a challenge it is in practice. Assuming we only have one life, however, and we don't spend it in a Buddhist monastery, and perhaps don't even go on meditation retreats, what are the odds of us achieving anything like this?

It's possible that things aren't as bad as the discussion of the four scenarios may have suggested. The problem they suggested may partly have been of the 'don't think of an elephant' variety. If someone tells you not to think of an elephant, it's nigh impossible not to think of an elephant. Perhaps somebody encouraging you to think about how your sense of self is an illusion is not a helpful way to enable you to let go of the sense of self. A self is, of course, an altogether more curious and intimate a thing than an imaginary elephant, and it doesn't have to be conjured into existence using the magic of words. But words can nonetheless reinforce it. Being told to let go of it can make it seem all the more present.

Just as it's perfectly possible to not think of an elephant simply by putting yourself in a situation where there's no reason to think of an elephant, perhaps it's possible to have no sense of self, by putting yourself in a situation where there's no reason to have a sense of self. The question is, what sort of situation would that be? Deep meditation is an obvious answer (I'll discuss this more in Chapter 10), or 'being awakened', but possibly, also, just carrying on with ordinary life in the right frame of mind. Possibly.

This is one justification for the kinds of Buddhist practice that are not about 'seeing through' illusion, or about intellectual reflection, but instead involve paying close attention to what *is*. For example, meditating on the breath, or on thoughts arising and passing away, or indeed 'living in the moment'. Perhaps living in the moment – or what that phrase is intended to encourage people to do – may be a perfectly reasonable and useful approach to living in a more Buddhist way, and the last thing you should be doing in the moment is dwelling on my knit-picking criticisms of exactly what it means. There's definitely something to be said for spending time experiencing how simple and unproblematic it can be to 'just be', letting go of judgement, attachment, aversion, even reflection.

An awful lot of life, however, outside of the monastery or the retreat, does not lend itself to being carried out in a mindful, let alone an 'awakened' way. The more you act in the world, the more you inevitably focus on your own life and experience. After all, the experiences of the particular person you are, are the only ones you can remember rather than imagine. It's only the actions, decisions, and experiences of 'this person' that can be directly affected by this consciousness. You're the only person who will definitely be affected by changes to the way you understand your self. And the more you're focused on your own interaction with the rest of the world, the more that sense of a separate self creeps back in.

I'm not sure that a realisation of no-self is a realistic thing to expect, but I'm okay with less-self. And to achieve that, maybe aiming at no-self isn't a bad approach. You might compare a realistic approach to Buddhist practice to the approach you might have to your health. Aiming for perfect health is probably a little ambitious. But if you have any grasp of the significance of healthy living to your quality of life, you'll make some effort to eat well and exercise. Meditation may be a good way of bringing about positive change. Analytical thinking may also help. Perhaps different approaches suit different people. Whatever the best approach, Buddhism offers good reasons to think that the most desirable future, for yourself and for the world, will be one with more compassion, and therefore less sense of having a separate, persistent self.

*

There is a Zen story that tells of a monk who is travelling along a path, when he sees an old man walking towards him carrying a heavy bundle on his head. As the man draws closer, the monk recognises him as a great Zen master.

The monk greets the Zen master and asks him if there is any guidance he might receive that would help him to become awakened. In response, without saying a word, the Zen master removes the heavy bundle from his head, holds it out to his side, and allows it to fall to the ground.

As is so often the way in Zen stories, it is this simple, wordless action that somehow serves as a trigger that brings everything together for the monk. All the years of studying Buddhism, of practising meditation, suddenly fall into place, and he sees the reality that they were all pointing towards. He experiences what it truly means to let go and be released.

The monk stands for a while, experiencing this new way of being, and then, as his awareness of the wider world returns, he looks to the Zen master and asks the obvious question, 'Now what?'

In response, without saying a word, the Zen master casually picks up the heavy bundle, places it back on his head, and continues walking along the path.

6. CAPITALIST GROWTHS

Capitalism encourages people to act on the basis of their own material self-interest. It assumes that people will tend to do this anyway, and it works in various ways that make them more likely to do so. As Adam Smith says:

> It is not from the benevolence of the butcher, the brewer, or the baker, that we expect our dinner, but from their regard to their own interest. We address ourselves, not to their humanity but to their self-love, and never talk to them of our necessities but of their advantages.[1]

On this view, even in pre-capitalist societies, people only cooperated because they could see ways it would be to their mutual advantage. But the organisation of society provided limited opportunities to do so. The development of the market changed that.

With the growth of the market economy, people could purchase an increasing number and variety of commodities that they could never have produced for themselves. The market provided a way that people pursuing their self-interest could lead to social cooperation on a scale that would have been difficult to imagine happening otherwise.

The operation of the market, meanwhile, gave capitalists reason to want to accumulate ever more, to invest in expanded production of more and better products. The route to wealth was through beating your competitors, so companies were driven to accumulate more in order to be able to accumulate even more.

Since everything was being produced with the aim of selling, it was in everyone's interest for people to want to buy as much as possible. A whole advertising industry was created to encourage consumers to buy more, to convince people to desire whatever was being sold, or to want the latest update or alternative to what they already had.

As capitalists compete to make more profits, and they encourage consumers to believe that, to be happier, what they need is more and better things, a society has developed that is increasingly focused on possession and desire. People are encouraged to believe that their sense of worth comes from how wealthy they are compared to others. And as the exchange of commodities is mediated by money, and money becomes the measure of wealth, so there's no limit to how wealthy the wealthiest could become: even those who already own more than they could ever spend can hope to become even richer, even more successful.

When you consider the dynamism of capitalism, its constant drive to increase production and productivity, and when you consider the success with which it has transformed the world, and how it has been driven to encompass almost every part of the globe, one of the strangest realities of capitalism, as it exists today, is that so many of those nations to which it has spread seem to produce far less than they're capable of.

Looking at the objective, technical requirements for growth, there would seem to be no good reason for this. Almost any nation on Earth, for example, should be capable of competing in the profitable market for motor vehicles. Anywhere, from Albania to Zimbabwe, would at least have the necessary real estate and workers. The vast majority would have their own home-grown engineers, designers, technologists, administrators and other necessary employees. If there were any skills they were lacking, they could invest in appropriate training. Access to required raw materials shouldn't pose too much of a problem. At worst, they might have to import some advanced machinery, but if we assume (rather rashly perhaps) that the free market really means something, that shouldn't be a problem either, should it?

The resulting cars, rolling off the production lines, might not be quite as good as the latest models from Germany, Japan or the United

States, but surely they couldn't fail to be a match for some of the shamefully not-the-latest-model cars that many people – short on money or self-respect – audaciously drive around on the very same roads as those latest models.

Any nation should be able to produce the sorts of cars that would have had automobile aficionados drooling at the mouth a few years ago, and they should be able to do so with a level of efficiency that would have made Henry Ford's jaw hit the pavement. But for most such nations, those cars would be completely useless. Not in the literal sense, but in the capitalist sense: valueless.

What few nations are likely to be able to do is produce cars whose balance of features and price could compete with those from major car-producing nations. They wouldn't be quite as feature-laden as their competitors, they'd be slightly more expensive, they wouldn't benefit from being an established brand, they wouldn't have benefited from years of investment in that most productive of industries – advertising. And, unless they were far more confident of success than they had any right to be, they wouldn't benefit from the same economies of scale. So nobody would buy them. They'd sit, uselessly, in the car showrooms or warehouses. And if cars can't be sold, then what good are they? It's not as though you can just produce things for people to use, is it? That would be silly.

You could reasonably point out that having even more makes of car to choose from would hardly be a great gift to the world, and I'd have to agree. And so, indeed, would the advocates of the international division of labour that capitalism encourages. The capitalist ideal is that each nation should focus on producing whatever it can produce most efficiently. They should export products for which they have a 'comparative advantage', and they can then import products like cars from the most efficient foreign producers, and everybody is better off.

For successful economies, this makes sense. The problem is, if you're one of those nations that came late to the capitalist table or was forced to spend most of its history serving at the table of its imperialist rulers, you're going to struggle to compete in the production of any of the most profitable consumer products. What applies to car production applies to the production of the majority of goods, especially any goods that are likely to be competitive on the international market. This is why so many developing nations have been dependent on exporting raw materials or providing cheap labour to foreign companies.

This includes, ironically, providing cheap labour to be used in car production plants: in a sense, the whole argument about car production made above was unnecessary, because there are, in fact, modern car plants in places like Thailand and Mexico. They're generally owned, however, by companies based in countries like Japan and the United States. They were located there to take advantage of the one commodity developing nations have in abundance, and at knockdown prices: labour-power. And most of the products and profits created in those car plants make their way back to the wealthier nations with a speed and ease that can only be envied by those whose labour-power produced them.

In an apparently unimaginable world, where people consciously co-operated towards a common purpose, the solution to this situation would be obvious. If one country or company had some technology, some new invention, some technical expertise – anything that other people would find useful – they'd share it. It's the obvious thing to do, isn't it? After all, from the viewpoint of the world as a whole, if everybody is producing more efficiently, then everybody is better off – there's more for everyone to share.

But in the apparently only sensible way of organising the economy, around competition, only a fool would do any such thing. If you want to compete, you should keep your advantages to yourself, patent as much as possible, guard your trade secrets. If you help your competitor, then you clearly don't understand how the world works.

This is not to say that it's impossible for new nations to make their way into the economic big leagues. Just as it's possible for a few exceptional people, despite being born with few advantages, to work their way up and become part of the world's wealthiest one per cent, it's not unheard of for new nations to join those that were lucky enough to get a head start to success. The obvious example is China. Over recent decades, China has demonstrated that introducing the market and private ownership can still bring about spectacular economic growth. Some would point to this as an argument against Marxism, but Marx never denied that capitalism could create economic growth. Indeed, it was an essential part of his understanding of how history developed. The question is, under what circumstances and for how long will this continue, and are there better alternatives? The circumstances of China's success are certainly interesting.

In the 1980s and 1990s, China had a number of advantages over other nations. First of all, although China was to become the most striking example of success, it was not the first. It was able to learn lessons from previous successes, such as South Korea and Taiwan. This was not an option for most developing nations. As Ha-Joon Chang makes clear in his book *Bad Samaritans*,[2] the strategies that South Korea and Taiwan followed between the 1950s and the 1970s, which allowed them to avoid the more negative effects of the international market, were closed off to others from the 1980s onwards, as the most powerful capitalist nations and institutions imposed neoliberal orthodoxy on the world.

To be able to develop the kinds of diverse and profitable industries that exist in more advanced economies, nations like South Korea had nurtured certain industries through tariff protection, subsidies and other forms of government support, until those industries grew enough to withstand international competition.

This was, in fact, the same approach that had been taken by every country that had managed to develop into a major capitalist power. The United States, for example, was the most protectionist country in the world throughout the nineteenth century. US tariffs on manufactured imports between the Civil War and the First World War were between forty and fifty per cent, the highest of any country in the world, and this was a period when it was also the fastest-growing economy. Neoliberals argue that this growth was due to specific advantages of the US, and happened despite, not because of, the protectionism. But as Chang points out, there are plenty of other examples of countries that grew rapidly behind protective barriers: he names, Germany, Sweden, France, Finland, Austria, Japan, Taiwan and Korea.[3]

In the decades after the Second World War, organisations like the

International Monetary Fund (IMF) and the World Bank had allowed such approaches, largely leaving developing countries to follow their own course. But with the neoliberal turn of the 1970s and the insistence that the free market was always right, these organisations interfered more and more in how developing nations behaved. As Chang says:

> ...the roles of both the IMF and the World Bank changed dramatically. They started to exert a much stronger policy influence on developing countries through their joint operation of so-called structural adjustment programmes (SAPs) ... They branched out into areas like government budgets, industrial regulation, agricultural pricing, labour market regulation, privatization and so on.[4]

And this happened alongside the problem of third world debt, which left such countries especially open to pressure to do as they were told. China's situation was different. It was entering the world market after decades as a centrally planned economy, so it was able to ignore the advice and pressure. It had greater freedom to make its own decisions about how it would increase its involvement with the world market.

The second advantage that China had was that it was given a very clear lesson on why it should ignore the advice of the IMF and of other economists who claimed to know how best to gain from the benefits of capitalism. The lesson came from witnessing the experience of other centrally planned economies that had introduced capitalism: the nations of Eastern Europe and, in particular, Russia.

When the Soviet Union collapsed, it happened in a disorganised and unpredictable way. To the relief of Russia's new elite, however, there were lots of generous economic advisors from the capitalist world eager to explain how it could best benefit from its wise decision to embrace capitalism. A group of lawyers and economists from Harvard University were happy to set up shop in Moscow and advise the Russian government on how to proceed. They suggested the best way to reinvigorate Russia's economy was to adopt an approach which they quite happily referred to as 'shock therapy'. State enterprises should be privatised, the market should be allowed to set prices and competition should be introduced wherever possible. In the short term it would be a shock, but then the invisible hand of the market would guide the nation to a brighter future.

Shock there certainly was; therapy, not so much. Between 1992 and 1995, Russia's GDP fell by forty-two per cent. And as bad as that sounds, it actually underestimates the shock for most Russians, because alongside this precipitous fall in overall production, there was a sharp increase in inequality. While those in a position to do so snapped up the former state enterprises at knockdown prices, the poorest faced unemployment accompanied by austerity, and the welfare provisions they'd taken for granted became more difficult to access or disappeared entirely. Violent crime increased more than fourfold, the suicide rate doubled, and deaths from alcohol abuse tripled. But at least the Russian people finally got to see shops with shelves full of inviting consumer goods.[5]

By the time Russian society began to recover from the trauma of capitalist renewal, many people were only too happy to accept the promises of Vladimir Putin, former Lieutenant Colonel of the KGB, who offered a recovery from national humiliation and a more suitably confrontational approach to the West.

Despite constant encouragement to do so, China did not choose to follow the same route as Russia. Actually, China had begun its economic reforms much earlier than Russia, but they had done so cautiously. More than once, they'd considered following the encouragement to pursue 'shock therapy', but on each occasion, differences between political leaders, over politics or economics, led to them backing away from the decision.[6]

It's impossible to know what course China might have followed if the developments elsewhere had gone differently, but once they had witnessed shock therapy in action, surely nothing would have tempted them to consider it again. Instead, all the significant financial institutions in China, and most of its major enterprises, remained under state control.

China had recognised, however, that under central planning the economy was stagnating, and had accepted that introducing some market forces could help promote economic growth. The challenge was how to allow the market to have a positive effect without handing over more control than they had to.

Another challenge was how to gain access to modern technology and to learn the latest engineering and management techniques. To do this, they put in place ways of attracting foreign companies to set up export manufacturing plants inside China – first by creating 'special economic zones' and later through the 'coastal-development strategy'.

In effect, what China offered had much in common with what Britain had offered in the nineteenth century: a large supply of very cheap labour, being sold by workers with very few rights, alongside an increasingly impressive infrastructure with which to exploit them. Unlike Britain, however, it also benefitted from having wealthy potential export markets in places like the United States, Europe and Japan, and pre-existing companies ready to move their production to wherever labour was cheapest.

For foreign companies, the price of admittance to this capitalist utopia was a willingness to provide technologies, production techniques and management skills that could help China's domestic companies to grow. Either through formal measures such as joint venture requirements, or via informal arm-twisting, the Chinese government made technology transfer a condition for access by foreign firms.

At the same time, unlike those countries that were in hock to the IMF, China could use tariffs and state support of favoured sectors, along with control of financial measures such as low interest rates, an undervalued exchange rate, and capital controls. As the economy grew, there was a gradual decrease in the cheapness of labour-power but a corresponding increase in consumer demand from potentially the biggest domestic market there's ever been.

The result has been nothing short of spectacular. Hundreds of millions of people have been lifted out of poverty, a middle class has been created where none existed, and China now has more billionaires than any other country. Assuming these developments continue, China may well achieve levels of wealth and inequality similar to the longer established successful capitalist nations – albeit with far more state ownership and more authoritarian government. But then what? Sooner or later, one way or another, we come back to the same question: once you have an advanced capitalist economy, what do you do then? Do you keep on trying to make it work better, despite all its contradictions and injustices, or do you investigate whether it has created the possibility of organising society in a better way, one that builds on its strengths but is designed more in the interests of people than profits?

The capitalist world gained immensely from China's engagement with the international market. Without it, the economic crises of recent years would have been more severe, and the 2008 crash would have been far worse. So, naturally, other nations have reacted to China's success with outrage and condemnation! This is what capitalism is like – everything that is good is also bad, everything desirable is also regrettable. Companies want the economy to do well, but their competitors to do badly. Nations want other nations to be able to provide resources and to buy their exports, but not to be able to sell competing exports of their own. This sort of contradiction also applies to the relationship between employers and employees, capitalists and workers.

Believe it or not, capitalists want workers to be paid as much as possible. Of course they do, because workers are consumers. Companies need customers with money to buy what they're selling, and the most significant source of demand comes via workers' wages. Even if a company isn't selling directly to workers, they depend indirectly on those that do. If workers are paid as much as possible, then everyone will have lots of money to spend, leading to lots of profits and successful companies able to hire more workers and pay them more. It's a virtuous circle.

There's just one unfortunate little wrinkle in this potentially rosy picture. Whilst all employers want workers to have as much money as possible, they make an exception in the case of the workers that they themselves have to pay. All workers are potential consumers and therefore sources of profit, but the wages paid to a company's own workers reduce its own profits. So every capitalist would like to see everybody else's workers being paid higher wages – just so long as it didn't give their own workers the idea that they should be paid more as well.

The problem, as so often under capitalism, comes back to the fact that it isn't enough to produce use-values. Commodities have to be sold in order to realise their exchange-value. This can be a major problem for capitalists. It can be an even bigger problem if the commodity you're trying to sell is labour-power. The labour-power a worker has to offer may be highly skilled, may be all-singing, all-dancing, multitasking, the most workaholic, flexible labour-power ever known, but it's worthless if nobody wants to buy it.

One of the ways in which labour-power is different from other commodities is that it will continue to be produced regardless of whether it can be sold. People will keep on having children. Children will continue to grow into adults. The majority of adults, even if they can see no prospect of finding a purchaser for their labour-power, will prefer living on the scrapheap to jumping off a bridge.

Recognising this problem, the more reasonable of the more successful capitalist nations have put in place measures to make life more bearable for those who can't sell their labour-power, or whose earnings from their labour-power leave them too far below the poverty line. The available help may be anything from the degradation of homeless shelters and food banks, to the dizzy heights of a universal basic income. But whatever form it takes, those providing it are faced with a dilemma.

On the one hand, they want to provide sufficient support so that life is bearable – whether out of concern that doing otherwise might lead to social unrest and political radicalisation, or out of simple humanity. But on the other hand, they're reluctant to make life for the unemployed *too* bearable, because they need workers to be motivated to find employment, and they want those in employment to have reason to put up with relatively low wages. They also don't want to have to raise taxes to pay for whatever they provide. For all these reasons, it would be irresponsible to make the lives of unprofitable people too comfortable.

Those workers born in nations that didn't get into the capitalist competition at the start, and which have failed, or been prevented, from catching up, are doubly unlucky. Not only are they less likely to find anyone able to make a profit from their labour-power, they're also unlikely to be offered much material help or support.

For those who are most entrepreneurial, or desperate, or both, one solution is to try selling their labour-power on the export market. Of course, another oddity of the commodity labour-power is that you can't export it without going along to deliver it minute by minute, hour by hour. For this reason, the champions of neoliberalism, who've done everything they can to allow capital and commodities to travel across borders with as few restrictions as possible, make an exception in the case of the commodity labour-power.

If such workers try to get into a country where there's more demand for their labour-power, they won't be congratulated on their entrepreneurial spirit, but rather condemned as 'economic migrants' – a rare example of people being condemned for doing what the market encourages them to do. If they do manage to get in, they'll face hostility from some of those already living there, who've been told, their whole lives, by politicians and media, that the reason they themselves face economic challenges is nothing to do with the economics or politics of their own nation, and everything to do with foreigners 'coming over here' taking what they have no right to.

Most of the problems and contradictions we've been looking at in the chapter so far concern the circulation of capital, money and commodities – the processes by which commodities are sold to realise their exchange-value, how exchange-value is represented in money, and how money capital is turned into productive activity – or the way in which these things fail to happen. Marx describes these processes, and the contradictions they can lead to, in Volume 2 of *Capital*.

In Volume 1, Marx had focused on the production process. In order to do this, he imagined a world, most unlike the real world, in which circulation proceeds without any problems. It's understandable that he would take this approach, because he wanted to make clear how surplus-value is created through exploitation – how capitalist profits are created within the production process, from the surplus-labour of workers, and not, as it can appear, in the circulation process, where commodities are bought and sold.

There's no point in producing commodities, however, unless their value can be realised through the process of circulation. So in Volume 2, he makes the unrealistic assumption that the production process proceeds with no problem, and focuses on problems of circulation: on the need for commodities to be sold, for capital to circulate, and for different, interdependent sectors to somehow coordinate the production of machinery, consumer goods and so on – all of which has to work in order for the process of accumulation to continue.

Even fewer people read Volume 2 of *Capital* than read Volume 1, which is regrettable, because unlike the account of the production process in Volume 1, where the whole point was to describe something that is difficult to see, the contradictions described in Volume 2 are much easier to see being played out around us. Indeed, they can be seen to be fundamental to the major economic developments that have taken place over the past century.

The challenge presented by the long depression of the 1930s led to something truly new: an economist and admirer of capitalism coming up with a genuinely innovative way of making capitalism work more effectively and fairly. Although he had little interest in Marx's critique of capitalism, John Maynard Keynes did recognise that companies would not invest so long as they could see there was no demand in the economy, and there would be low demand so long as nobody was investing. One of the solutions he advocated was for governments to be willing to go into debt in order to provide investment and employment. This would provide demand and so encourage private companies to invest. Once government spending had stimulated the economy and it began to grow, the increased tax revenues would allow governments to pay off their debt.

This approach was widely adopted, and it helped to create what is sometimes called the 'golden age of capitalism'. The decades following the Second World War saw continuous economic growth. Capital controls and other measures were put in place to prevent financial speculators from doing too much damage. High employment and the development of the welfare state meant that workers were in a stronger bargaining position, which led to a larger proportion of national income shifting in favour of wages rather than profits. The wealthy in society were willing to accept this as long as it went along with growth for the economy as a whole.

But the 'golden age' did not last. In the 1970s, it developed into 'stagflation': stagnating growth alongside increasing inflation. The most obvious explanation for this, from a Marxist perspective, was that rising wages and the taxes needed to pay for the welfare state had increasingly undermined profits. There were certainly other factors, such as the increase in energy prices due to the actions of the OPEC countries. And there are other suggested explanations. But whatever disagreements there are about the causes, the solution that those in power all agreed on was clear enough: a shift in power and wealth away from the working class, and a strengthening of capital to allow profits to increase.

The neoliberal era was ushered in, most emphatically by Thatcherism in the UK and Reaganomics in the US. Powerful trade unions were taken on and defeated, and trade union rights were limited to embed the shift in power. As trade union power diminished, so did pay rises, and for many workers, a long period of stagnating wages began. Economy and society were subjected to deregulation, privatisation and cuts in welfare provision, alongside increased freedom for capital and the financial sector. Levels of inequality that had been shrinking for decades began to grow again. But whilst this led to profit margins increasing, it also brought back the old problem: as wages stagnated, workers had less money to spend on the goods companies needed to sell to them. The way this was solved was through the massive extension of credit.

Marx outlines the importance of credit in Volume 3 of *Capital*, but even he could not have envisaged the extension of credit on the scale that took place over the following decades. Personal debt rose as credit cards and loans were handed out, mortgages were given to people with little or no collateral, student grants were replaced with student loans, and every opportunity for encouraging people to borrow was promoted. As Grace Blakeley describes it:

> Rather than adopt the Keynesian approach which, as we have seen, gave workers too much power for the bosses' liking, the

architects of finance-led growth opted for a different model: privatised Keynesianism. Instead of state spending, demand would be propped up by debt, creating a class of indebted and individualised consumers in place of a class of powerful workers.[7]

Despite stagnating wages, workers were able to buy, and capitalists were able to sell. The only problem was that everyone went further and further and further into debt, until it became unsustainable – and we arrived at the events of 2008.

As everyone knows, in 2008, the world economy crashed. Except that, in a sense, it didn't. On the day after the 'crash' – or the week after, or whatever the appropriate time is for how long a 'crash' takes to happen – all the requirements of a functioning economy remained in place, just as they had been before. You would have searched in vain for the rubble or the wreckage, the injured or the maimed.

The same workers who had been working before the crash were just as capable of making their way to the same factories, workshops or other workplaces, where they would have found the walls and ceilings as solid as ever, and the machinery still fully functional. They were no less able to use the same equipment to transform materials from the same sources into the same varieties of products, which could be distributed via the same trains, travelling along the same intact train tracks, or the same lorries driving along roads no more potholed than before, to be distributed to the same people (or to different people, as appropriate).

All the plumbers and electricians, the painters and decorators, the hairdressers, the children's entertainers, physical trainers, and other service providers, were just as able to go along to the same (or different) places, and provide their various services to people in the same way as they had done before the crash.

But the economy was not organised around people providing goods and services for those who wanted or needed them. It was organised around people providing goods and services for the market. And whilst 'the economy' had not crashed, the market had. All the requirements of a functioning economy were in place, but the capitalist way of organising them was no longer functioning as its advocates insisted it should.

The relationship between people producing things for sale, and other people wanting and being able to buy those things, had broken down. And as tends to happen when the market mechanism begins to falter, it became manifest first of all in those parts of the market that are most divorced from the production of things people have real use or need for: the crash announced itself as a financial crash.

A financial crash is calamitous for capitalism whenever it happens. The financial sector plays an important role under capitalism, because the decisions about what to produce and how it should be distributed are decided by private individuals and companies, operating in the market, and those individuals and companies are limited in what they can do by the amount of money that's available to them. Without a financial sector to provide credit, this would impose serious limitations.

By extending credit, the finance sector allows entrepreneurs to create companies, and companies to make investments, without having to amass all the wealth needed to do so in advance. The money borrowed, plus interest, can be paid back later from profits. Similarly, finance allows people to buy expensive items, like houses and cars, earlier than they'd otherwise be able to – by giving them the option of also paying for a loan.

In this way, the finance sector is supposed to provide the oil that keeps the cogs of the capitalist machine turning. But by 2008, the financial sector was more like an oil spill through which companies and consumers were sliding.

The basis for the 2008 crash had been put in place by the developments of neoliberalism over the previous decades. The changes to the financial sector in the 1980s had not only enabled workers to keep buying by going into debt; they had also given more freedom and power to capital. International bodies put pressure on developing nations to allow free movement of capital. In the US, the Glass-Steagall Act, which had enforced the separation of commercial and investment banking, was repealed. In the UK the 'Big Bang' of 1986 changed rules for the London Stock Exchange, deregulating the financial markets.

Capitalism encourages people to innovate, to find new ways of making profits. But creating innovative companies and producing commercial commodities is difficult. With the changes that had been made, there was an obvious place for the sensible entrepreneur to focus their efforts – in the financial sector. Why complicate the profit-making process unnecessarily? Let the production of goods be done by someone else. The keenest minds, the most agile innovators, could find a home for themselves far from the places where surplus-value was actually created. By dealing only with the monetary manifestation of surplus-value, they could focus their efforts where money could be made most efficiently – directly from money.

Many of capitalism's most imaginative innovators applied their talents to the financial sector, and the results were impressive, especially when you consider how little they had to work with – no metals, plastics or wood, no chemicals or machinery, just numbers, currencies and legal contracts. And yet their innovations were endless. From insuring each other's insurance policies and speculating on each other's speculations, they moved on to creating innovative financial instruments that allowed them to bet other people's houses on what they felt sure were sure things, while hedging their bets by buying credit default swaps to insulate themselves from debt obligations that they collateralised by dividing loans into tranches and apportioning them to portfolios with options and futures and derivatives of different derivations via carefully structured investment vehicles that could be driven through legal loopholes allowing fiduciary infidelities that leveraged everything available and wrapped it all in terminological and mathematical intermediations that ensured that nobody knew what they were doing, including, it turned out, themselves.

The financial sector grew to dwarf the real economy. Why would those working in it doubt for a moment that they were doing something worthwhile? The value of all those innovations was there for all to see in the statistics. What they were producing may not have amounted to anything more concrete than numbers. But, oh, what numbers!

The only annoying complication was that buried within, or beneath, or somehow connected to, those financial products, there had to be loans to actual companies producing actual commodities, or to actual consumers buying concrete products – to those people not clever enough, or wise enough, to have become part of the financial economy. So they made it as easy as possible for those companies and consumers to take advantage of simpler opportunities. They offered them financial products suited to their levels of sophistication, loans and mortgages and financial options with nice sounding names and not too complicated apparent advantages. They had something for everyone. A lack of collateral posed no problem. There was always something subprime to help out the less fortunate.

But then, increasing numbers of those people they had offered such good deals to, mysteriously seemed to be unable to pay their debts. They were clearly trying to perform the making money from money trick. They were paying off mortgages by taking out loans, paying off loans using their credit cards. But they couldn't seem to get the hang of it. The debts kept mounting.

On the face of it, there was no obvious reason why a relatively small number of not very important people being unable to pay their mortgages would cause the entire world economy to enter one of the biggest crises in capitalist history. But it occurred to some people in the financial sector that the number of loan defaults was worryingly high, and then other people in the financial sector heard about this and they worried that the value of their financial assets, which depended above all on the confidence of others, might not be sustained. So they sold them. And seeing these sales of assets that had been considered valuable by people who, everyone agreed, knew how these things were supposed to work, others lost confidence, and they sold up as well. And since capital and confidence, and the lack of them, can spread so much more easily from nation to nation, than people or goods, in no time at all, billions of dollars that had been magically created, magically disappeared.

The market mechanism broke down, revealing some of the most useless people in the world – in terms of contributing anything worthwhile to society – to be some of the most useless people in the world, in the sense of lacking the competence to do the job they were supposed to be doing. And over the following months and years, contracts were cancelled, redundancy notices were sent out, mortgages were foreclosed and tenancies terminated, companies were shut down, spending was cut for schools, for hospitals, for social care, and millions more joined the unemployed or underemployed, prevented from doing the useful work they were willing to do, from making the contributions to society that they were capable of making.

The only possible explanation for people allowing this madness to continue is that the great majority of people have been convinced that it's unreasonable, that it would be unrealistic, to expect anything better, that all those authoritative sounding economic experts, despite their occasional displays of embarrassing ineptitude, regardless of the repeated inadequacy of their predictions, and even though their ability to learn from hindsight is so clearly limited, are nonetheless the most insightful guides we can hope to find – that the economic system they insist we stick with is the only practical one possible. Which is odd, when you consider that the evidence to the contrary has never been clearer.

For socialists, one compensation for capitalism surviving as long as it has, is that the longer it survives, the more evidence it provides that it's no longer needed. In the twenty-first century, some of the clearest evidence is provided, ironically, but not surprisingly, by some of the most successful capitalist companies. Leigh Phillips and Michal Rozworski make this case in *The People's Republic of Walmart*. They present many reasons to believe that economic planning could – or already does – work better than the market, and they recount various attempts and experiments that suggest it could work more democratically. They begin, however, by looking at some of capitalism's greatest 'success stories', starting, you will not be surprised to hear, with Walmart.

The authors are at pains to stress that they have no love for Walmart, which built its brand on low wages and union-busting. But they can't help admiring Walmart's 'operational efficiency [and] logistical genius' – in much the same way that 'an epidemiologist concedes an irrefutable genius to the wicked evolutionary dexterity of drug-resistant tuberculosis'.[8] Walmart is the third largest employer in the world. The only larger employers are the United States' so-called Department of Defense, and

China's so-called People's Liberation Army. (Both of which, incidentally, are publicly run, and not exactly famed for their inefficiency or ineffective planning.) Walmart stocks products from more than seventy countries, operating over 11,000 stores in twenty-seven countries. If its revenues were described as 'Gross Domestic Product', it would have a GDP similar to Belgium or Sweden, bigger than that of Austria, Ireland or Norway – or indeed the majority of nations in the world.

Yet, remarkably, Walmart manages to organise its nation-sized economic activities without dividing them up into separate organisations or sub-companies, competing with each other to see which can make a profit. The way it organises its economic empire is through sophisticated central planning. In effect, Walmart is one of the most successful planned economies ever. If Walmart can do it, why can't Belgium?

And if the positive example of Walmart isn't persuasive enough, Phillips and Rozworski also provide a counter-example. Sears, Roebuck & Company was similarly nation-sized, but it occurred to its chairman and CEO, Edward Lampert, that there was no reason a nation-sized company should have to make do, as capitalist companies have always done, with organising their internal operations through planning. A nation-sized company could gain from all the same advantages as a capitalist nation. Accordingly, he reorganised the company, creating competing units as part of an internal market. The result was disaster. Instead of working together, the different sections undermined each other and became uncoordinated. The company lost billions, and in 2018 it filed for bankruptcy.

You might object that a company like Walmart can't be compared to a national economy. The fact that they can so effectively plan the range and scope of activities they're involved with, certainly brings into question why mainstream opinion suggests it's so necessary to rely on the market to organise the economy. But perhaps there are some aspects of economic development that capitalism does better.

If there's one thing we all know a vibrant market economy provides, it's that all-important stimulus and motivation for entrepreneurs and private companies to innovate – to develop new technology in order to outdo their competitors. Except that it doesn't. Actually, the evidence suggests that most private enterprises want returns on their investment as soon as possible, and they are reluctant to invest in the sort of long-term research and development necessary to create real innovation.

And why should they, when the state does it for them, and does it better? In her book *The Entrepreneurial State*, Mariana Mazzucato describes the extent to which most innovation comes not from private industry but from the state. She cites a study from 2011 which found that:

> ...between 1971 and 2006, 77 out of the most important 88 innovations (rated by *R & D Magazine*'s annual awards) – or 88 per cent – have been fully dependent on federal research support, especially, but not only, in their early phases – and the *R & D Magazine*'s award *excludes* IT innovations.[9]

Mazzucato provides an extensive list of examples, showing how the state has been responsible not only for specific innovations, but for creating entirely new sectors, such as the internet, nanotechnology, biotechnology and clean energy. But pride of place amongst her examples is that supposed icon of private company innovation – Apple's iPhone. Mazzucato goes through the twelve technologies that made the iPhone possible, from microprocessors and memory chips to micro hard drives and liquid crystal displays, from the internet and cellular networks to GPS and voice recognition, and shows how every one of them was only developed thanks to state funding.

Mazzucato's intention is not to argue against private companies, but to highlight how state support has often been essential to their development. She suggests companies like Apple should be required to feed more of their profits back to the government, to support further state-funded research that could help other companies. Her conclusion ignores a rather obvious question, however – why do we need private companies at all?

Are we seriously supposed to believe that whilst researchers and scientists funded by the state can somehow find the motivation to come up with all the technologies that went into the iPhone, the only way a product like the iPhone itself could be created is thanks to the unique genius of entrepreneurs driven by the profit motive? That the only way to be sufficiently motivated to the heights of genius required to put existing technologies together, in the form of an iPhone, was thanks to the prospect of being able to farm out production to underpaid Chinese workers, and hire super-skilled advertising companies to convince people to pay for every overpriced upgrade, in order to earn billions of dollars, that could be hidden away in tax havens?

Or is the reason it happened like that because the capitalist state is happy to invest taxpayers' money in research that can be used, for free, by profit-making enterprises, but if someone were to suggest that state employees could develop a practical device like a smartphone, then those in control of the money would shake their heads at such foolishness and explain, 'No, no, no – that isn't the sort of thing the state should get involved with. That's clearly something that could make money. That should be done by private companies, because... capitalism!'

So we know entrepreneurs are not very keen on investing in the sort of research and innovation that has the potential to create a better society, when there's no guarantee of making a profit, but fortunately, there are people who are very good at doing so, when the state is willing to fund their research. And we have evidence that it's possible to plan economic activity on a nation-sized scale, but only as part of an authoritarian capitalist company. But that still isn't enough. It's not as though we have any plan of how we might organise a whole economy differently, do we? Actually, yes, we do.

In the wake of the collapse of the centrally planned economies of the twentieth century, many Marxists have been attracted to the idea of 'market socialism'. This approach takes the view that the market itself is not the problem. The development of an economy guided by the market may have been necessary before capitalism could come into existence, but the real problem was that it did so in a way that involved private ownership of the means of production and exploitation of workers. There's no reason the market can't be retained as a way of organising production and distribution, whilst finding a way to replace all those roles that are purely parasitic on the parts of the economy that produce things people actually need. In this way, we could eliminate the need for private company owners and shareholders, landlords, most of the finance sector, and so on.

David Schweickart, for example, considers it regrettable that the term 'market economy' is often used interchangeably with 'capitalism', because:

> The term 'market economy' highlights the least objectionable defining feature of capitalism while directing attention away from the really problematic institutions, namely, private ownership of means of production and wage labour.[10]

In *After Capitalism*, Schweickart provides a detailed description of how market socialism could work. In what he calls 'Economic Democracy', the market is allowed to function to guide production and distribution, but it's combined with worker self-management of enterprises. Capital is not owned by workers but by society as a whole: it's effectively leased by each enterprise, which pays the equivalent of tax on capital assets, with the money from this tax then going towards all new investment through a network of public investment banks.

Schweickart examines seven topics: inequality, unemployment, overwork, poverty, economic instability, ecological degradation, and lack of democracy. For each one, he then outlines why the problem is endemic to capitalism, and how moving to Economic Democracy would either mitigate the problem or overcome it entirely.

Clearly, Schweickart's model has never been implemented at a national scale, but as he points out, something like it has been done on a smaller scale – although, really not that small. Mondragon is the sixth largest company in Spain. It's made up of a federation of more than two hundred cooperative enterprises, each of which is wholly owned by its workforce. The workers elect a board of directors, which appoints the management. Senior managers are paid, at most, five times as much as the lowest-paid workers. By comparison, the average CEO of a FTSE 100 company earns 129 times as much as their lowest-paid employees.

Mondragon also has its own bank, a social security scheme, a supermarket chain, and various educational institutions including a university, along with a number of technology and R&D centres.

Although it operates within the market, it makes decisions that are more reflective of the priorities of its workers. One of its central missions is job creation, rather than profit maximisation. Funds are made available to individual cooperatives to help them through bad times. As Schweickart says:

> Capitalists do not manage the Mondragon cooperatives. Capitalists do not supply entrepreneurial talent. Capitalists do not supply the capital for the development of new enterprises or the expansion of existing ones. But these three functions ... are the only functions the capitalist class has ever performed. The Mondragon record strongly suggests that we don't need capitalists anymore...[11]

It's difficult to see how the economic model Schweickart outlines could fail to be an improvement on capitalism. Some, like Schweickart, see such a system as a reasonable end to aim at, whilst others would view it as a practical step in the process of transitioning to a system that doesn't need the market at all. For the foreseeable future, there's no reason for these views to be in conflict. If this sort of change could be implemented, it would then become clearer whether there's good reason to go further.

Personally, I suspect that after a market socialist system was introduced, there would be an increasing recognition that, even with cooperatives and public investment, the market is not quite such an effective way of organising production and distribution as some advocates of market socialism seem to think. At the same time, more and more alternatives would be developed and implemented, until people would start to debate how marginal the market needs to become before it counts as a shift from 'market socialism' to 'socialism with markets', and then to 'socialism with market elements', and eventually there would just be a 'Market Day' once a year when everyone dresses up in comical suits and ties, or uniforms and other silly costumes, and re-enacts the funny old days when people related to each other by buying and selling.

For some people, the sooner we can get rid of the market the better. According to Robin Hahnel:

> ...market relations not only fail to provide means for people to take the interests of others into account, they systematically punish any who attempt to practise solidarity. In other words, markets 'work' by stimulating greed and fear while undermining trust and solidarity needed to build the economics of equitable cooperation. In short, markets are cancer to the socialist project.
>
> I use the word 'cancer' ... because cancer begins as a small malignancy, a cellular dysfunction, which spreads until it destroys an entire organism. And that is the image I wished to convey for why we should fear permitting markets to continue to play a role in a truly desirable economy.[12]

In the 1990s, Hahnel, along with Michael Albert, developed a detailed economic model to replace capitalism – and the market – called Participatory Economics (sometimes shortened to Parecon). This system aims to organise the economy around democracy, justice and solidarity using four major institutions:

1. Self-governing democratic councils of workers and consumers where each member has one vote,
2. Jobs balanced for empowerment and desirability by the members of worker councils themselves,
3. Compensation according to effort as judged by one's workmates, and
4. A participatory planning procedure in which councils and federations of workers and consumers propose and revise their own interrelated activities without central planners or markets, under rules designed to generate outcomes that are efficient, equitable, and environmentally sustainable.[13]

The two main criticisms that tend to be made of Participatory Economics are that it would involve endless meetings and that it would not, in fact, end up being efficient. Hahnel insists that this is not true and that it reflects a failure to understand what is being proposed. I have to say that, if it is a mistake, it's an understandable one. Reading the details of how Participatory Economics would operate does not inspire confidence that living in such a society would be a liberating experience.

But that may well be unfair. Textbooks offering a detailed description of how the human body works don't, I imagine, set anyone's pulse racing, and yet we're all very happy to have a healthy body with a pulse that can occasionally race. Perhaps living in a society organised along the lines of Participatory Economics would be far more enjoyable than reading about it. It would certainly be nice to have the chance to find out. As Hahnel says, it will only really become clear:

> ...after many progressive mass movements have waged many successful struggles over many years, and after millions of people have created a multitude of real world experiments in different forms of equitable cooperation even while global capitalism persists.[14]

Obviously, there are many possibilities between market socialism and a fully planned economy, and many possible ways of organising either of these and everything in between. There are other thinkers who've suggested alternative approaches. But, frankly, not many. Which is odd, isn't it?

You might compare it to a situation where people worked out how to build flying machines, then came up with lots of ways to improve them – added propellors, fuselages, perfected their aerodynamic design, then invented jet engines, and developed all sorts of other impressive technologies to make flying a practical and enjoyable experience – but hardly anybody showed any interest or curiosity in whether it might be possible to travel beyond the Earth's atmosphere. Considering the number of economists there are in the world, you'd think a few more would have the intellectual curiosity to wonder whether it might be possible to design an alternative economic system to capitalism – even if only as an interesting thought experiment. But evidently not.

Far from being surprised by how few suggestions there have been for economic alternatives, most people would be surprised to learn that there are any alternatives at all. Since the 1980s, economic debate has been shaped by the assumption, or the assertion, that Margaret Thatcher famously put into words: 'There is no alternative.'

The left was not prepared for the success of neoliberalism. Most assumed that some form of Keynesianism would continue to work, either remaining much as it was in the post-war decades, or gradually leading to greater improvements. Some, bizarrely, held on to the idea that the Soviet Union was in some way progressive, only to see it collapse. Those who were arguing for any other alternative lacked influence and ended up being defeated.

In reality, there have always been alternatives. What's been missing is an opposition capable of effectively advocating for them. Through the 1980s, the Labour Party, like other Social Democratic parties, shifted rightwards, and left-wingers were marginalised. When the Conservatives finally lost an election, it was to the 'New Labour' of Tony Blair that Margaret Thatcher had understandably declared to be her greatest achievement, a Labour Party that had fully accepted the neoliberal logic.

One of the first acts of New Labour in government was to make the Bank of England independent, sending the clear message that the best people to trust with the economy were economists and bankers, not politicians. Labour would invest more in education and the health service, but at the same time would extend Conservative policies of academisation in education and internal markets in the NHS. They preferred 'private finance initiatives' to public ownership. They introduced a minimal minimum wage, whilst boasting that Britain retained the most restrictive trade union legislation in the Western world. Their approach to the financial markets, on the other hand, was to practise 'light touch' regulation that would contribute to the financial crisis to come.

The denial of alternatives had become so ingrained that even the financial crash of 2008 ended up being paid for by the poorest, while the bankers were soon back to receiving their bonuses. As late as 2013,

David Cameron felt confident enough to claim that 'there is no alternative' to austerity. His confidence proved justified when the Labour Party responded by asking if that could include 'austerity lite'.

It took a long time, but the effects of the crash, on top of growing inequality and insecurity, finally gave rise to opposition and resistance. The left began growing again in significant movements in Greece, Spain and France, and around the campaigns of Jeremy Corbyn and Bernie Sanders. At the same time, however, right-wing movements became increasingly threatening across Europe, the United States and elsewhere.

When Margaret Thatcher proclaimed 'there is no alternative', it was an expression of strength, of confidence that she was representing the way forward. When David Cameron said it, it was more of an assertion that people were just going to have to put up with the way things were. More recently, it's less likely to be said out loud, but it's always there as an assumption, an assertion, underlying political and economic arguments, because the pathetic reality is that it's the strongest argument opponents of socialism have. It's the lie they rely on to convince people to accept the status quo.

When enough people realise that, not only are there alternatives, but that exploring those alternatives will mean taking more control over their own lives, then the apologists for twenty-first century capitalism will find themselves in the novel and unnerving situation of having to find a positive argument for why people should prefer to stick with the way things are. It will be interesting to see them try.

7. Interlude – So Far

A long time after the beginning, after energy and atoms, after stars, after explosions of stars, after water had flowed across earth, after matter had breathed into life, something miraculous happened – a creature opened its eye.

One could say, instead, over millions of years, species evolved, brain capacities expanded, sense organs became more specialised. But compared to the time that had gone before, it all happened of a sudden, and each eye that opened achieved the same miraculous thing: it created light.

From out of the energy that had been streaming out from the Sun, a few wavelengths split away. They scattered down through the atmosphere, ricocheted across objects, passed through the absence of the pupil, were transformed through the still more mysterious path to the mind, and the world was suddenly something to behold.

Up until then, everything had been what it was and nothing more. Now, some parts of the world were what they were, but were also expressions, representations, of other parts of the world. The world had begun to reflect on itself.

And as the eyes grew sharper, and the minds grew keener, the world took shape. Lines became more clearly drawn. Shapes sharpened into objects and stood apart from their surroundings. Patterns persisted. Perspectives shifted.

Plants grew out of the Earth and apart from each other. Trees rose up higher, branches spread out against the sky. Movement became more fluid. The blur amongst the branches resolved into a shivering of leaves.

As night followed night, the grey night sky sank back into blackness and stars flickered into existence. As day followed day, the Sun and the Earth and the mind conspired to paint the world in greens and browns, in mixtures of yellows and reds, in oranges, blues and purples, deepening and brightening as clouds covered and uncovered the Sun.

Until there were eyes looking out on a world that appeared much as the world appears to us today. But that world was quite unlike the world we know, because that world was almost entirely devoid of meaning.

*

The first glimmers of meaning were there, as creatures explored the world, as they dealt with their hungers and fears, as they hunted and searched, some guided by parents, some cooperating or competing with others.

But for the world to begin to resemble the world that now surrounds us, creatures had to appear whose minds could transform those first glimmers of meaning, as their ancestors' eyes had transformed the first glimmers of light.

And such creatures arose. They took the step back. They looked at the world around them, and they saw how the world held meaning for them. And they looked into each other's faces, and they smiled, and they frowned.

And as they interacted with each other and the world, a world of meaning spread out around them. It sparked from their fingertips. It spilt from their tongues, as they gave voice to all that had been unspoken, gave shape to new, or newly found, realities and realisations.

They introduced new wonders to the world – beauty and ugliness, good and bad, love, kindness, cruelty, meaning and meaninglessness, friendship and enmity, gratitude, forgiveness, envy, ignorance, wisdom, greed, compassion, pride...

And they agreed and disagreed about how to make sense of the meanings they had created. And they taught their thoughts to their children, and their children wondered at the world they had been born into, and the possibilities that it might contain.

*

The world could not have sparked spontaneously into consciousness, so consciousness had crept into the world creature by creature, each sensing the world around it as separate from it, as something outside of itself.

Each consciousness of each creature, created by the changing world around it and the changing mind within it, sensed itself as the still centre of a changing world.

And as consciousness brought meaning into the world, it divided the world into separate parts whose interdependence was hidden. It enabled insights and it created illusions. It hid the process of change behind abstractions.

And creatures began to categorise the world. They divided it, first, into what was wanted and what was to be avoided, with the rest relegated to unimportance. Then, later, finding importance in more complicated ways, they sorted it further.

And as the world expressed itself in words, commonalities enough were found to allow communication, and differences enough were encountered to create confusion. And people asked themselves and each other what they should make of it all.

*

As cooperation developed, society gained a sense of itself, and it studied nature as something separate from it. People made use of the tools that nature provided, and then fashioned more complex tools of their own. They ceased fleeing from fire and learned how to create it and to cultivate its uses. They extracted metal from stone, blended metal with metal. They forged new tools and fashioned jewellery.

They changed rivers, and then oceans, from barriers to travel into means of travelling, and they travelled to every part of the world. And when they encountered others like, and yet unlike, themselves, they clashed or cooperated. Goods and ideas were exchanged or taken.

They adapted themselves to new environments, and they adapted environments to fit their needs. They designed their dwellings, created settlements, built villages, towns, cities. They domesticated plants and animals, developing new varieties and breeds.

Adding ever more to the sum of knowledge, each generation learned from those who came before and passed its learning on to those who followed. They created testimonies to themselves and their pasts, in stories, in paintings, in monuments, in sculptures, in libraries.

They made sense of the world with logic, with mathematics, with imagination, with science. And using the concepts with which they made sense of the world, they reshaped the world, and the changing world gave them reasons to rethink.

They identified the elements of nature, worked out their commonalities and their distinctions. They identified different forces and forms of energy. They measured the depths of the oceans, the mass of atoms, the speed of light.

*

While finding new ways to indulge their age-old urge to stargaze, the realisation arrived that the light they were looking at had started its journey before the world was born.

And they took their understanding of atoms and energies back to within moments of the moment of creation, and worked out how atoms coalesced into clouds, ignited into stars, combined into molecules, into mountains, into oceans, into life.

They investigated how life could have come into being and evolution unfolded. They followed the fossil trail to their own beginnings. They excavated the earliest civilisations, deciphered ancient texts, uncovered the first stirrings of philosophy and science. They traced their own histories and puzzled out the reasons for paths taken and not taken.

And after contemplating all that human beings had built, had learned and created, they turned from that short period of their past, in which they had achieved so much, and tried to imagine the virtual infinity of the future. And they wondered at what wonders they might yet create.

They imagined a world of people working together to deepen their understanding of themselves and each other and the world, aiming to enable everyone to do and to be as much as they were capable of doing and being.

They looked forward to the seeming certainty of moving beyond poverty, of providing everyone with security, care and comfort, to creating a world of plenty.

They wondered how long it would take to eradicate diseases, to be able to undo every kind of injury or infirmity, to allow everyone to live long and healthy lives.

They imagined a world where they would work on what they wanted to, while automation would take over ever more of the menial, the tedious and the routine.

They wondered what developments would be created in leisure and recreation, in culture and art. And they laughed at the limitations of their imaginations.

They imagined a world of people who would take for granted what was now almost beyond imagining, and who would imagine more.

*

But then, they looked back to the time when the world had become increasingly interconnected, when the accumulation of wealth and understanding had accelerated, as their production was dispersed across continents, creating interdependence and integration, enabling greater efficiency, encouraging innovation and invention.

And looking back, they saw how there had been no possibility of consciously bringing this process about. There had not been the abilities or the organisation to deliberately put such a system into place. So instead, mechanisms had emerged that encouraged, and then required, that people produce things for others, in cooperation with others, and as efficiently as possible.

They saw how the world had been brought together without the intent to do so, how the process that bound people together appeared as something separate from them, how people cooperated in order to compete, and each person was encouraged to work with others only for the sake of what they could gain for themselves.

They saw how the world had become more social for the sake of selfishness, and the means by which it was brought together created conflicts and contradictions.

Inventions were made and then patented to prevent them from being shared. Wealth was created and then hoarded, while millions went without. Work became more productive, yet there was always the demand to get more work done. Money and goods moved freely, while borders kept people apart.

And even as everyone had relied increasingly on everyone else, they had become more divided and isolated and alienated from each other and from the world.

And people looked at the world around them and the possible futures facing them, and they imagined divisions deepening and descending into wars, imagined cities burning, nations fracturing, civilisation disintegrating, spirits broken and hopes destroyed.

They saw the possibility of the human part of nature tearing the nature on which it depended apart, of science that could save the environment, destroying the environment, of poisoned minds and poisoned bodies on a poisoned Earth.

And they saw the possibility of a return to a world where everything would continue, as ever, to change, but a world where there would be no understanding of what was happening, no understanding of what had happened, and nobody left to care.

8. To Be Determined

It seems obvious that you have free will, doesn't it? It's surely absurd to suggest otherwise – you've been making your own decisions all day long. All your life long. It's not as though somebody or something has been holding a real or metaphorical gun to your head as you've been going about your business. Search as they might, no one will find your hidden strings. Your whole life has been a series of choices. How could it be otherwise?

And yet every decision you've made was dependent on the situation you were in and the person you were at that moment. But that situation depended on the situation a moment before that, and the person you were then. And how you acted then depended on the situation a moment earlier and the person you were then. And so on, right back to before you existed and were capable of being in any situation at all. So at what point did you make a choice not determined by what came before? There would seem to be nowhere for freedom to creep in. Obviously, the sense of having free will must be mistaken. Your life is just a step-by-step sequence of cause and effect.

Both these conclusions seem to make sense, but they also seem to contradict each other. They can't both be true, can they? If all your decisions are determined by what came before, shouldn't it be possible for you to stand back and wait to see what this process of determination dictates you'll do next? If you do so, of course, what will happen is this: you'll stand back and wait to see what it has been determined you'll do next. Because that is what you decided to do. (Although, of course, those who don't believe in free will, would argue that your decision to do so was determined.) Whatever the case, you'll never find out what it is you were supposedly determined to do until you stop waiting to see what it is, and decide to do something. Could anyone choose not to find this confusing?

Those who argue that there's no such thing as free will have been greatly encouraged by the results of experiments conducted by Benjamin Libet in the 1980s. Libet asked subjects to choose a random moment to carry out a simple physical activity, such as pressing a button or flexing a finger or wrist. He measured the associated activity in their brain and compared it with the time they felt the intention to move. He found that the 'readiness potential' – the unconscious brain activity leading up to the action – began, on average, around two hundred milliseconds before the subject consciously felt they had decided to move: the subject's belief that their action occurred as a result of their conscious decision was shown to be false.

This clearly contradicts what we assume about the relationship between conscious intentions and actions, and it's absolutely devastating news for anyone who has believed, for their whole life, that they're capable of making meaningful decisions in less than two hundred milliseconds. On the other hand if, like me, making the decisions that matter to you – and even some that don't matter that much – tends to involve thinking for a while, considering the pros and cons, weighing things up, settling on a decision, but then maybe changing your mind, then deciding to leave the decision till later, then finally coming to an almost certainly final decision and then maybe – just maybe – acting on the decision, then it's not entirely clear why Libet's experiment would matter to you.

There are plenty of decisions I've made that I didn't become aware of until long after I'd made them. I seem to remember it wasn't until I'd been thinking about how to organise the chapters of this book for weeks that I realised I'd come to the decision that I was seriously going to try to write it. It never occurred to me that this meant the decision to write it was not really my decision.

Libet's results certainly contradict what was always assumed about how thoughts and actions are related. But now that we know the truth, how much difference does it really make? When you carry out actual hand movements in real life, when you delicately brush an eyelash from somebody's cheek, or flip someone the finger, does it matter to you whether you became aware of your decision before or after you began to move your hand, and by how many milliseconds? If you do, for some reason, decide to reflect on the sequence of what just happened, is there so much difference between believing that you made a decision to carry out an action that then followed, as opposed to realising that you made a decision to carry out an action and then became conscious of it? Presumably, the action, the decision and your consciousness of both will all play a part in what unfolds next, regardless of what order they happened in.

To see this sequence as meaningful is a bit like saying that, in a democracy, the decision about who forms a government is not actually made by the electorate, because that electorate does not get to find out who it elected until long after its votes are cast.

I can see how it would seem like a problem, for someone who thinks of the decision-making part of themselves as being a persistent self, somehow separate from the body and the brain, rather than as part of that complicated, constantly changing, physical and mental process. But that's not how modern scientists think of the self, is it?

The debate about free will and determinism matters to Marxists, because Marxism is often portrayed as a determinist doctrine that would – first philosophically, and then in more dastardly ways – deny people their freedom.

Marx's understanding of history is sometimes referred to as 'historical determinism'. It isn't a term Marx ever used; he preferred 'the materialist conception of history'. But it isn't unreasonable. Some of his writings certainly justify it. Probably the best-known example is this passage from the preface to his 1859 work, *A Contribution to the Critique of Political Economy*:

> In the social production of their existence, men inevitably enter into definite relations, which are independent of their will, namely relations of production appropriate to a given stage in

the development of their material forces of production. The totality of these relations of production constitutes the economic structure of society, the real foundation, on which arises a legal and political superstructure and to which correspond definite forms of social consciousness. The mode of production of material life conditions the general process of social, political and intellectual life. It is not the consciousness of men that determines their existence, but their social existence that determines their consciousness.[1]

If Marx really believed that people's consciousness was quite so determined by material reality as some people read this passage as suggesting, then you have to wonder why he put so much effort into writing and political activity, with the apparent aim of influencing what people thought and did. In reality, it's clear from his writings as a whole that this attempt to briefly sum it up oversimplifies the process he's describing.

Part of the reason for this is probably that he wished to differentiate himself from some other socialists, who he believed were not giving enough importance to the material, economic and social context in which political developments took place. But the unfortunate result is that many who've read his work – and not only his critics – see it as being more deterministic than it is. In later life, Engels would try to correct such misunderstanding, for example in a letter to Joseph Bloch, written in 1890:

According to the materialist conception of history, the *ultimately* determining element in history is the production and reproduction of real life. More than this neither Marx nor I have ever asserted. Hence if somebody twists this into saying that the economic element is the *only* determining one, he transforms that proposition into a meaningless, abstract, senseless phrase. The economic situation is the basis, but the various elements of the superstructure: political forms of the class struggle and its results, to wit: constitutions established by the victorious class after a successful battle, etc., juridical forms, and then even the reflexes of all these actual struggles in the brains of the participants, political, juristic, philosophical theories, religious views and their further development into systems of dogmas, also exercise their influence upon the course of the historical struggles and in many cases preponderate in determining their *form*.[2]

It seems to me that part of the reason people find the idea of materialism objectionable, or unrealistic, results from the way Marx often presents it as though consciousness is something passive, acted upon and shaped by material reality. The point, surely, is that consciousness and material reality are parts of the same thing, each affecting the other. Conscious human action is inseparable from material change. Some of Marx's writings do express this, for example:

> History does nothing; it 'possesses no colossal riches'; it 'fights no fight.' It is rather man – real, living man – who acts, possesses and fights in everything. It is by no means 'History' which uses man as a means to carry out its ends as if it were a person apart; rather History is nothing but the activity of man in pursuit of his ends.[3]

Admittedly, this is from 1844 and, it could be argued, represents the young Marx, not the supposedly more 'economically determinist' Marx of later years. But how about this description of the labour process from the book he put more time and effort into than any other, Volume 1 of *Capital*:

> A spider conducts operations which resemble those of the weaver, and a bee would put many a human architect to shame by the construction of its honeycomb cells. But what distinguishes the worst architect from the best of bees is that the architect builds the cell in his mind before he constructs it in wax. At the end of every labour process, a result emerges which had already been conceived by the worker at the beginning, hence already existed ideally. Man not only effects a change of form in

the materials of nature; he also realizes his own purpose in those materials.[4]

I suspect some people dislike Marx's ideas because of the materialism, at least as much as the determinism. We tend to associate what's most human, what most expresses our sense of freedom, as being bound up with our consciousness – 'the free play of ideas'. Stressing materiality seems to undermine this, and to reduce what is mysterious and uncertain to a simple mechanical process.

The experience of consciousness is undoubtedly mysterious, but there are many kinds and levels of mystery in the world, and it isn't clear how their mystery is undermined by their being a part of material reality. Consider, for example, a leaf turning, as some leaves do, toward the light, as the Sun moves across the sky. The sunlight is not moving the leaf. What *is* moving the leaf? There's no consciousness. It's just cause and effect, but the cause and effect is certainly not simple. It isn't like waves smashing against rocks, or rocks falling into the sea. It's a collection of dumb atoms, but is what the collection of atoms are doing so dumb?

Or consider something more complex, something where there is, presumably, consciousness – certainly there's a brain – a spider, spinning its latest wonder of a web, sitting at its centre. What conceptions does the spider have, if any, of the world it's making or that made it? Having spun the web from itself, does the spider know where its body ends and the web begins? When it feels the web's vibration, does it conceive of something fly-like, something food-like, struggling? Does it consider whether, or when, to retrieve its prey?

Or take a still fancier predator – a fox. Like the spider, it's a product of long evolution, a collection of instincts, a body and mind perfectly shaped to fill its niche in the natural world. But it clearly has the ability to hold an incredibly complicated model of the world in its mind. It wasn't only shaped by evolution. It learned from its mother, learned from playing with the world, and maybe it learned a few tricks of its own which, if they were taught, were taught by trial and error or even thinking things through for itself – it's a cunning fox.

When the fox crouches down in the long grass, does it conceive of the way its prey might see its surroundings? Does it grasp the difference between the way it sees the world and the way the world is seen by its prey? If so, how impressive is that! Even young children have difficulty grasping that other people don't know the world in the same way that they do.

There may be nothing in the universe so impressive as the human mind. No wonder we who possess them are inclined to think of our own mind's workings as adding up to a different order of reality – all those thoughts, those perspectives, those complex possibilities, the most impressive mental juggling act in existence. But our ideas are inseparable from the material world, just as much as the fox's cunning, the spider's web, the leaf's turning. They are all part of the material world unfolding.

I doubt anyone, on encountering Buddhism, has felt that it suffered from an excessive focus on the material world. The very first line of the popular Buddhist text, *The Dhammapada*, begins, 'All experience is preceded by mind, led by mind, made by mind.'[5] There's even a Mahayana school of philosophy, the Yogacara, that views reality as 'mind-only'.

Buddhist practice, furthermore, is all about developing the mind and learning to see more clearly. Its main practices involve developing a more meditative mind and seeking insight. One practice the Buddha gives a lot of importance to is progressing through the 'four jhanas'[6] – developing successively deeper levels of calm and concentration. But supposing a meditator were to progress all the way to the fourth jhana, what should they do with their perfectly focused mind? According to the accounts of the practice in the earliest Buddhist texts, they should do this:

> When one's mind is thus concentrated, pure and bright, unblemished, free from defects, malleable, wieldy, steady and attained to imperturbability, one directs and inclines it to knowing and seeing. One understands thus, this is my body, having material form, composed of the four primary elements, originating from mother and father, built up out of rice and gruel, impermanent, subject to rubbing and pressing, to dissolution and dispersion, and this is my consciousness, supported by it and bound up with it.[7]

This sort of focus on the physical, especially the physical as experienced by body and mind, constantly appears in Buddhist teachings. Material form is one of the five aggregates that make up a human being. If there's any teaching on meditation that's seen as more central than the four jhanas, it's the *Satipatthana Sutta*, which guides the meditator through contemplation of four 'foundations of mindfulness', the first of which is the body. Indeed, by far the most common start to any meditation practice involves focusing on the breath. In a 'mind-only' world, why would the breath be seen as a particularly good focus for meditation? In a mind-only world, why are people even breathing?

What about free will and determinism – what is the Buddhist view? What might we conclude, for example, from this explanation, by the Dalai Lama, of why we should accept that there is no self, that everything is empty:

> Through the twelve links of dependent origination, Buddha teaches that all things and all events, including all elements of one's individual experience, come into being merely as a result of the aggregation of causes and conditions. Understanding this, in turn, can lead us to see that all things are by nature interdependent, originating entirely as a result of other things and other factors.
>
> Buddha teaches that the very fact that something is dependently originated means that it is necessarily devoid of an essential, or independent, reality. For if something is fundamentally *dependent*, by logical necessity it must be devoid of having a nature that is independent of other phenomena, of existing *independently*. Thus it is said that anything that is dependently originated must also be, in actual fact, empty.[8]

No doubt there are some Buddhists – quite possibly including the Dalai Lama – who would argue that what is being described here is not 'determinism'. But it is though, isn't it? Or certainly as much so as some Marxist writings that are widely interpreted as being determinist.

The 'twelve links of dependent origination' that the Dalai Lama mentions refers to another of the central teachings of Buddhism. There are different variations of these links in the suttas. Rupert Gethin offers this as a representative account:

> Conditioned by (1) ignorance are (2) formations, conditioned by formations is (3) consciousness, conditioned by consciousness is (4) mind-and-body, conditioned by mind-and-body are (5) the six senses, conditioned by the six senses is (6) sense-contact, conditioned by sense-contact is (7) feeling, conditioned by feeling is (8) craving, conditioned by craving is (9) grasping, conditioned by grasping is (10) becoming, conditioned by becoming is (11) birth, conditioned by birth is (12) old-age and death – grief, lamentation, pain, sorrow, and despair come into being. Thus is the arising of this whole mass of suffering.[9]

It hardly needs to be said that this is confusing. If there were any doubt on that score, you only have to consider that Buddhists disagree about whether this sequence applies to a single life or is spread over three lives – and those who believe the latter, disagree about where exactly the breaks between different lives occur! If ever there was a likely example of something that did not survive those centuries of oral transmission very well, this is surely it.

In *Dependent Arising in Context*,[10] Linda Blanchard does actually manage to make a persuasive case for how it could make sense, if it's understood partly as a commentary, or satire, on Vedic mythology and rituals that would have been familiar to the Buddha's audience, and if it's seen as describing not a human life (nor three), but the coming into being of the illusion of self. This is certainly not, however, the way most Buddhists have understood it (or failed to understand it).

Whatever we make of the details of the sequence, two things are clear. Firstly, it's notable that it displays no attempt to separate material reality and consciousness, no indication that the relationship between them, or the primacy of one over the other, was of any interest to the Buddha.

Secondly, it's a description about cause and effect. The problem is suffering, so we need to look for the cause of this, and then the cause of that cause, and keep tracing the sequence back to the underlying problem that can be addressed. And then, if we can change the root cause, it will result in the sequence of cause and effect changing and the release from suffering. Indeed, everywhere this appears in the suttas, it's followed by the 'opposite' sequence, where ignorance is overcome and, as a result, suffering does not arise.

The root cause is ignorance or delusion (*avijja*), which in this context refers to seeing permanence in the impermanent, believing there is a self where there is none. But the point of describing the sequence is to explain to people why they should choose to follow the eightfold path, so as to overcome their habitual ignorance and free themselves from suffering. It is, in effect, a demonstration of how understanding the way in which reality is conditioned, and having the ability to choose to change that reality, are seen as part of the same thing.

Although later Buddhists would put a lot of time into arguing about issues which would now be thought of in terms of idealism, materialism, free will and determinism, it's clear that the Buddha did not give great importance to such philosophical questions. He did not see them as useful. Rather, he focused on whatever could bring about practical results. This is made particularly clear in the *Culamalunkya Sutta*.

This sutta recounts how a monk named Malunkyaputta demands clear answers from the Buddha on a number of philosophical questions, such as whether a Buddha continues to exist after death, and whether the soul is the same as the body – but the Buddha refuses to give answers. The sutta makes clear that the Buddha believes giving any answer will only encourage Malunkyaputta to give such questions undue importance; he should, instead, be focusing on the insight and practices that will free him from suffering. Malunkyaputta is compared to someone who's been struck with a poisoned arrow but refuses to let anyone remove it until he knows the name of the person who fired it, their family, how tall they are, and so on.

Suppose someone were to give due consideration to the well-known conundrum that asks which came first, the chicken or the egg, and they decide, for some reason, that it was the chicken: it seems unlikely they would conclude from this that eggs should be dismissed as unimportant epiphenomena, and that they should, from then on, focus their interest on the fundamental question of how chickens create chickens. Similarly, if you see material reality as having come before, and given rise to, consciousness and ideas, there's no way to then make sense of reality without understanding the part that consciousness and ideas play, as they're shaped by their material context, and as they guide the way people choose to interact with the rest of the material world.

Marx and the Buddha both saw ways in which the world had created new positive possibilities, but also how those very developments had created contradictions and illusions. In each case, they saw how the same process that caused the problems also created the motivation needed to develop an understanding of how to overcome them.

The Buddha saw how the way in which consciousness developed – built out of the experience of separate creatures interacting with the world, and through people abstracting from the complexity of the world to understand how its different parts interacted – led to the sense of having a separate self. This led in turn to suffering and discontent, which led to the attempt to understand why that suffering existed, and then to the recognition that the sense of self was an illusion, and finally to the development of ways to overcome or undermine the illusion and the suffering that it caused.

The reason Buddhism is more open to idealist interpretations is because it's more concerned with people's experience of the world than with changing the material reality that we experience. But the reality we experience is a material one. The only way to understand our experience is to see through the conceptual illusion of a self, and to recognise that each person is actually a collection of changing, interrelating skandhas – the body, feelings, perceptions, mental formations and consciousness.

Marx saw how the way in which capitalism came into being had led to the development of technology and the division of labour, which created the possibility of eradicating poverty and of creating a world where alienation could be overcome. But the way it did so also involved alienation for all, and exploitation of the majority. The exploitation and alienation provided the motive for people to develop an understanding of the way in which capitalism worked, and how they could replace it with something better.

For Marx, materialism mattered because the form of alienation he was concerned with was bound up with how people produced and distributed the things they needed to live. But that alienation led to people misunderstanding their relation to society. The way forward involved developing a better understanding of the way society was organised, which is why he worked to change people's ideas – to enable them to change society.

Consciousness isn't determined by the material world in the sense of being something separate from it and passively determined by it. Rather, the most consequential way in which people use their consciousness is for making sense of the material reality in which they live. They don't get to choose the reality they're trying to make sense of. And it's those thoughts that most accurately grasp that reality, which best understand the practical possibilities, that are the ones that lead to people acting in ways that bring about change.

This ability to understand the contradictions that we face, and work out how to overcome them, seems to me to be an expression of freedom. Which brings us back to the question we started with – can we talk meaningfully about freedom when the choices we make are part of a process of cause and effect?

Before attempting to answer this, I think it's worth asking the opposite question – can we talk meaningfully about freedom if the choices we make are *not* part of a process of cause and effect? There are certainly some ways of making decisions that are free from being part of such a process – decisions made at random: flip a coin, stick a pin in a map. This would certainly undermine determinism, but I don't think anyone would see the result as an expression of free will. At best, it would be an expression of the freedom not to decide something for yourself. But if a decision is not left to luck, and if it's not part of the process of cause and effect, then where could such a 'free' choice come from?

The only answer I can see, is that such a concept of free will is bound up with the idea of a separate, independent self. It is the self, standing aside from the process of your life, that makes supposedly free decisions. But just as it's difficult to see why anyone would value having a separate self that is unaffected by their actual day to day, year by year unfolding reality, it's difficult to see why anyone would see a decision coming from somewhere outside of that unfolding life as being an expression of their freedom.

If the concept of freedom refers to something meaningful, it must surely relate to that part of the world that has been growing in significance ever since parts of the world found themselves having to make choices – ever since the process of cause and effect arrived at a point where the accumulation of causes pointed towards more than one possible result. The reason there was more than one possible result, was that the process of cause and effect had created a consciousness, and that consciousness could see more than one possible course of action. There was no way for the world to continue that did not involve that consciousness deciding which path to follow.

The first such choices that were made would have been made by minds that were barely aware they were making choices, hardly aware of why they decided in the way they did. So it's easy to argue that there was still no freedom, that it was just a new expression of cause and effect. But something had changed. The world had been set on course to something new.

Those parts of the world that were making choices grew in number, they interacted and became more complex. They began to better understand their circumstances, to see more possible courses of action. They began to develop a sense of themselves, their circumstances, their past decisions, the decisions of others, of how the choices they made would have consequences for their future, until they were able to see not only how one choice rather than another was more likely to satisfy their genetically determined desires, but to think about what their desires really were, and why, and whether they had to act on them at all.

If we call this freedom, then it's not a freedom *from* cause and effect, but rather a freedom that has been created *through* cause and effect, the freedom of a process that was blind and meaningless changing into a process that is conscious and purposeful. It's because we possess consciousness, and because that consciousness was created from our material reality and is capable of developing a deeper understanding of the reality from which it was created, that it's possible for us to choose to change the world we live in, and to choose the way we experience that world.

If we view freedom in this way, then it's worth distinguishing between two kinds of process in which our choices can make a difference. On the one hand, there are processes that would continue as they were if we did not consciously intervene to take advantage of the opportunities they offer: from straightforward processes like water flowing or crops growing, to processes that require deeper knowledge to intervene in, like chemical reactions, and to complex challenges that are more difficult to understand and influence, like genetic inheritance, habitual patterns of behaviour or market forces.

On the other hand, there's the process of our own conscious life, a process which inevitably includes our continually making choices, a process that involves us asking – and answering – questions such as: What do I want to do now? Am I the sort of person who would do that? What would people think if I did this? Would they be right? Should I care? Or even: Do I believe in free will, and how is my answer to that question relevant to the decision I now need to make?

As we increase our understanding of the world, we increase our freedom. And again, we can make a useful distinction between the two kinds of process. The more parts of the world we're able to make decisions about, the more freedom we have. That doesn't mean we want to make choices about everything possible. In some cases, we may choose not to intervene. For example, our greater understanding of genetics means we could decide the gender of our children, but we might decide not to.

Similarly with the economy, some of us would argue that the greater the degree to which economic decisions are made by individual or democratic choice, the better. Others might argue that it makes sense to leave some choices to the market. At the very least, however, if we want to seriously claim to care about freedom, we should want as many people as possible to be as well informed as possible about how the market works – or about different understandings of how it works – and the implications for other aspects of society, so that people can democratically decide what role the market should play, if any, or what experiments with alternatives should be explored.

We also gain more freedom as we develop a better understanding of ourselves – how we fit into the world, shaping it and being shaped by it. The more we understand, the less likely we are to be misled by the effects of an evolutionary process for which the experiences of the species that survived was never what mattered, or by the illusion that we have a separate self, or by a social system that encourages greed and selfishness and hides how much we have to gain from working together and how much we have to offer each other. The better our understanding is, the more likely it is that our choices will reflect our best interests.

Every decision is part of the process that we call the world. Every time somebody makes a decision about their life, they're on the leading edge of the world deciding what it wants to become. And when enough people, with enough influence, see new possibilities – either because the parts of the world outside of their consciousness have changed, or because the part of the world that is their consciousness has arrived at new conclusions – and they act on those new possibilities, then the trajectory of history shifts.

Arguments about free will and determinism sometimes suggest that an action can be considered free if the person acting in a particular way could have done otherwise. It's an interesting definition. The most obvious problem with it is that it looks for freedom of action in retrospect. But there are reasons for every non-random decision you make, so if you had enough knowledge about the past, you could always look back at any decision and identify what the determining factors were.

If freedom is to be found anywhere, it's in the present and the future, where you choose which factors to be affected by, which factors are going to be the determining ones. You consider all the factors that seem relevant, including, of course, the process that led to the current possibilities, and the context in which the possibilities exist. If enough time is available, you take as long as you need to be as sure as you can about coming to the right decision. But no matter how long you take, none of those factors is going to step forward and let it be known that they are the determining ones. Nothing is going to reach out and nudge you in one direction or another. You are the part of the world that makes the choice.

And after you've done so, if you're so inclined, you can look back at those factors, and conclude that they were the factors that determined the choice you were going to make. But then, you have to turn back to the present, and to the possible futures facing you, and decide for yourself what comes next.

Another interesting aspect of this definition of freedom is what it implies about the relationship between freedom and meaning. If you try to think of examples of choices where you might have chosen otherwise – the sort of choices that, according to this definition, can be seen as most likely to be free or containing the most freedom – then the most obvious examples would be choices where there's no strong reason for choosing one option over another, or where the choice doesn't matter too much to you: 'Would you like sprinkles on that?', 'Given the history of the last century, would it be less misleading to call Marx a socialist rather than a communist?', 'What's your favourite episode of *Buffy the Vampire Slayer*?'

On the other hand, if you try to think of examples of choices that, according to this definition, are *least* likely to be free, or to contain the smallest amount of freedom, they'd have to be choices where there's a good reason for making one choice rather than another, where the choice matters to you: 'Racism – for or against?', 'Shall we just keep using fossil fuels, and trust that any problems will sort themselves out?', 'Would you like me to take you seriously?'

If freedom is what matters most to you, and you agree with this definition, then by all means, fill your life with as many inconsequential and unimportant choices as possible. No doubt there's pleasure to be had there. Roll around in all that lovely freedom. Make one free choice after another. Occasionally do something really liberating, like changing your allegiance from Coke to Pepsi.

Freedom sounds wonderful and the lack of it terrible, but which would you rather be faced with: a choice so inconsequential you could just as easily choose one thing as the other, or a choice that matters so much to you, and where the reasons to make one choice are so clear, that the idea you could seriously make a different choice is absurd? Personally, I'd give up a 'free' but inconsequential decision for a 'determined' but meaningful one any day. How about you?

Of course, there are some decisions that matter to you, but where the choice is not obvious: 'Is writing a book likely to be worth the effort?', 'Given the first-past-the-post electoral system, is there no better option than the Labour Party?', 'Is this love that I'm feeling?' Perhaps it's in making the choices that matter that we create, or discover, the meaning of our lives. If this is the case, however, I'm not convinced that, of those decisions that matter, the difficult ones are more meaningful than those where you hardly feel you have any choice at all.

The nice thing about a religious morality is that it's clear: here are the rules, and here's what happens if you obey them or break them. Perhaps followers of particular religions would argue there's more to it than that, but still, the straightforwardness is part of the attraction, isn't it? It's only a problem if, for some strange reason, not everybody in the world believes in the same religion.

If that's the case, then a religious morality is a divisive morality. There's really no way for such a morality to avoid making a significant distinction between the moral worth of believers in the religion (if they follow the rules), and everyone else. Non-believers are, at best, incapable of appreciating how to be good and of recognising the rewards for doing so. At worst, they're plain bad and headed for hell. If the religion gives importance to how non-believers behave, steps should be taken to convince or force people to abide by the religious morality.

Most religious people don't want to be divisive. They don't want to tell people who don't share their religion that they don't know how to be good. In the twenty-first century, most religious people, asked why they think someone should behave in a particular way, are unlikely to respond by quoting scripture. Their most likely reaction is to explain why such behaviour would be good for people and society. They assume that, since the religion they believe in is good, its morality must make sense as a way of contributing to a better world.

When they do this, however, they have effectively ceased to promote a religious morality. Instead, they're arguing for a morality on the basis that it makes sense for society. It just happens to also be the morality revealed by their religion. Those of us who aren't religious can join the discussion about the morality's merits, without worrying about the whole religious distraction.

You might argue that religious people are particularly resistant to arguments against their moral beliefs, because if they come to see any flaw in them, they may have to engage in some sort of complicated reappraisal of their religious texts, so they can be interpreted as compatible with their new beliefs. But if we're honest, it isn't only religious people who should, ideally, be more open to alternative points of view.

Buddhism sits rather oddly in relation to all this. It has its own rules, or precepts, and they're pretty much what you'd expect from any major religion: don't kill, don't steal, don't engage in sexual misconduct, and so on. Most people who grow up in traditional Buddhist societies would relate to such rules in much the same way that Christians would relate to the ten commandments. This would only be reinforced by the traditional, and most widespread, understanding of *karma* as a supernatural force that ensures people are rewarded or punished for how they behave.

The most interesting difference is that the precepts of Buddhism were not handed down from a deity. The Buddha made them up as he went along, and he made no bones about it. He formulated them in the course of developing the monastic sangha. They were aimed at encouraging the way of behaving and relating to others that would create the state of mind most suited to becoming awakened. For those who formally joined the sangha, who chose to dedicate themselves to awakening, there were a whole mass of rules, and when the rules didn't seem to work as intended, or backfired, the Buddha would change them or drop them. As part of presenting Buddhism to the wider world, the most important rules were selected as the ones most suited for lay followers or for society as a whole.

As with other religions, those who don't consider themselves Buddhists have no reason to accept what it says about morality, unless it makes sense to them. But whereas many religions view those who aren't followers of the religion as lacking a basis for being good, for Buddhism, anyone is free to accept or reject its explanation of why and how it makes sense to follow the path it describes.

The traditional view of karma was adopted, or adapted, by Buddhism from the Brahmanic teachings that were dominant in India at the time. The idea of karma as a supernatural force or law is certainly present in Buddhist teachings, and it has become a fundamental part of the religion. But the Buddhist teachings also contain a more down-to-earth account of karma.

In this account, karma describes the process of cause and effect, but from the viewpoint of how people's choices shape the sort of person they are and, therefore, the way they experience the world. In a sense, this account appears so ordinary and unremarkable that it hardly seems to merit the amount of attention it gets as a part of Buddhist practice. But the point of that attention is to make clear how every choice is significant. It's no use saying, 'this isn't the sort of thing I'd usually do, but...' Every choice matters. As Andrew Olendzki puts it:

> There are patterns of cause and effect that can be seen in experience and traced over time to explain the dynamics at work shaping each moment of consciousness. The word for this is *karma*, and it does *not* mean fate.
>
> ...Every thought, emotion, intention, attitude, or aspiration is shaping how ensuing experience will unfold. This means that every single moment of consciousness is a moment of practice, whether we like it or not. We are practising to become ourselves. The important question is really just how much we want to participate in the process.[1]

So karma reminds us that our choices determine what follows. This provides a response to those who argue that, if people's actions are just part of a process of cause and effect, then their actions are not under their control, so they have no responsibility for those actions. But even if your choices are shaped by your past, you can still have an understanding of how the future is likely to be shaped by those choices.

If there's no self, then the responsibility a person has is not about accepting their past as though it defines who and what they are, but rather to recognise that, whilst their past actions shaped what they are now, they are now choosing how to react to that past, and how to change what they become. The past that created someone is clearly relevant to that person, and they may relate to it with regret, with gratitude, with equanimity or in some other way, but the real responsibility is in deciding what to do now – how to shape the future.

If a person has a persistent self, then it appears reasonable to punish them for their past actions – the self experiencing the punishment is the same self that carried out the acts for which they're now being punished. But how should people be treated if you see a person as a changing process?

When it comes down to it, everyone always does what makes sense to them or feels right to them, given the situation they're in and the way their past has led them to interpret, to experience, that situation. How could we expect anyone to do otherwise? It follows that, if we want someone to behave differently in the future, we should either change their situation, or offer them good reasons to interpret their situation differently.

Of course, in a sense, that's how society always acts: putting someone in prison certainly changes their situation, and convincing someone that they bear all the responsibility for their actions would shape how they interpret their situation. The problem with these ways of treating people is that they encourage people to view themselves as defined by what they've done in the past, and to see their likely future behaviour as determined by 'who they are'.

Nobody, in fact, bears all of the responsibility for their actions. Those who insist individuals should take such responsibility are effectively demanding that they themselves, and society as a whole, should not have to take any responsibility for the situations that people find themselves in, for the influences that helped create them, or for what could be done to give people positive reasons to behave differently in the future.

It's reasonable enough to judge a person by their actions. Those actions express what the person's past has led them to do; they are the most obvious guide, other things being equal, to how they're likely to act in the future. But the best way to judge their actions is to understand the process of change that led them to where they are, and the possibilities for how they could change for the better in the future. And to do that adequately, individuals can only be judged in the context of all the other parts of the world with which they have been, and will be, interacting.

In Europe, for centuries, the overriding moral rules were those supposedly written in stone and handed down to Moses – supplemented by the moral messages of the New Testament and the interpretations of later Christian thinkers. But as enlightenment and humanist ideas gained influence, the moral authority of religion and tradition began to wane. In place of feudal hierarchy, the organisation of society was increasingly understood in terms of self-interested individuals interacting with each other as legal and social equals. Liberal thinkers were faced with the problem of how to provide a moral basis for social behaviour in a world of egoistic individuals.

One of the key concepts they developed was the idea of the 'social contract'. There have been a number of advocates of this, from Hobbes and Locke to Rousseau and Rawls, but all share the conceptual assumption that society can be viewed as an aggregation of individuals. The idea of the social contract starts from the view that individuals can be viewed as though they exist distinct from society. Whilst living in this way offers great freedom to the individual, it also leaves everyone at the mercy of everyone else. So people make the rational decision to enter into a social contract, giving up some of their freedom, so as to benefit from security and order.

Different liberal thinkers have developed different ideas about how reason can be used to justify a morality that individuals should accept. One of the most influential approaches has been utilitarianism, which argues that morality should be based on the criterion of whatever produces 'the greatest happiness of the greatest number'. Everyone seeks pleasure and avoids pain, so the sum total of pleasure and pain for everyone affected should be calculated, and choices made on the basis of whatever would result in the maximum happiness.

Immanuel Kant took a very different view. He rejected the idea that happiness could be the basis for morality, and instead saw moral behaviour as expressed by a willingness to overcome or reject our desires and inclinations in order to follow our duty. He argued that a justifiable moral rule should be based on the 'categorical imperative' – that one should 'act only in accordance with that maxim through which you can at the same time will that it become a universal law'.

There have been many criticisms of these ideas, and many attempts to defend them or to suggest ways in which they could be modified or developed to take the criticisms into account. To my mind, however, one of the most interesting questions about them – and one which seems to get strangely little attention – is how they're expected to have a significant effect on the way ordinary people actually behave.

Say what you like about religious moralities, it was clear enough how their advocates expected to make people aware of them and to take them seriously. The advocates of different liberal moral approaches show strangely little interest in how to do the same. The social contract is something people are assumed to have implicitly entered into by becoming a member of society (which is to say, by being born). There is, apparently, no need for most people to know their contract exists, let alone for them to be consulted on it.

As for utilitarianism or Kantian ethics, if they're expected to have an impact, presumably it's via the decisions of well-educated legislators, judges, or others involved in the legal professions. Or perhaps they're intended mainly as discussion points for those justifying or critiquing the actions of actually existing governments or citizens, who in practice base their decisions on the practicality of living together in society.

All the liberal approaches to morality have two things in common. Firstly, they focus on 'the individual' as though individuals can be understood in the abstract, separately from the society in which they're living. Secondly, they're based on ideas of freedom and equality, but they decide on what terms freedom and equality should be available, and they show little interest in engaging those people who are considered to be free and equal in deciding how the terms should be understood, let alone what sort of society might make the terms most meaningful.

One of the most influential people who declined to accept liberal morality on the terms offered was Friedrich Nietzsche. Nietzsche didn't waste a lot of time with detailed criticism of the flaws of utilitarianism or Kantianism. Instead, he took a simpler approach by expressing a view of the world that effectively said to the advocates of those philosophies, 'Why should I care what you think?' As far as Nietzsche was concerned, moral authority had died along with God, and it was hardly going to be reinstated in a university philosophy department.

Nietzsche saw morality as having become the triumph of 'slave ethics'. It had promoted the idea that weakness, self-denial and self-sacrifice should be considered good. Anyone who accepted it was agreeing to be part of the herd. The people who really deserved to be admired were those who showed the ability and courage to reject it, to make their own decisions and assert their 'will to power'.

Nietzsche rejected liberal morality, but he accepted its focus on the individual. The most fundamental criticism of liberal morality, however, is that it's simply not true that individuals could ever be understood separately from society. They may create society, but society also creates them. The idea of the social contract makes no sense, because only people who had already been shaped by their social existence would be capable of meaningfully entering into such a contract.

As Kenan Malik points out, this criticism reflects Hegel's understanding of the world, in which everything is interconnected and any part is only understandable in terms of its relationship to everything else, so individuals can only be understood in the context of society:

> Philosophers before Hegel had simply assumed the existence of the human subject. Hegel insisted that the human subject had to be created. An isolated individual could not be truly self-conscious, nor act as an agent. I become conscious of my self only as I become conscious of others and of my relationships with them.

Humans are not individuals who become social but social beings whose individuality emerges through the bonds they create with each other. Psychological dispositions and desires are not fixed but are shaped by those bonds, as are the answers to questions such as 'What are my goals?' and 'How should I live?' Freedom can never be simply that of the individual, but must also be at the same time social.[2]

Marx, naturally, agreed with Hegel that human beings are intrinsically social, but he understood the society that gave rise to liberal morality as a society divided into classes with different relations to the means of production, and therefore different interests.

Like Nietzsche, Marx had no time for liberal morality, but for very different reasons. For Marx, since society was divided into classes whose interests were in conflict, an appeal to morality could not be effective as a way to justify action. As Alistair MacIntyre explains, in Marx's view:

Within bourgeois society there are two social groups ... constituted by the dominant and dominated class. Each of these has its own fundamental goals and form of life. It follows that moral precepts may find a role within the social life of each class. But there are no independent, transcendent norms which are above those issues which divide the classes. Certainly, many of the same precepts will occur in the moralities of each class, simply in virtue of each class being a human group. But these will not serve to determine the relations between classes.[3]

An additional reason why Marx rejected arguing in terms of morality was to distinguish his approach from other socialists who couched their criticisms of capitalism in precisely such terms. Their condemnation of capitalism implied that the problem lay in the immoral behaviour of capitalists. Marx wanted to stress the importance of understanding and explaining how capitalist exploitation was not the result of moral failings, but followed necessarily if you understood how the capitalist economy worked.

But whilst rejecting moralism as something that could not be usefully applied to class society, Marx clearly does talk about capitalism in ways that imply moral condemnation of its injustices and exploitation, and he clearly sees the solidarity and cooperation that are a necessary part of the struggle against capitalism as being worthy of praise. In effect, he seems to be morally condemning capitalism for creating a society where a consistent morality is not possible.

Capitalism gives people good reasons to reject liberal morality. Liberalism promises individual freedom and equality, but most people are expected to accept a social contract they apparently signed without knowing it. And that contract requires them to accept an organisation of society where they have to spend their working lives following the orders of people who are exploiting them. Those who fail to make the most of their supposed economic freedom are held to be individually responsible and are morally condemned for laziness or for failing to develop their 'personal capital'.

If people reject the idea that society is organised to benefit everyone equally, but they accept the individualism on which liberalism is based, then it makes sense for them to embrace an attitude much like Nietzsche's – whether or not they actually know anything about Nietzsche. Why should they not view accepting such moral demands as something like 'slave mentality' and try to find an expression of individual freedom in something like a 'will to power'?

But for most people, such an individualist reaction is a dead end. It's a route to nihilism and further alienation. It may lead them to reject the whole idea of equality, and to look for some kind of community amongst people wanting to assert their will to power – probably at the expense of other groups.

For Marx, the appropriate reaction to alienation is not to reject society but to play a part in changing it. He suggests that a meaningful morality would be possible in a classless society, and in so doing, makes implicitly moral criticisms of capitalism. But Marx's antipathy to liberal morality, and his wish to distinguish his materialist politics from the moralism of others, meant that he did not offer a coherent approach to morality of his own. According to Alasdair MacIntyre, as a result, later Marxists have, in practice, fallen back on utilitarian or Kantian moral arguments.

MacIntyre agrees with Marx that capitalist society makes it impossible to have a morality that everyone has reason to accept, but he takes a far more serious interest in the question of how a meaningful morality could exist. In *After Virtue*, he argues that morality has become increasingly meaningless ever since it moved away from the 'virtue ethics' of ancient Greece.

For the ancient Greeks, morality did not exist as a separate topic in the way that has become the case since. The term 'good' was not used in a way that was divorced from specific subjects. Something was good if it served its purpose effectively. Just as a good boat was one that was seaworthy, a person was seen as good according to how well they fulfilled their purpose.

In MacIntyre's view, once morality became separated from the actual life of people in society and the socially accepted understandings of the roles people should play, it became increasingly empty. He argues that there's no meaningful basis for a concept of 'the good' as something that can be applied to anyone, regardless of the society they're a part of. A meaningful morality has to emerge from established traditions and values.

There's a problem, however, in applying this to the modern world. Philosophers like Aristotle could view ethics in this way because they lived in a society with widely accepted ideas about the purposes of different people. This included the appropriate virtues of slaves and of women, each different from the virtues of a citizen.

We obviously don't want to accept the traditions of ancient Greece. Some advocates of virtue ethics suggest we need to develop a new account of what human well-being should mean. MacIntyre, however, agrees with Marx that the conflicts inherent to capitalism make this impossible. He sees no possibility of a meaningful morality until some sort of newly agreed upon tradition or community can develop with a shared understanding of the good for both individuals and society.

As Kenan Malik argues, however, there is an alternative basis on which to develop a virtue ethics approach:

> We can, however, while rejecting the idea of morality as being created by isolated individuals, also think of social embeddedness in a different way to MacIntyre, in terms not of tradition but of *transformation*. Movements for social transformation are defined less by a sense of a shared past (though most draw upon historical traditions) than by the ambition of a common future... With the coming of modernity, as the necessity of traditions gave way to the possibilities of collective change, so a new question was posed. People now asked themselves not simply 'What moral claims are rational given the social structure?', but also 'What social structures are rational?' What kind of society, what types of social institutions, what forms of social relations, will best allow moral lives to flourish?[4]

One of the implications of this approach is that – as for Aristotle – morality cannot be separated from politics. The question of how a person can be good or virtuous is inseparable from the question of how to create a good society. Politics and morality, the individual and society, all mutually constitute each other.

One reason MacIntyre doesn't see things in these terms is, perhaps, because he accepts an assumption that runs through discussions of morality from Aristotle to religious moralities and on to liberalism – that, for morality to be meaningful, it must be universally applicable; it must be possible to imagine it being accepted by everyone. Even those moralities that are founded in society, such as virtue ethics, assume a tradition everyone is expected to accept. Debates about morality have generally been debates about where the authority for morality resides – in tradition, in religious revelation, or worked out on the basis of reason.

The reality is, however, that there is no objective, given, authority to look to. The enlightenment was right to reject tradition and religion, and to argue for human beings to act on the basis of reason. But abstract reason cannot arrive at an objective conclusion about what the correct morality is, because morality is socially created, and societies change.

If a society is to construct an effective morality, then the first thing it needs to do is recognise that this is in fact what it's doing. A real rejection of tradition rejects not only existing claims to moral authority, but also the idea that individuals can only be socialised through a morality that is external to them. Morality can't be handed down from the authority of God, nature or abstract reason. A meaningful morality is not something to be discovered or asserted; it's something to be discussed and developed, something that members of society engage with as they work out how they can practically relate to others, and how to convince others to relate to them.

Disagreement amongst people about morality, far from being a problem that undermines moral authority, is part of morality being created by society – and changing as society changes. If there are fundamental divisions within society, you would expect there to be conflicting ideas about morality. We don't see people having different ideas about politics as evidence of politics failing to operate. We don't look for an ultimate authority that can tell us what politics to accept. Why should morality be any different?

If people become more consciously engaged with constructing morality, they may see utilitarianism, Kantian ethics, or different social contract theories as providing useful guidelines for developing practical approaches to moral behaviour – but as guidelines rather than rules. They may find other reasons for developing morality. Some might even be so presumptuous as to suggest their own alternative moral guidelines. And in that spirit, why don't I have a go at coming up with a guide to moral action of my own? How about this:

> An action might be seen as good according to the degree to which it contributes to undermining the reality or the illusion of separation or conflict.

What do you think? I'm not entirely happy with 'separation or conflict', which seems to imply too clear a separation between 'separation'

and 'conflict'. Undermining either one would presumably also undermine the other. But it's hard to see how to dispense with either.

It seems to me that, ideally, a moral rule or guideline should offer a
practical guide that people can make sense of and that they can see a relatively straightforward way of applying. If that was the only consideration,
then it would probably make sense to offer a simpler version of this rule –
something like, 'a good action is one that contributes to reducing conflict'.
But if you want to appeal to something more than people's common
sense – or what you hope they will agree is common sense – then a moral
guide should also have some basis in a way of understanding the world
and social relations. Hopefully, the basis for my suggestion is clear
enough, reflecting, as it does, the Buddhist or Marxist understanding of
everything as change and interconnection, and especially the Buddhist
aim of overcoming the illusion of a separate self. Undermining separation indicates something of that understanding but can also be seen as
relating to the more practical aim of undermining conflict.

Some might question how well the idea of undermining conflict sits
with Marxism, which is not exactly famed for its conflict-avoidance. But
the problem is more apparent than real. While there are, no doubt, some
Marxists who are rather more enthusiastic about the idea of 'class war'
than there's any reason to be, it's clear enough that the actual aim of
Marxism is a classless society.

Undermining conflict doesn't mean avoiding it, or always seeking
compromise. If conflict is to be undermined, then the first thing required is to identify where it exists and clarify what the basis of it is, and
then to consider how it might be resolved or prevented from recurring.[5]
In some circumstances this may involve compromise, but in others it
certainly won't. In the conflict between racism and anti-racism, for example, it's clear only one side could lead to an end of conflict.

Marxism argues that class conflict is inseparable from capitalism.
Only by replacing capitalism can such conflict be resolved. In addition,
capitalism acts as a barrier to resolving other conflicts – conflicts between nations, divisions on the basis of gender or race, and so on. A
morality that seeks to undermine conflict has to resolve the conflicts that
are bound up with capitalism.

This doesn't mean trying to create a society in which everyone wants the same thing, but rather a society in which, as much as possible, one person pursuing what they want does not stand in the way of anyone else doing the same – or better still, complements their doing so. In Marx's words, 'In place of the old bourgeois society, with its classes and class antagonisms, we shall have an association, in which the free development of each is the condition for the free development of all.'[6]

As pointed out earlier, one of the curious aspects of academic discussion of morality is the extent to which it is just that – academic. The focus is on philosophical argument. Surprisingly little attention is paid to the question of how, and if, such moral arguments might be likely to influence the behaviour of ordinary people in everyday life.

And it's not as though people aren't interested in moral thinking. We do it all the time. Every time we think about our actions not just in terms of what we want, but whether they're the right things to do, every time we judge the actions of others not in terms of how they directly affect us, but in terms of whether they should be approved of.

We do this constantly because we don't only care about our material self-interest. We also care about our place in the social world, our views of others and their views of us. We want to think of our views and actions as expressing more than our prejudices or desires. In other words, we are more than self-interested individuals. We are moral, social beings.

This is why the idea of some Marxists – and, to a large extent, of Marx – that we should avoid discussion of morality, seems to me both unrealistic and counter-productive. It's just not the way people relate to the world. Everyday morality is everywhere.

Most moral thinking, in fact, goes on between ordinary people in everyday situations. When someone suggests, or denies, that Jeff Bezos is 'just doing what anyone would do if they had his kind of money', or argues about attitudes to immigration, they're engaging in moral debate which is every bit as meaningful, and probably more consequential, than when an academic philosopher submits an essay to a philosophical journal arguing the merits or flaws of utilitarianism or some other ethical system.

If we want to develop a more meaningful and effective morality, the most likely way to do so is not by presenting morality as a rule, or set of rules, that people are expected to accept, nor as a matter of learning about other people's academic arguments, but by making it clear that everyone is already involved in a process of working out what sort of morality and what values can be agreed upon – and how to create the sort of society where such a morality would be most likely to work.

10. AWAKENINGS

If you want a taste of what Zen Buddhism has to offer, I can recommend reading *Fukanzazengi* or *Universal Recommendation for Zazen* by the founder of the Soto school of Zen, Eihei Dogen.[1] The first time I read it, I hated it. There were two reasons. The first was partly down to bad timing. I'd been attempting to develop a meditation practice and – on the premise that if you're going to try something of questionable value, you should at least try to do it properly – I'd been attempting to sit in the half-lotus position. After many meditation sessions, my left knee had made contact with the floor, and my right knee was inching – or rather millimetring – down, session by session, with the prospect of someday joining it. My back was staying straight for minutes on end, before starting to slouch. Then, one day, whilst engaged in the relatively unchallenging task of walking along a pavement, I somehow managed to sprain my ankle.

There was a thought that had recurred regularly, throughout those early meditation sessions. But each time it had appeared, I'd followed the procedure that my understanding of meditation suggested – noting it, letting it be, letting it go, returning my focus to the breath. But now, as I faced the prospect of an enforced break from adopting a posture remotely lotus-like, and the likelihood of my progress in that direction being reversed, that thought – accompanied by emotions entirely unsuited to a meditative frame of mind – returned full-force: *how the hell can sitting in a particular, ridiculous, impossible-to-sit-in posture be important to gaining any kind of awakening?*

I could think of no good answer. Giving up any attempt to sit Buddha-like, I switched to sitting up straight, in an upright chair, and I renewed my efforts to find better guidance on what exactly I was supposed to be doing, and what exactly I was supposed to be gaining from it, and why, and how. Which brought me to *Fukanzazengi*, a highly praised, concise guide to practice, a seminal text of Zen Buddhism, and a few lines in I find this:

> Sit either in the full-lotus or half-lotus position ... place your right foot on your left thigh. ...place your right hand on your left leg and your left palm (facing upwards) on your right palm, thumb tips touching... Be sure your ears are on a plane with your shoulders and your nose in line with your navel...

Are you kidding me! The text is only short, and a whole section is devoted to a detailed description of precisely how to sit in a position that no normal person could sit in.

The second reason that *Fukanzazengi* annoyed me was that so much of it made no sense at all. This sort of thing:

> ...the bringing out of enlightenment by the opportunity provided by a finger, a banner, a needle, or a mallet, and the effecting of realization with the aid of a *hossu*, a fist, a staff, or a shout...

It turned out this line references a number of 'well known' Zen koans. I probably should have found a copy with footnotes. Although, I'm not sure knowing this, let alone reading the koans, would have helped make things clearer. And there were some lines that no footnote, nor anything else, could have added any sense to:

> Think of not thinking. How do you think of not thinking? Non-thinking in itself is the essential art of zazen.

If all *Fukanzazengi* had to offer was confusion and advice on how to sit, perhaps I would have reacted by just being bemused as to why it was so well thought of, and moved on to something else. But there were also lines that left me wondering whether Dogen had something worthwhile to offer that I was missing:

> You should therefore cease from practice based on intellectual understanding, pursuing words and following after speech, and learn the backward step that turns your light inwardly to illuminate your self. Body and mind of themselves will drop away, and your original face will be manifest.
>
> ... intelligence or lack of it does not matter; between dull- and sharp-witted there is no distinction. If you concentrate your effort single-mindedly, that in itself is negotiating the Way. Practice-realization is naturally undefiled. Going forward [in practice] is a matter of everydayness.

I now have rather a soft spot for *Fukanzazengi* – partly, perhaps, because of the irony of how the reaction it first provoked in me was precisely the opposite of what I now believe was intended. It seems to me now that, whilst Dogen may well have given a questionable importance to exactly how to sit, another purpose of that description of sitting was as an example of a simple, straightforward, step-by-step activity – which, presumably, is what sitting like that would have been for his intended audience. In this way he was trying to set, or reflect, the tone of the whole text.

If Dogen had been writing for the likes of me, I suspect he might have thought it worth setting aside the importance of describing the best sitting posture, and perhaps instead described another common Buddhist practice, walking meditation – using a similarly, simple description such as this:

> Stand, with your back straight, lift your left foot, heel first then toe, place it in front of your right foot, then lift your right foot... place your left palm on your right palm, thumb tips lightly touching...

He might even have added a few lines just for me:

> Read a line of *Fukanzazengi*. If you understand the line, then
> understand it. If you do not understand the line, then do not
> understand it. Then read the next line...

What purpose would it serve to be frustrated at not understanding, to waste time deciding whether to aim your frustration at the person who failed to explain matters more clearly, or at yourself for being incapable of grasping what was being explained? Or, indeed, at the world for being so damn confusing? Either you understand, or you don't. Either you will, or you won't. Let it sit in your mind like a koan. Become one with it (and don't worry about not knowing what that means). Just be what you are now. Try to see as clearly as you can what you are now, what the world is now. See this moment and see what follows. Do what follows. Be what follows. As Dogen says:

> It is never apart from one right where one is – what is the use of
> going off here and there to practise? And yet, if there is the slight-
> est discrepancy, the Way is as distant as heaven from earth. If the
> least like or dislike arises, the Mind is lost in confusion.

As with *Fukanzazengi*, there are many Buddhist writings where it's important to remember that they were not written for the likes of you or me. For example, there are texts suggesting that anyone who wants to pursue the Buddhist path should put their absolute maximum effort into it. At the most extreme, these texts effectively say, 'If you're not going to put everything into attaining awakening, then why follow the path at all?'

For someone who's abandoned their home and joined the sangha, dedicating themselves to becoming awakened, this may well be an effective way to encourage them not to let their resolve falter – to motivate them to practice diligently. For someone who's curious about Buddhism but also has a good internet connection and a Netflix subscription, or a toddler tugging at their sleeve, a more reasonable reaction might be to conclude that Buddhism probably isn't for them.

Such a conclusion would be a sad mistake. Frankly, even if someone were never to meditate at all, it seems likely to me that their lives could still benefit from taking some time, occasionally, to think about the insights that Buddhism has to offer and what it says about the choices that are most likely to lead to them being free from suffering or discontent.

Another recurrent theme of Buddhist writings is the importance of finding a good teacher. Stories of significant figures in Buddhist history often include accounts of them finding their 'true teacher' – the person who provided the key to how they should practise. Dogen, for example, studied with a number of teachers in Japan before travelling to China and spending years studying with different Chan masters at different monasteries, before finally finding the person he considered to be his 'true teacher'.

A lot of present-day Buddhist teachers seem to agree – presumably having themselves found good teachers. No doubt it's my own failure to find (or, to be honest, to even look for) an appropriate teacher that explains why I'm not, at least at the time of writing, a fully awakened master of meditation!

On the other hand, it does seem to me that finding a teacher or a school of Buddhism that you feel comfortable with can be a mixed blessing. For those who find the personal contact valuable, no doubt a good teacher is useful, but every teacher and every school of Buddhism offers some teaching that might be useful, alongside other teachings that might not suit everyone. Maybe the instruction in Zen that says you should keep your eyes open while meditating doesn't suit you as well as the view of other schools that suggest your eyes should be closed. Maybe the teacher you've found who's provided you with valuable guidance on how to establish mindfulness is not offering the best approach to taking your meditation further.

One of the advantages of learning about Buddhism today is that you don't have to go trekking off to distant lands to find alternative teachings. You can access a wide variety of approaches through books or the internet. And if there is a problem, it's not so much in finding teachers and teachings, it's in choosing between them. Personally, I think one indication of a good teacher is that they themselves have knowledge of multiple traditions and are open to different approaches.

For the atheists and sceptics amongst us, if we somehow develop an interest in Buddhism, I imagine the tradition most likely to attract us is Zen. It appears so clearly to be the least religious, the most heretical, most irreverent. What other school – what other religion – would offer the equivalent of the saying, 'If you see the Buddha on the road, kill him'? This view that being delusional is far worse than being disrespectful, this insistence on the centrality of fathoming the here and now, seems to offer the possibility of a breakthrough to a better way of being that doesn't require signing up to some set of beliefs, that requires nothing more than your own mind and body: it's right there in front of you, or inside you, if you can just see it.

I read two entire books about Zen whilst labouring under the illusion that there must have been some formal, doctrinal break, like the Protestant break from Catholicism, when Zen Buddhists dumped all the stuff about rebirth and supernatural karma. It never happened. Read enough Zen, and you'll come across uncritical mentions of past lives and any other belief from the traditions Zen was built on. It's just that most Zen teachers don't give such matters much importance.

Zen was partly a reaction against other schools of Buddhism, and in particular against the way in which Buddhism had become a matter of scholastic debate and intellectual discussion rather than something to be intimately experienced. As such, some of its innovations were a refreshing new attempt to reconnect with the need to ground practice in direct experience. But it also meant that there was a tendency to be antiintellectual, to reject the need for clear thought and explanation, even a tendency towards mysticism.

As a result, if you're looking for a rational explanation of the Buddhist understanding of the world, you may be better off asking a Theravadin monk or even someone who believes they're the reincarnation of a Tibetan Lama. Tibetan Buddhists may believe in oracles and prayer wheels, but they generally respond to a question with words you can actually make sense of.

Actually, that's unfair to some Zen teachers. The more accounts of Buddhism you read, the more it seems the differences between individual teachers outweigh the significance of which school of Buddhism they belong to. Of course, when it comes to more recent Buddhism, this may be partly because, with the much easier accessibility of texts and teachings, more and more teachers familiarise themselves with teachings from traditions outside those they're closest to.

Zen contains much that is valuable, and its allusive, indirect approach has clearly been effective for many people. But it seems to me that people are most likely to gain from it if they already have a good understanding of Buddhism. Zen embodies the reality that words and explanations can't completely convey what Buddhism is trying to lead people towards. If you manage to get what Zen is offering, then Zen teachings can clearly be effective. The problem is, if you don't get it, then they can just leave you clueless and wondering if you wouldn't be better off doing something else.

The lack of clear explanation that characterises much of Zen is evident, also, in the meditation practices it teaches. The form of Zen meditation people are most likely to have heard of is probably meditating on koans. If there's one form of meditation that I'm even less qualified to comment on than all the others, and which even I wouldn't consider practising without access to a suitable teacher, koan study is it. What I can say with some confidence, however, is that it probably doesn't involve providing people with clear, easily understandable explanations of what they're supposed to be doing and why.

The most widely practised form of Zen meditation is actually not koan study but *shikantaza*,[2] which takes a very different approach to not providing meditators with a clear explanation of what they're supposed to be doing. Shikantaza translates as 'just sitting', and much of the guidance on how it should be practised isn't much of an advance on the name. What guidance there is seems to suggest that the appropriate way of 'just sitting' consists of something more than, or distinct from, literally 'just sitting'. It's just not clear exactly how it's different.

Most Buddhist schools see meditation as a key part of the path to awakening. But approaches to meditation vary significantly. If you've been learning about meditation from the Zen tradition, and you then read something like *The Mind Illuminated* by Culadasa (John Yates) and Matthew Immergut, you may suffer something of a culture shock. Culadasa does not disagree with the Zen belief that what practice is aiming at cannot be put into words, but he belongs to that tradition within Buddhism that believes words, in the form of clear instructions and explanations, can be useful in helping to move beyond them.

To this end, amongst other things, he draws from various early Buddhist teachings and later commentaries to provide ten clearly described stages of meditative development. He supplements this with some insights gained from recent neuroscience and cognitive psychology, and he provides not just one, but three, models of conscious experience that can be helpful in clarifying how to practise. And he doesn't shy away from saying that some ways of just sitting are just a waste of time:

> Stable, hyper-focused attention without mindfulness leads only to a state of blissful dullness: a complete dead end. But ... the opposite is also true. ... Until you have at least a moderate degree of stability, 'mindfulness practice' will consist mostly of *mind-wandering*, physical discomfort, drowsiness, and frustration.[3]

The traditional accounts of meditation practice that Culadasa bases his book on make many distinctions about different factors and approaches that are involved. Particular importance is given to the distinction between the practices of *samatha* and *vipassana*, and the relationship between them. Vipassana is generally translated as 'insight meditation', which seems to me to be yet another problematic translation – although I confess I can think of nothing better. (Apparently, the most literal translation is something like 'special seeing'.) The problem with the term 'insight' is that it seems to imply grasping something completely new.

Some modern descriptions of the practice do, in fact, imply that this might happen, although they often sound like they've been influenced as much by Freud as by the Buddha. The 'insights' that are traditionally seen as being most important are not likely to come as much of a revelation to anyone who has learned the basics of Buddhism. As Culadasa describes it:

> The five most important of these are Insights into imperman-
> ence, emptiness, the nature of suffering, the causal interdep-
> endence of all phenomena, and the illusion of the separate self ...
> the fifth, Insight into no-Self, is the culminating Insight that
> actually produces Awakening.

This quote is preceded, however, by a description of the real point of the meditation:

> The Insights called *vipassana* are not intellectual. Rather, they
> are experientially based, deeply intuitive realizations that trans-
> cend, and ultimately shatter, our commonly held beliefs and un-
> derstandings.[4]

The point, again, is that merely intellectual understanding does not really change the way we relate to the world. The aim of vipassana seems to me to be something more like confirmation, deepening or realisation of the intellectual insights that Buddhist teachings try to explain.

There are different descriptions of what sort of experience this insight is, and how it's arrived at. Some, as in Culadasa's description above, suggest a revelatory experience, whilst others suggest a more gradual process of integrating Buddhist understanding into a person's character and habitual way of relating to the world. To some extent, these two descriptions relate to different understandings of the relationship between vipassana and samatha.

Samatha is often translated as calm or calm abiding. Some people translate it as concentration, although others insist that this needs to be accompanied by qualities like tranquillity and equanimity. You might say that samatha is to concentration, what freewheeling is to carefully keeping your balance on a bicycle. Or what sinking is to diving – once you've moved beyond the need to pay attention to the breath.

One account of the way these practices relate to each other explains that it's only after developing deep levels of samatha that it's possible to experience the sort of insight that can truly transform the way you experience the world. According to this account, you should practise the four jhanas (as mentioned in Chapter 8) until you reach levels of such deep concentration that all conceptualisation and even sensory awareness disappear. With your mind emptied of thoughts and distractions, it's impossible to carry out vipassana at the same time. Only after emerging from the jhanas with a profoundly clear mind can one directly see the reality of impermanence and no-self with a clarity that's transformative.

One reason to be sceptical about this is that every account of the path through the jhanas mentions how people are likely to experience 'supernormal powers' such as being able to float, or pass through walls. Buddhists don't give a lot of importance to these experiences or suggest that they're great achievements. They're generally seen as distractions from developing the real insights that are the aim of meditation. But on what basis are these supernormal experiences, reached while developing the jhana states, judged to be unimportant, or illusory, while 'directly seeing' impermanence or no-self are seen as realising important insights? Surely the reason is that one fits with the intellectual insights of Buddhism and the other doesn't – that you already know, in at least some sense, what you're trying to see?

I don't think this necessarily undermines the value of trying to see the insights in this deeper way. There are other contexts in which people consider it reasonable to go to great lengths to experience, in a new way, something that's already known intellectually. Most of us, I would assume, can imagine that seeing the Earth from space could bring home, in a new way, the reality that the Earth is a fragile sphere floating in space. The experience would not tell us anything we didn't already know, but it could be made more real to us. Perhaps seeing Buddhist insights about reality with a suitably transformed state of mind could work in a similar way.

Much of the guidance Culadasa provides could be useful to anyone trying to develop a meditation practice, but he clearly accepts the view that it's only possible to gain the kind of insight that can create awakening after developing deep states of concentration.

Meditation teachers vary in how much effort they think is necessary to develop the jhanas. Compared to some, Culadasa is optimistic, reassuring us that all that's required is a year or so of practice, during which time all we have to do is:

> a regular daily sitting practice of one to two hours per day in combination with some of the supplemental practices described in the appendices. Meditation retreats are quite helpful, but ones lasting months or years are certainly not necessary.[5]

He also assures us that the level of concentration and insight needed for awakening can be achieved by anyone. He can confirm this, he says, because he takes an empirical approach to meditation:

> It is a science in the sense that it is objectively verifiable through repeated testing and replication of results. Everyone who accurately performs the same 'experiment' in meditation reports the same results.[6]

The sample on which Culadasa bases this, however, is self-selected, to put it mildly. I do wonder whether a similar level of success would be achieved by people who were engaging in this amount of practice despite having serious doubts about whether it was likely to work for them, let alone by people who would have to be forced, bribed or somehow cajoled into doing the practice, because there's no way they'd devote that much time and effort to it voluntarily – which, let's be honest, is most of us!

There's good news, however, for anyone who wants to follow an authoritative or traditional approach to Buddhist meditation but who has reasonable doubts about how far they're likely to be able to progress. Some Buddhist scholars have made a convincing case that the version of the relationship between samatha and vipassana described above is actually a development specific to the Theravada tradition. By contrast, earlier Buddhist texts describe a different approach in which, instead of having to develop samatha first, samatha and vipassana are developed together, with each helping to develop the other.[7]

There's no reason to assume, of course, that the approaches to meditation described by the Buddha must be the correct or best ones. It's perfectly possible that new ways of becoming awakened could be developed that could be just as good or even better. Perhaps developing deeper samatha first is very effective. Maybe koan meditation is a superior approach. Different approaches might be suited to different people.

But developing the two together seems to make sense. Anyone who has tried to practise vipassana meditation (or *any* kind of meditation) will recognise that developing a greater level of calm or concentration is a necessary part of moving the practice forward. And if you're deepening your ability to concentrate as part of Buddhist meditation, it would seem strange if doing so didn't involve something that could reasonably be called insight, or vipassana. How, for example, could observing the way any object of concentration changes, and the focus of the mind changes, not be seen as relating to seeing the reality of impermanence?

There are now a bewildering number of guides to Buddhist meditation that attempt to be as accessible as possible. Some take their influence from a particular Buddhist tradition, others from a wider range of approaches, and they vary in the importance they give to the terminology and practices of past Buddhists.

One of the most influential attempts to make Buddhist mindfulness more accessible was developed by Jon Kabat-Zinn. His own influences included Zen and 'insight meditation' as taught by the Insight Meditation Society, which in turn was influenced by teachings from the Theravada tradition. Kabat-Zinn presented his approach as a scientific practice in a medical context, free from any religious associations. Describing it as 'mindfulness-based stress reduction' (MBSR), he first introduced it at the Stress Reduction Clinic he opened at the University of Massachusetts Medical School in 1979. In the decades since, it's inspired a range of related approaches to scientific 'mindfulness'.

This type of practice is sometimes summed up as 'present-centred, non-judgemental awareness'. There are two main objections that might be made to this description. First, there's the implication that there can be some sort of neutral, direct awareness of the present moment as it really is, sometimes described as 'bare attention'. The Theravada Buddhist monk Bhikkhu Bodhi, while conceding that this practice may be useful as a pragmatic approach for beginning a meditation practice, highlights a problem with it:

> ...it is questionable whether any act of attention, or any other mental act, can literally be 'bare'. As I see it, virtually any intentional act is necessarily subject to a vast set of determinants, internal and external, that governs the way it functions. It occurs *embodied* in a particular person with a unique biography and personality, and it occurs *embedded* in a particular context – historical, social and cultural – that gives it a specific orientation on which its very identity depends.[8]

In the case of mindfulness practice, one of the most significant contexts is the understanding the practitioner has of what they're doing, and why. For Buddhists, this is the context of everything they've learned from Buddhist teachings. The idea that someone introduced to the practice as a way of releasing stress, and without any wider knowledge of Buddhism, is engaging in the same activity but 'free of religious trappings', completely ignores the significance of this context.

The idea of being non-judgemental is also questionable. The attitude encouraged by MBSR is not, in fact, a neutral, non-judgemental one. It clearly encourages meditators to see some emotional reactions as undesirable. Whilst you could say that it encourages people not to be judgemental towards themselves, not to condemn themselves for having the wrong emotions, the emotional reactions themselves are clearly supposed to be judged on how much importance should be given to them.

Many Buddhist teachings are explicit about judging, and trying to change, the way we relate to experiences. The 'right effort' of the eightfold path is sometimes described in terms of welcoming and cultivating ways of reacting to experience that are described as 'wholesome' (*kusala*), whilst letting go of, and preventing the arising of, those that are unwholesome (*akusala*).

There's no reason to object to people using MBSR to let go of stress – Buddhism has no patent on mindfulness. It's regrettable, however, and misleading, if such practices are presented as though they're the same practices that Buddhism describes. This is why the Buddha described an eightfold path. Pursuing one part separately from the others is not 'right mindfulness'.

In a sense, it's unfair to blame mindfulness-based therapies for suggesting mindfulness can be separated from a wider understanding of Buddhism. The truth is that, to a degree, this approach reflects practices that are part of some mainstream Buddhist traditions. A number of approaches within Buddhism seem to me to underestimate what the Buddha accomplished. They give the impression that anyone who spends enough time practising non-judgemental awareness, or just sitting, or whatever else, will inevitably gain the same insights as the Buddha. Presumably, people who believe this must assume that, at the time of the Buddha, a lot of others who were engaging in similar practices had the same insights as him. They just didn't found religions.

So much of Buddhist teaching stresses that intellectual insight is not enough, that it's easy to lose sight of the fact that a significant part of the Buddha's awakening did, in fact, involve a major intellectual insight. Practising right effort, right mindfulness and right concentration may well lead you to develop a deeply concentrated mind, but no matter how long you direct that focused mind towards your changing experience, I can see no reason to see why that, in itself, would be sufficient to lead to the insight that you have no self – no more than if someone applied such a concentrated mind to studying the sunrise and the sunset, they'd be likely to arrive at the insight that the Earth travels round the Sun. Things are not the way they appear.

I do think it's possible for meditation to contribute to seeing these insights more directly, to experience the world in a way that is more in line with how things really are. But unless you're as insightful as the Buddha, you first need someone to try to convey to you, as best they can, what it is you're really looking at, what you're trying to see more clearly and less conceptually. Most Buddhism does aim to do that. Even Zen Buddhists do so, albeit in an indirect and sometimes confusing way. But at the same time, however, much Buddhism unnecessarily disparages the usefulness of doing so.

Supposing someone were to spend lots of time and effort trying to keep in mind how the Earth fits into the solar system, trying to bear in mind how the Sun is not moving across the sky, but rather the Earth is turning, and to keep in mind how the changing seasons relate to the orientation of the Earth as it travels round the Sun. I don't think it's unreasonable to believe they could, in time, come to be more habitually aware of the realities of the solar system, and to change their everyday experience of how they, the Earth and the Sun relate to each other. The reality would often be forgotten, for a time, as the illusion of walking along a flat Earth, with the Sun moving overhead, returned. But increasingly, the world could be experienced in a way that more accurately reflected reality.

I see Buddhist practice as working in a similar way, gradually overcoming the habits of a lifetime and the way things normally appear, continually trying to notice how the same reality we're accustomed to interpreting in one way can actually be better understood and experienced in another, and developing the habit of seeing things in a way that accords more closely to what actually makes more sense, and which allows us to let go of a cause of suffering.

Inevitably, you continually fall back into the habitual way of seeing things, and most of the time, doing so is not a problem. But then occasionally, the suffering that often accompanies that sense of self will become more noticeable, and you realise what's happening, and why. You take a breath, and adjust to the reality that allows that suffering to be let go of, and hopefully slightly reduces the likelihood of it recurring.

A person, of course, is far more complicated than a solar system. Nobody can be expected to consciously hold in mind a 'correct' understanding of what they are, even if such a thing could be defined. A practical approach to developing a Buddhist practice can involve a range of approaches aimed at developing concentration, or compassion, or identifying and overcoming habitual mental and emotional reactions.

For someone who's contemplating beginning Buddhist practice, it can be bewildering trying to work out what the best approach for them is. And trying to work out how to choose between them is a potential new source of suffering! For somebody who just wants to get on with *something*, I can see how an approach like 'just sitting' or MBSR might be reasonable enough, but only after they've gained some intellectual understanding of the Buddha's insights.

There are many aspects of Buddhism that are difficult to make sense of. Perhaps the most obvious is how the importance of letting go of the idea of a self relates to the importance given to rebirth. Surely the strangest of all, however, is that, according to early Buddhist teachings, the ultimate aim is not to achieve a favourable rebirth, but to not be reborn at all. Seriously! Being a good Buddhist leads to a good rebirth, but the ultimate aim is to become fully awakened, after which you live out the remainder of your final life, and then achieve *parinirvana*, never to be reborn again. As for whether something somehow exists after parinirvana, the question is generally treated as either meaningless or unimportant.

I confess, I struggle to make sense of this. I can see two ways of approaching something vaguely resembling an explanation, although neither one strikes me as particularly convincing. Looking at it logically, one possibility would be that the countries in which Buddhism developed contained a shocking number of manic-depressives who saw life as so awful that they wanted to end it all, but who had accepted a belief in rebirth, which meant that death did not offer a release. Buddhism would have offered the answer! I'm not aware, however, of any evidence for this other than the Buddhist aim of not being reborn.

A more likely possibility is that the Buddha, or his early followers, tried their best to follow the logic of the four noble truths, combined with rebirth, from an approach to overcoming suffering, to an all-encompassing religion about the nature of existence, and this was where the logic seemed to lead them. Presumably, if this was the case, most Buddhists would have taken the idea of parinirvana seriously but wouldn't have *really* taken it seriously. In much the same way that generations of

Christians apparently took the idea of burning in everlasting hell seriously, but clearly didn't *really* take it seriously, or there's no way they would have kept on sinning.

There is one way you could make a sort of sense out of the idea of being released from continual rebirth. Instead of applying it to the person, it could be applied to the illusion of self in this lifetime. That illusion of a self is born as you become a conscious being. You might say that it dies when you're asleep or when you're living in the moment, or absorbed in some activity, but it's continually reborn. It dies a more significant death in the course of Buddhist practice, in moments of awakening or in deep meditation. But then, as you engage in everyday life, it's reborn, in a slightly more awakened state. But ultimately, if your practice develops far enough, it dies completely, never to be reborn, leaving you able to live your life free of illusion.[9] That makes sense to me, but it certainly isn't what the major Buddhist traditions have meant by rebirth.

One of the innovations of Mahayana Buddhism was to criticise the aim of not being reborn as displaying a lack of compassion. Instead of aiming to become an *arhat* – someone who has gained awakening and will not be reborn again – Mahayana suggested the compassionate Buddhist should aim to become a bodhisattva, who chooses to forgo parinirvana in order to devote their future lives to helping others overcome suffering – for as long as it takes, until all sentient beings have become awakened.

I wouldn't wish to cast aspersions on Mahayana Buddhists, or on their compassion, but I can't help suspecting that one or two Buddhist monks, on hearing about the idea of the bodhisattva, may not have been entirely dismayed at the idea of giving up the possibility of not being reborn, and instead looking forward to countless future lives spent helping others.

It isn't only people considering their future lives who question whether Buddhism shows compassion in an effective enough way. Despite the importance that compassion plays in Buddhist thought, when it comes to evidence of it in practical action, something seems to be missing. By comparison, Christians, for example, have put more effort into setting up schools, hospitals, charities and so on. Partly in reaction to this, as Buddhism has become more popular in the West, a movement of 'engaged Buddhism' has developed.

This has found form in organisations like The Buddhist Peace Fellowship in the United States and the Network of Engaged Buddhists in Britain. There are many other examples. No doubt such organisations have done worthwhile things, but I suspect even those involved with them would admit that their impact has been disappointing.

It isn't easy to know what conclusions to draw from this. Realistically, I'm not sure there's any way to know how much effect Buddhism – whether of a specifically 'engaged' variety or more generally – has had on people's practical expressions of compassion. There's no reason people whose involvement with Buddhism leads them to social involvement would necessarily do this as part of a specifically Buddhist organisation. Personally, I can't imagine why they would. If you want your social action to affect as many people as possible, why would you link this to a particular religion?

Ironically, the Buddhist-related movement that might be seen as having 'engaged' most successfully with wider society has done so in a way that has focused on meditation and mindfulness. Over the past few decades, the mindfulness-based stress reduction program, started by Jon Kabat-Zinn at the end of the 1970s, has given rise to a veritable 'mindfulness industry' that provides courses, training and 'mindfulness-based interventions', not only in different branches of health, but in education, in the workplace, in developing leadership skills, even in helping train the military.

In his book *McMindfulness: How Mindfulness Became the New Capitalist Spirituality*, Ronald Purser describes how many of those offering mindfulness-based training try to juggle the advantages and disadvantages of its association with Buddhism. One minute they're describing how their Buddhist teacher inspired them to find ways to express their compassion and bring the dhamma to the world, and the next they're pitching their product to corporate CEOs as a scientifically proven way to overcome workplace disengagement and increase corporate efficiency.

Purser argues that one reason mindfulness has become popular is that it fits comfortably with the neoliberal view that people should see everything in terms of individual responsibility. It encourages people to respond to problems by looking inside themselves, rather than questioning wider society.

This is particularly clear in the workplace. When an employer in a capitalist business is willing to devote time and money to providing their employees with mindfulness training, you have to suspect that any concern with their employees' wellbeing is probably related to the hope of getting their employees to focus more on their work and to learn to be at peace with their working conditions and their wages.

If you really want to reduce the stress, or the suffering, of workers, a good way would be to get rid of private ownership and create a cooperative. Better still get rid of capitalism. Or, if you insist on being more realistic, organise a trade union that can ensure people aren't overworked or underpaid. And if this leads to lower dividends for employers or shareholders, and they're unhappy about that, they should definitely be sent for some mindfulness training to help them accept the situation with equanimity.

It's easy to see why Purser is so critical of the mindfulness movement, especially when you consider some of the more absurd ways that those involved present what they're doing. Chade-Meng Tan, for example, who developed *Search Inside Yourself*, a mindfulness-based emotional intelligence training at Google, says, 'My goal in life is to create the conditions for world peace by making the benefits of mindfulness meditation accessible to humanity.'[10]

As Purser makes clear, in reality all these practices actually teach is a particular mindfulness approach that has little to do with Buddhism and little likelihood of bringing about real change other than in the attitudes of individuals – which includes accepting their situation.

In his attempt to present a case against this, however, Purser presents an account of mindfulness which leads him to suggest that 'Truly revolutionary mindfulness is liberating, social, and civic. It depends on critical thinking, not non-judgemental disengagement',[11] and that 'Mindfulness could be an empowering and emancipatory practice, exploring ways to change social conditions and priorities.'[12]

Honestly, I'm not sure that it could. There are, of course, different understandings of Buddhist mindfulness and different activities that might be described as 'mindfulness' whatever their relation to Buddhism. But Buddhist mindfulness as I understand it would hardly be suited to 'exploring ways to change social conditions'. Rather, it focuses on how we experience the world from moment to moment. To the extent that it begins with a conceptual understanding, it aims to move beyond it – for example, to replace the intellectual recognition of no-self with a change in the way we habitually relate to the world.

Dealing with causes of suffering such as exploitation are almost the opposite of this. It is, of course, the subjective experience of social suffering that is why it matters, and it's important to try to understand people's subjective experience. But to solve the problem, we actually need to step back from personal experience, and to abstract from it, in order to try to understand society and to work out how best to bring about social change.

Purser implies that part of the problem with the mindfulness movement is that it ignores other important aspects of Buddhism. But it seems to me that many of his criticisms could be applied equally well to Buddhism as a whole. It's true that Buddhism stresses how mindfulness and meditation should be practised as part of a path that also includes insight and morality. But it isn't clear how these wider teachings of Buddhism would be any less compatible with capitalism.

In particular, Buddhism has always been focused on bringing about change at the level of the individual – on changing the way people experience the world, rather than changing the world itself. This is most obvious in the meditative practices. Even loving-kindness meditation – the closest you can get to 'engaged' meditation – is still more about the meditator's state of mind than about contemplating real-world engagement.

But even when we look beyond meditation, things are not so different. Seeing that desire can cause suffering, or that there is no self, are both fundamentally about individual experience. There is obviously a relationship between an awakened person – or a person trying to become awakened – and society, but even where the relevance to society seems most significant, such as in the ethical guidelines, or the organisation of the sangha, more often than not it seems that the details of how people live together are judged on how conducive they are to people becoming awakened. Other aspects of what makes a good society are not a priority.

You could argue that the Buddha was perfectly clear about what he had to offer. He said, on a number of occasions, 'All I teach is dukkha and the ending of dukkha.' I assume most Buddhists imagine him saying this in a profound Buddha-like 'dispensing wisdom about what matters most' kind of a way. Although I can't help imagining him saying it in a more defensive tone: 'Guys, I only promised freedom from suffering. I never said I could tell you what to do with your lives or how to organise society!'

There's nothing in the Buddha's awakening that implies anything about the future of society. If there were such a thing as a Buddhist Utopia, so far as I can tell it would consist of people approaching each other with one saying, 'Please allow me to help release you from your suffering', to which the person being addressed would reply, 'No need! No need at all. I have already been released from all suffering. Is there anything I can do to release *you* from *your* suffering?' And that would basically be it.

'Actual existing Buddhism' has, of course, created all sorts of valuable art, culture and social institutions, as anyone can see by looking, for example, at Tibet, or at the influence of Zen in Japan. But none of this is the aim of Buddhism. They are, if anything, means to the goal of release from illusion and suffering.

It's understandable that Buddhism would not present a positive vision of a future society, or more broadly pay attention to the question of how people's lives could be better in the future. The Buddha's insight was all about how people experience the world, not about the world itself. It would be relevant regardless of the form of society. And perhaps more significantly, the way the Buddha tried to teach his insights was by focusing on the value of letting go of desire, which is not likely to be helped by presenting a positive future for people to contemplate.

On the other hand, the aim of Buddhism is to help people see clearly the way things really are. Whilst that includes recognising that the self is an illusion, it must also mean seeing the reality that lies behind that illusion. The main way Buddhist practice does this is by paying attention to the constantly changing process of that selfless person. But what actually exists is more than this. No individual can be understood separately from the society they're a part of. And society is more than just a collection of individuals. Changing how society is organised can change how individuals experience themselves and their relation to each other.

Although the Buddha's focus was on individual experience, it was clear to him that his views did have some implications for society. It was obvious that his understanding had no place for the caste system. And whilst he wasn't immune from the prejudices of his time about gender,[13] he recognised that women were as capable of awakening as men. Many Buddhists today recognise that aspects of society, such as consumerism and greed, conflict with the aims and values of Buddhism. But whilst some Buddhists make the effort to address the question of how society can be changed for the better, I don't think it's unfair to suggest that the closest most Buddhists get to a 'political analysis' of society is believing that the world would be a happier place if everyone was nicer to each other. Which is true, of course. But it's difficult not to be struck by the contrast between the amount of detailed attention paid to the challenges of changing individuals, and the comparative lack of such attention paid to society.

Understanding how society could be changed for the better has never been more important. More than any previous form of society, capitalism encourages ways of relating to the world that directly contradict what Buddhism teaches. Given the challenges that we currently face, for people today, and for those born (or reborn) in the future, the likelihood of finding an end to dukkha – or other kinds of suffering – is likely to be affected more than ever by the economic and political changes of the coming decades.

Moving from the skandhas, to the individual, to social beings, to societies in general, and to the specific society we live in, I'm not sure whether we move beyond what Buddhism, as Buddhism, should concern itself with. You wouldn't expect Buddhist teachings to directly teach you about yourself as a unique individual. Rather, it addresses individuals in general, and provides ideas and practices that can allow individuals to come to a better understanding of themselves.

What about specific forms of society? In a sense, it's appropriate that Buddhism doesn't pay detailed attention to the organisation of society, because the sort of society that is possible changes over time, and there's surely more than one good way that society can be organised. But whilst I don't think it's unreasonable for Buddhist teachings to pay little attention to questions about society and politics, it does seem rather odd when those who've been influenced by such teachings take little interest in how the politics of the society they're living in is relevant to how people experience and act in the world.

Practising Buddhism means accepting the present as it is, avoiding the suffering that follows from greed or anger, attachment or aversion. But it also means having compassion and loving-kindness and wanting less suffering for everyone in the future. Any realistic plan for a better future needs to understand the social forces that influence people – that people can either recreate or choose to change. Seeing more clearly what actually is, opens the possibility for deciding more meaningfully and successfully what we want to become, and what sort of society we want to create.

The reasons why human beings are able to become more awakened, to see reality more clearly and escape unnecessary suffering, are the same reasons why we are capable of creating a better world – a world where people recognise that they're better off working together, where they can put an end to as many causes of suffering as possible, including poverty, exploitation, oppression, and every kind of alienation.

11. REVOLUTIONS

There's something surreal about mainstream economics. To see how this is the case, it's useful to compare it with another sphere of knowledge that aims to improve our understanding of the world so as to create a better future, and which has seen significant change over the last century. Let's go with technology.

Suppose you were to ask an averagely intelligent person – let's say, for example, a mainstream economist – how they imagine the world will have changed a century from now, as a result of technological developments. They would presumably look back at the developments of the last century, at developments in radio and television, in all kinds of transport, from planes, trains and automobiles to space travel, at satellites enabling global communication, at the developments in atomic energy and solar energy, at computerisation and the internet, at phones moving from desktops to briefcases to pockets, at robotics and artificial intelligence, and so on. Having considered all this, they might then engage in some educated speculation about developments that seem likely to make an impact in the future. But they would almost certainly also add that, in all likelihood, developments will happen that we're in no position to predict now, any more than people a century ago would have been likely to predict the significance of, for example, the internet.

Now suppose you were to ask the same averagely intelligent mainstream economist how they imagine the world will have changed a century from now, as a result of economic developments. They would presumably look back at the developments of the last century, at the abandonment of the gold standard, at the Wall Street crash and the depression that followed, at the development of Keynesianism, its success in the post-war decades, and its breakdown in the 1970s, at the third world debt crisis, the rise of neoliberalism, the financial big bang, the collapse of the eastern bloc economies, the dotcom boom, the development of the European Union and the rise of China, at the 2008 crash and the austerity policies that followed, and they'd probably reply, 'I imagine it will be more or less the same as now, but hopefully with lower taxes.'

This may be a little unfair. The truth is, there's little to suggest many mainstream economists ever think in such challenging timescales. Economists are generally comfortable with large numbers, happy to think in the trillions when it comes to dollars or pounds, euros or yen, but when it comes to future decades, most seem to struggle with anything beyond about two. Maybe three.

In the 1990s, when people were talking about 'the end of history' – the idea that 'liberal democracy' was the final form of human society – I always wondered what sort of timescale *they* were thinking in: decades, centuries, millennia, tens or hundreds of millennia, millions of years? Barring bad luck with asteroid strikes, or destroying ourselves, human beings *could* be around for millions of years, so if 'history has ended', that would mean that millions of years from now society will still be organised on the basis of liberal democracy and capitalism. Could they seriously have meant that? Perhaps they were just assuming that human beings would not survive for long – which is, of course, a perfectly reasonable assumption if you're determined to stick with capitalism, although I'm not sure that's the point they were trying to make.

It isn't difficult to see why mainstream economists would be reluctant to engage too seriously with such challenging concepts as 'the future' or 'human ingenuity'. Suppose they were to concede that, at some point in the future, human beings might work out a way of organising the production and distribution of the things people want that – miraculously – works *even better* than private companies competing on the market to see who can make a profit. This could presumably lead to some slightly awkward follow-up questions, such as, 'Do you have the remotest clue how that might work?' or 'Do you think, if you were to devote just a teensy-weensy bit of your precious time and undoubted economic expertise to thinking about that question, it might help us move to that better system sooner rather than later?' It certainly makes things simpler if you stick to a timescale where you only have to convince people that there is no alternative, and not that there never could be.

Marx knew that he and his ideas only existed because of the specific history of which he was part, including the revolutions that ushered in capitalism, and without which he could never have come to understand history and the world in the way that he had. He hoped and believed that he and his ideas would help lead to another revolution, one that would enable the world to build on all the developments that capitalism had driven, realise the positive possibilities it had created, and leave behind the limitations that were inseparable from it.

Marx used the term revolution in two different ways. The most commonly used meaning refers to the overthrow and replacement of those in political control, usually involving some degree of violence. Marx used it in this sense, but the kind of revolution he was most interested in was not a merely political revolution but rather a social revolution – a transition from one economic system or mode of production to another, as in the move from feudalism to capitalism or from capitalism to communism. Such a revolution would affect every aspect of society: economic, political, institutional, cultural, people's sense of themselves and how they relate to society and to each other. For most of his life, Marx took it for granted that this latter kind of revolution would require the former kind, although the political developments he saw later in life suggested the possibility that some countries – he named 'America, England, and [possibly] Holland'[1] – might make the transition by peaceful means.

Marx saw the possibility of revolution arising when 'the forces of production' come into conflict with the 'relations of production'. So, for example, within feudalism, developments in technology and the organisation of production led to new possibilities for producing more efficiently and taking advantage of the growing market. This development in 'the forces of production' went hand in hand with the growing influence of those who benefitted from it, the emerging bourgeoisie or capitalist class. But the 'relations of production' under feudalism prevented them from taking full advantage of the opportunities. For example, serfdom meant there was not a suitable supply of people selling their labour-power. As the bourgeoisie grew in wealth and influence, it increasingly came into conflict with those defending the feudal order.

This does not mean that the revolutions that overthrew feudalism followed straightforwardly from economic causes. Those who played a role in the revolutions were trying to make sense of the changing world they were a part of. While this naturally included seeing opportunities for more wealth and power, they were also influenced by wider ideas such as those that developed through the protestant reformation and the enlightenment.

Political developments were also shaped by the nature of the feudal order that the bourgeoisie were opposing. The ideas of freedom and equality, around which the bourgeois revolutions were focused, could motivate broader sections of society. It was no coincidence, however, that the kind of equality most people gained was a strictly formal, legal equality, and the freedom most people gained was the 'double freedom' Marx described as belonging to the working class – freedom from being bound to a feudal lord, but also freedom from ownership of the means of production, leaving them with no choice but to sell their labour-power in order to live.

As capitalism became established, the pace of economic and social change accelerated. Competition drove capitalists to improve productivity, and to develop new products to sell. But along with the improvements in ways to compete and make profits, capitalism also created 'its own gravediggers' in the shape of an ever-growing working class that had reason to resist exploitation. Capitalism also developed the very technologies and knowledge that made it easier to envisage a way of organising society that would provide for everybody's needs without private ownership of the means of production and wage labour. In other words, the capitalist relations of production changed from something that aided economic and social development into something that stood in its way.

There are important differences, however, between the situation facing those who wanted to move beyond feudalism and those who want to move beyond capitalism. Firstly, it was possible for capitalism to grow within feudalism. By the time they started to express their political demands, the capitalist class were already powerful by virtue of the economic significance of capitalist enterprises. Whereas, for the working class, although they became the most significant actors in the economy, the wealth they created gave more power to their employers than to themselves.

Objectively, the working class have more power within capitalism than the capitalist class did within feudalism. Feudalism could have carried on just fine if the capitalists had disappeared, whereas it would be impossible for capitalism to continue without the working class. You would expect this to make the working class stronger, and in a sense it does, but only if the working class is organised, conscious of its power, and agreed on the changes it wants to bring about.

So long as capitalism continues, however, workers are dependent on capitalism functioning in order for them to be able to make a living. Any challenge to capitalism can be presented as a threat to the working of an economy, and to the profitability of companies that the working class are reliant on to provide them with jobs and wages. Transitioning from a situation where working-class organisations are focused on improving or protecting their wages and conditions, to one where it's possible to replace capitalism, is fraught with challenges and contradictions.

One of my least favourite quotes from Marx appears at the start of *The Eighteenth Brumaire of Louis Bonaparte*. Marx is describing the events that led to Louis Napoleon Bonaparte declaring himself Emperor Napoleon III in 1852, and comparing this to how Louis' uncle, Napoleon Bonaparte, became the first Emperor of France in the course of changing European and world history. Marx writes:

> Hegel observes somewhere that all the great events and characters of world history occur twice, so to speak. He forgot to add: the first time as high tragedy, the second time as low farce.[2]

This is invariably misquoted as, 'History repeats itself, first as tragedy, then as farce', and, frankly, why not? Quote and misquote share the same essential quality: they're complete codswallop! Why repeat twice? Why not three or four times? Why tragedy and farce? Why in that order? If 'all great events' in history occur in these two ways, that must mean that no great event could ever happen that is *neither* tragedy *nor* farce – well ain't that just dandy!

It's clear enough that Marx is just having a rhetorical dig at Louis Napoleon, somehow failing to foresee how many people, in future generations, would consider him worth (mis)quoting every time they wanted to have a dig at some subsequent historical figure or event. This would hardly matter if it weren't for the fact that both quote and misquote reinforce the impression that Marx saw history as following some neat, predictable pattern. This reflects a widespread assumption about Marx's understanding of history that is, in fact, wrong – an assumption that Marx promptly goes on to contradict in the rest of *The Eighteenth Brumaire of Louis Bonaparte*.

Marx begins by putting that opening quote into a context that transforms it from complete codswallop into codswallop that vaguely relates to a quite interesting point about the way history sometimes develops. He describes how people find themselves in completely new situations (because history does *not* repeat itself), and they struggle to make sense of these new situations, and as a result:

> ...just when they appear to be revolutionizing themselves and their circumstances, in creating something unprecedented, in just such epochs of revolutionary crisis, that is when they nervously summon up the spirits of the past, borrowing from them their names, marching orders, uniforms, in order to enact new scenes in world history, but in this time-honored guise and with this borrowed language.[3]

In this way, the leaders of the French Revolution cast themselves in roles from the Roman Republic, and Louis Napoleon cast himself (more farcically) in the role of Napoleon Bonaparte.

What people in such situations *should* do, however, is to recognise that history is not, in fact, repeating itself, and come to terms with the newly developed reality. Marx compares this to the way a language learner masters a new language:

> Likewise a beginner studying a new language always translates it back into his mother tongue; but only when he can use it without referring back, and thus forsake his native language for the new, only then has he entered into the spirit of the new language, and gained the ability to speak it fluently.[4]

It is this entering into the 'spirit of the new language' that Marx thinks needs to be done to engage adequately with any actual historical development, and this is what he tries to do in *The Eighteenth Brumaire of Louis Bonaparte*.

Whatever their flaws, all of Marx's writings are intended to provide people with an understanding of society that will help them to change it. But this involves a constant balancing act. On the one hand, he wants to provide analysis that will continue to be relevant over the medium or long term. But on the other hand, he needs to make it clear that the form in which things develop is always new and requires developing a further and deeper understanding.

When he's addressing the fundamental nature of the capitalist mode of production, in *Capital* and elsewhere, Marx aims to provide an understanding of the ways in which it will define social relations for so long as it exists. So, when it comes to class, his main focus is on the two most important classes defined by their relationship to the means of production – the working class or proletariat who have to sell their labour-power in order to live, and the capitalist class or bourgeoisie who own the means of production.

When Marx turned to examining particular historical events, as he did in *The Eighteenth Brumaire of Louis Bonaparte*, it would never have occurred to him to use only those categories that were applicable to capitalism as a whole. He examined the way in which these were manifested in the particular circumstances, taking into account all the cultural, political and economic complexities. So he referred not only to the proletariat and the bourgeoisie but also to landowners, the finance aristocracy, the petite bourgeoisie, the manufacturing bourgeoisie, the peasantry and the lumpenproletariat, along with groups defined less by their economic relations than by their ideas and loyalties – distinguishing, for example, between the role played by the democratic-republican petite bourgeoisie compared to the republican bourgeoisie.

History does not repeat itself precisely, but there is an undeniable predictability in the way, every few years, or decades, some rising academic star will notice that class structure is actually quite complicated, and will write a celebrated book or article that points out how, since this reality bears no resemblance to Marx's simplistic reduction of class to the proletariat and the bourgeoisie, Marx was either always wrong or is now obsolete and, either way, has nothing to say to the modern world.

In reality, Marxists have always paid attention to the complex ways in which class relations develop. Part of the challenge is to understand the changes that matter and the challenges and opportunities that they present. One of the most significant changes over recent decades has been the decline in traditional industries in which workers had relatively stable long-term employment, a situation that lent itself well to organising trade unions. As these types of jobs have declined, there's been a growth in the number of workers in increasingly insecure conditions. This is sometimes described as the *precariat* – a term popularised in particular by Guy Standing, who describes their situation like this:

> The precariat ... consists of millions of people obliged to accept a life of unstable labour and living... Their employers come and go, or are expected to do so. Many in the precariat are overqualified for the jobs they must accept: they also have a high ratio of unpaid 'work' to labour – looking and applying for jobs, training and retraining, queueing and form-filling, networking or just waiting around. They also rely mainly on money wages, which are often inadequate, volatile and unpredictable. They

lack access to rights-based state benefits and are losing civil, cultural, social, economic and political rights, making them supplicants if they need help to survive.[5]

Most Marxists would recognise this description, which highlights some of the challenges of politically organising the working class today. I can't imagine many would agree, however, with some of the conclusions Standing draws. He sees the precariat as a distinct class, separate from the working class, who will form the basis of any organisation for change in the future, while the traditional working class, along with existing trade unions, he sees as a spent force. Changes in the nature of work are undoubtedly a challenge, but a more likely way forward is for trade unions to find ways to adapt to those new challenges – as many are attempting to do.

There are other significant developments in the class structure, such as the growth of the middle class (or different sections of the middle classes), or the conflict of interest between small businesses, multinationals and the financial sector. It's always worthwhile to develop an understanding of the relevance of different class forces as well as other divisions within society, but in a sense, the more significant question at the moment is how to create support for socialism amongst any group of workers at all.

Marxists and socialists have always tried to develop more effective ways to engage in politics and to take account of the ways that capitalism and society are changing – with very varied results. Recent years have seen increasing numbers of people engaging in debates, getting involved in different movements and organisations, writing books and articles, trying to work out the best way to build an effective socialist movement.

If you think the argument in favour of Marxism that I've made here is worth pursuing in a more practical way, one book that I think would be an interesting complement to this one is *People Get Ready!* by Christine Berry and Joe Guinan. Although the values and aims expressed in that book and this one are much the same, the books themselves are very different. My subject matter has been capitalism in general, arguably a little too much about the capitalism Marx was familiar with and not enough about the way it has changed. I wouldn't say writing this book has been easy, but at least I never had to worry (sadly) about its subject matter becoming obsolete. I've been able to set my own deadlines, and I've been able to repeatedly fail to meet them. That the situation was different for Berry and Guinan is indicated clearly enough by the book's – in retrospect, perhaps, regrettable – subtitle: *Preparing for a Corbyn Government*.

That subtitle does, in fact, serve a useful purpose in reminding us just how quickly politics can change. In 2015, the British left seemed about as far from real power as it had ever been. Two years later, the totally unexpected victory of Jeremy Corbyn in the Labour Party's leadership election, followed by the almost equally unexpected progress during the course of the 2017 general election – increasing Labour's share of the vote by more than in any election since 1945, gaining seats for the first time since 1997 and depriving the Tories of their majority – meant that Britain was faced with the realistic possibility of a government led by socialists. A few years later and it's difficult to remember just how real that possibility was.[6]

Berry and Guinan wrote *People Get Ready!* in a few months, in the wake of the 2017 election – because it was clear to them that the left absolutely was *not* ready for the challenges that a Corbyn government would have faced. But don't be put off by the subtitle or how long it took to write. The authors were clearly drawing on years of learning and experience. Much of the book, as you would expect, addresses the measures that could be carried out from government, but alongside this is a continual consideration of the relationship between electoral politics and the building of a wider socialist movement. This is part of a debate that existed before Corbyn and continues today.

A socialist movement, as it attempts to grow, is faced with contradictory tasks. The long-term aim is to replace capitalism. But to convince people it can be trusted to work in their best interests, it must try to improve their lives while capitalism continues to exist. It must try to make capitalism work more fairly. The more such movements manage to find ways to do this, the more involved they become in trying to work out how best to make capitalism work, and the easier it is to focus on this, rather than more radical change.

This applies nowhere more so than when socialists get into government. If such governments don't want to appear to be failing, they have to make capitalism work. Compromises have to be made. Those who have the easiest access to power – representatives of business, the owners of most of the media, the finance sector, other governments and international organisations representing capital – will be putting constant pressure on them to focus on making capitalism work, and to be willing to compromise on the aim of making it fairer for those who are most exploited by it.

Barriers will be put in the way of even relatively mild changes, such as those that Corbyn's Labour Party were proposing, let alone any movement that sought to build on that and to seriously shift the balance of power in society. There's always the danger that elected representatives will give in to such pressure. There are many examples of this happening, from the decisions of Social Democratic parties on the outbreak of the First World War, through the Mitterrand government in France in the 1980s that abandoned plans for radical change, to Syriza's inability to deliver on its promises to the Greek people.

One way of reacting to this is to reject electoral politics altogether. Many on the left have done this over recent decades, sometimes taking more inspiration from anarchist than socialist politics. This could be seen in the anti-capitalist and anti-globalisation movements, and later the Occupy movement. But many who were involved with these movements came to realise that they offered no way of bringing about real change.

The success of the left in electoral politics, in the Labour Party, in the United States around Bernie Sanders and the Democratic Socialists, in Spain, France and elsewhere, have offered the promise of significant change – but for that promise to be carried through, they would have to be combined with a wider movement that supports them. As Berry and Guinan conclude:

...radical governments need a solid power base in wider society in order to implement their agenda – one that is both well informed and well organised. If the base lacks strength or depth, the radical agenda will not survive the inevitable battering from opposing forces.[7]

Such a movement only really existed in embryo while Corbyn was Labour leader. If there had been a Corbyn government, it's impossible to know how much it could have achieved. It would be nice to believe that it could have used its position to aid the development of such a movement, which could in turn have supported changes from government. As it turns out, such a movement is needed to get socialists into government in the first place.

In the post-war decades, social democratic politics succeeded in improving people's lives. Partly for this reason, socialists found it more difficult to build movements for more radical change. With the establishment of a welfare state and steadily increasing wages, the option of improving things within capitalism seemed realistic, and the value of bringing about radical change was less clear. As a result, when politics became more volatile in the 1970s, it was right-wing parties that were better prepared and able to seize the initiative.

One conclusion that could be drawn from this is that, if a socialist movement is to be sustained and grown in the way necessary to bring about real long-term change, then it needs to be built not only on addressing immediate material concerns, but on arguments for the sort of society we want to create and why socialist values are worth building on.

Suggesting this will always provoke objections from some on the left who will insist that the focus should be on the 'real, practical concerns' of workers, on 'bread and butter issues'. The most obvious reply to this is that nobody who's serious about socialism would argue a concern with values should *replace* addressing material concerns such as wages. The point is that such concerns should be linked with a debate about why such struggles are needed in the society we live in, and what sort of society it's worth trying to create. A movement that's focused entirely on short-term material conditions is never going to build a new society.

One reason some people influenced by Marxism might call for the focus to be on 'material needs' is a confusion about different meanings of 'materialism'. Marx was a materialist in that he saw material reality as providing the possibilities and limitations for change. He saw it as important to understand the way in which changes in material and social reality are relevant to the way consciousness develops. This is not the same as the common meaning of being 'materialistic' – of viewing your material well-being as what matters most.

In fact, *that* meaning of materialism fits far better with the liberal, capitalist view, which sees everyone as being guided by their self-interest. If Marxists don't believe human beings are capable of better than that, it's difficult to see how we expect to organise a worthwhile post-capitalist society. Marxism does see people's consciousness and motivations as being shaped by their material reality, but that reality is not only one of material need – it's also one of alienation, of people being deprived of control over their lives, treated like commodities and used to create the commodities their employers really care about.

Far from representing 'people's everyday concerns' or 'what workers really care about', arguing for a focus on material concerns is a misrepresentation of what people care about which, frankly, verges on the insulting. Obviously, it's true that people want material things, but even those concerns are bound up with wanting their lives to be about far more. This should not be controversial – the evidence is everywhere to be seen.

You only have to look at those people who choose to do jobs such as nursing or teaching, which they hope will be rewarding and give them a sense of doing something worthwhile, when they could direct the same talents towards better paid professions. The evidence is also there in the actual activity of trade unions, which have never been focused exclusively on wages, but also on providing workers with more freedom by reducing working hours – introducing the five-day week, paid holidays, and parental leave. And trade unions also provide their members with a sense of having more control over their own lives, and the rewarding feeling of working in solidarity, including solidarity with other progressive movements in society.

The evidence is also there amongst the very Marxists who may be insisting that 'material factors' are what really matter. If you look at the reality of Marxist history, it's clear that this has not been the motivation of Marxists at all. If it had been, then you would expect history to be littered with stories of Marxists who ended up bemoaning how they'd been sold a lie, how they'd been promised the world and experienced only struggle, how they'd been told they had nothing to lose but then gave much of their lives to struggles that brought no material gain.

Presumably such people exist, but they're curiously difficult to find. If you want a better guide to what has really motivated Marxists, you could do worse than read *The Romance of American Communism* by Vivian Gornick. Gornick interviewed people who were involved with the Communist Party of America, people who believed that allying with, and being guided by, the Soviet Union was the best way to advance the interests of workers against capitalism, and who ended up leaving the party, either after Khrushchev's revelations about the crimes of Stalin, or in reaction to the Soviet Union crushing the uprisings in Hungary and Czechoslovakia.

If anyone had a right to feel they'd been misled by Marxism, and that they'd have been better off devoting their abilities and hard work towards developing their own careers and earning a living, it's these people. But they express no such sentiment. The regrets they have are more about having lost the sense of meaning they had when they felt they were contributing to something worthwhile. Take Maggie McConnell, for example, who spent fifteen years as a party organiser in the trade unions. When Gornick asks her if she feels she sacrificed her life to the Communist Party, she smiles and replies:

> Sacrificed my life! Of course not. Hon, we were in the world-changing business. You can't get much better than that. What's better? Money? Position? Are you kidding?[8]

But in case you think I'm presenting Marxists, or the working class, as particularly immune from the focus on material things that capitalism encourages, let's consider someone who's about as different from

Maggie McConnell as you could hope to find: Ayn Rand. Rand is the self-proclaimed champion of 'The Virtue of Selfishness', much admired by economic managers of capitalism and Silicon Valley entrepreneurs,[9] widely reviled by much of the left. And yet if you read Rand's most popular book, the novel *Atlas Shrugged*, you encounter a very curious plot indeed. The central story involves some very rich people voluntarily destroying their own wealth and withdrawing to a remote valley to work hard at building a new society!

Rand loathed the Marxist idea of 'from each according to their ability, to each according to their need'. Her understanding of it, however, was in the context of a very odd view of the world. For most people, I'd assume (and hope), it's interpreted in the context of an understanding that everybody has needs, and everybody, at least for most of their lives, has abilities. So the aim is to bring these facts into harmony, ensuring that everyone has their needs met, and everyone has the opportunity to develop their abilities and to make good use of them to help themselves and others.

The wonderful world of Ayn Rand, however, is not like this at all. The people it contains might be divided up into three groups. Most important are the small group of Rand's heroes, whose remarkable entrepreneurial abilities give rise to all that is new, worthwhile and impressive in the world.

By stark contrast, there are the working masses, although you'd be forgiven for missing them, because, surprising as it may seem, they hardly make any appearance in *Atlas Shrugged*. They appear, occasionally, in walk-on parts, as bit-players, some of them 'decent hard-working people' (with no apparent connection to the unions who claim to represent them), others dishevelled, almost sub-human hovel-dwellers. Presumably, they have some varying share of basic abilities, but none significant enough to be worthy of attention. Their needs may be significant, but they themselves are too inconsequential to either meet their own needs or demand that others do so. They are instead represented by a third group – the real villains of Rand's world.

This third group seem to get all their needs met without having any worthwhile abilities at all. They're the people who most successfully ride on the coat-tails of Rand's heroes, the people those heroes are forced to do business with, to take account of, to attend tiresome social functions with,[10] people who spend all their spare time criticising the selfishness, greed and driven personalities of her heroes – insisting that they should care more about fairness, popular opinion, social responsibility, public relations, and good government.

These are the people who – in a not remotely communist way – embody the idea of 'from each according to their ability, to each according to their need', which in this context means the demand that the most admirable and able people in society should be required to give what they've rightfully earned to people who've done nothing at all to deserve it. And in order to force the heroes to behave in a more responsible way, these people spend their professional lives getting together in organisations, associations and governmental bodies to pass rules, laws and edicts to force the heroes to reflect these socially responsible values in ways that frustrate their ability to actually build the impressive and necessary businesses that they want to create, and that society actually needs.

Until, finally, the heroes become so frustrated by the barriers put in their way that they set fire to their own oil wells, collapse their copper mines, bankrupt their banks, and withdraw to their hidden valley where they can happily relate to each other through a self-interested exchange of the things they're so well-suited to creating, leaving the rest of the world to fall apart as it becomes clear how it can't survive without them.

Rand doesn't tell people that if they want to be happy they should get rich. She tells people who are already rich, or who are confident they have the ability to become rich, that they should be proud and unapologetic about building their wealth, because it's a reflection of the valuable and admirable people they are. She tells them that their desire to hold on to their wealth, and their resentment at anyone wanting to take it away, is not an expression of greed, but a demand for social justice!

The picture of the world that Rand draws may be ridiculous, but it reflects something meaningful about human beings – that we never relate to the world in a purely 'materialistic' way. Whether it's a homeless person feeling bad about having to beg for money, or a billionaire feeling good about having a few more millions to hide away in a tax haven, people always experience their material situation in terms of what it says about them and society, in terms of the way they understand the world to be – and the way they think it should be.

When it comes to the question of where to look for the values socialists should promote, a number of recent authors suggest the same answer: liberalism. That may seem odd, but it makes sense. The demands that liberals championed were a reaction against the absolutism and fixed hierarchies of feudalism. Those values were, and are, progressive. The problem is that liberalism was incapable of delivering them in a meaningful way. This was partly because it understood those values from the point of view of abstract individuals separated from society, but most of all it was because of capitalism.

In *How to Be an Anticapitalist in the Twenty-First Century*, Erik Olin Wright suggests that these values, as expressed in the slogan of the French Revolution, 'Liberty, equality, fraternity,' need to be developed in a more meaningful and socialist way. He argues that 'three clusters of values are central to the moral critique of capitalism: equality/fairness, democracy/freedom, and community/solidarity'.[11]

The value of 'fraternity', which those involved in bourgeois revolutions clearly found inspiring, always sat rather oddly with the liberal stress on self-interested individuals. It does not seem to have long survived contact with actual existing capitalism – except in the form of American male undergraduates getting drunk and thinking of ways to humiliate those who, for some strange reason, want to fraternise with them. Its underlying sense, however, is well expressed by Wright's 'community/solidarity', and it is most often expressed in contrast, or opposition, to liberalism and capitalism. Wright expands on these values:

> Community/solidarity expresses the principle that people ought to cooperate with each other not simply because of what they personally receive, but also from a real commitment to the well-being of others and a sense of moral obligation that it is right to do.
>
> When such cooperation occurs in mundane, everyday activities in which people help each other out, we use the word

'community'; when the cooperation occurs in the context of collective action to achieve a common goal, we use the term 'solidarity'.[12]

The liberty or freedom that liberalism called for was a rejection of the traditions and hierarchical rule of feudalism; it was a freedom seen in terms of the individual, the sort of freedom Ayn Rand wants for her heroes, setting them free to pursue their self-interest. What it ignores is all the ways in which capitalism *constrains* the freedom of most people, leaving them no choice but to sell their labour-power to others and spend most of their working lives following the orders of their employers. A socialist freedom involves promoting democracy in every sphere of life.

Jeremy Gilbert in *Twenty-First Century Socialism* argues that socialists should organise around a demand for 'radical freedom', and he sees this freedom as going hand in hand with the same values that Wright talks about:

> ...twenty-first century socialism is a philosophy and a politics of freedom. But it is also important to remember that, from a socialist perspective, a politics of freedom is always also a politics of equality, solidarity and democracy. This is what socialism has always meant; and it is still what it means today.[13]

Many people assume Marx gave a lot of importance to the value of equality, but this is not in fact the case. He saw the concept as suited much better to the liberal viewpoint, which understood it in terms of abstract individual citizens relating to each other as legal or political equals. He criticised this as ignoring the social reality in which people were anything but equal. Marx's vision of a communist society was better expressed by the idea of 'from each according to their ability, to each according to their need', which takes account of the variety of real individuals. It seems reasonable, however, to call for 'equality' as a shorthand way of calling for an end to unnecessary inequalities. This is a call that many will recognise as reasonable given the obscene levels of inequality that exist in the world today.

G.A. Cohen in *Why Not Socialism?* argues that socialism needs to realise two principles: an egalitarian principle, and a principle of community. He argues that the sort of egalitarianism we should aim for is a 'socialist equality of opportunity' where, 'differences of outcome reflect nothing but differences of taste and choice, not differences in natural and social capacities and powers'.[14]

So people might choose, for example, to work more than others in exchange for a greater share of what society collectively produces. But this would not only move beyond 'bourgeois equality of opportunity', removing formal inequalities of the type that existed under feudalism. It would also move beyond 'left-liberal equality of opportunity', which aims to mitigate inequalities resulting from a person's position in society by, for example, supporting people from deprived backgrounds, while accepting inequalities resulting from individual differences.

Just as capitalism has provided the material developments that enable the creation of a socialist society, liberalism has promoted the values that we should be building on. Socialists have no need to promote new, unfamiliar values. Rather, we should be calling for a more meaningful realisation of the values that our current society was built on, but which capitalism has always been, and will always be, incapable of delivering, values that only socialism can make truly meaningful.

There's an additional reason to focus on values, and to call out capitalism and 'liberal democracy' for their failure to deliver on the promise of equality. This is the importance of social movements that address various forms of inequality that are not about social class – inequalities based not only on exploitation, but on oppression of sections of society based on gender, race and other differences.

It's difficult to think of any movement against oppression or injustice, whether in relation to racism, sexism, gay and lesbian rights, anti-imperialism or anything else, where there haven't been Marxists trying to play a role, but the relationship of such social movements to socialist politics has always been in dispute. Some have seen socialist involvement as distracting from the oppression that they were focused on, and so getting in the way of bringing about change.

Advances made by such social movements have managed to simultaneously confirm and refute this criticism. On the one hand, significant advances have been made in improving the situation of women, racial minorities and others, demonstrating that such advances could be achieved without linking them to a critique of capitalism. But the more success there's been, the clearer it's become that capitalism shapes, and limits, the kind of advances that are possible; the most visible advances have been the growth of a Black middle class and increasing numbers of women and racial minorities in positions of power.

Positive though these changes have been, amongst the majority, who remain part of the working class, oppression continues, and they continue to be amongst the most exploited in society. The reality is that, since we're living in a capitalist society, all forms of inequality or injustice are shaped by the class divisions that are intrinsic to the economy. Challenging them effectively means challenging that system, and overcoming them completely would require changing it.

This also applies, of course, to the increasingly important ecological movement. It's true that the communist states of the last century showed that it isn't only capitalism that can be bad for the planet, but it's difficult to see how we can deal effectively with climate change or other ecological challenges within an economic system that is focused on producing whatever is most profitable for private companies, even when doing so is at the expense of what's good for society as a whole.

The first aspect of the capitalist worldview that all progressive social movements would benefit from moving beyond is the idea that, for anyone to win, someone else has to lose. Capitalism benefits from division, especially from divisions amongst those whose exploitation and oppression are integral to how it works. Socialists, along with everyone who doesn't benefit from capitalist exploitation, gain from overcoming such divisions. By uniting all such movements around shared values of equality and freedom for all, any advance for one movement can be seen as an advance for others.

Marxists place a particular importance on class, but this is not because exploitation is seen as more important than different forms of oppression, or because of some sort of glorification of the working class. It has nothing to do with rating different issues in importance, nor subordinating one to another. The reason class is important is because the best way to bring about change is to put the most effective pressure on those who have power and want to resist change, and the one group that can do this effectively is the working class on which capitalism is entirely dependent.

The aims of socialism are at one with the aims of every progressive social movement. The most likely way for any of them to succeed is to overcome divisions, to work together towards common aims, and to build a movement that can create a society that removes every kind of oppression, injustice, exploitation and alienation, a society where 'the free development of each is the condition for the free development of all.'[15]

When Marx and Engels published *The Communist Manifesto* in 1848, it was under the title *The Manifesto of the Communist Party*. It made sense to change the title, because the use of the word 'party' would become misleading. When the manifesto was written, the word did not have the same meaning it would later have. It certainly didn't refer to the kind of disciplined revolutionary party that Lenin argued was appropriate to the circumstances of Tsarist Russia. It didn't even have the meaning it would come to have as 'representative democracy' became less unrepresentative, and organised political parties came to reflect the interests of particular classes or ideologies. It referred not to an organised group but more a tendency or current of opinion.

The manifesto claims, in its opening words, that 'A spectre is haunting Europe – the spectre of Communism.' One sense in which it was a spectre was that it was still in the process of formation. The meaning of communism was being shaped by historical developments, and by the debates and disagreements amongst those who identified with its aim of creating a more equal and just society.

As members of this 'communist party', Marx and Engels were commissioned to write the manifesto by the small Communist League – formed a year earlier when the even smaller League of the Just merged with the Communist Correspondence Committee. Writing the manifesto was, in part, their own attempt to influence what communism should become, by presenting the ideas around which they believed it should be focused.

At the time it was published, the manifesto received little attention. The reason it came to be such a significant publication was because its authors went on to promote and develop the analysis they had provided, and to convince people that they offered the most coherent account of how capitalism worked – and why people should, and could, move beyond it.

Naturally, some aspects of the manifesto reflected the time and circumstances in which it was written. Even in the preface to the 1872 edition, Marx commented that, in the light of subsequent events, it had, in some ways, become 'antiquated'. Some parts of it were also just wrong. Probably the most significant – one for which Marx continues to be criticised – was the prediction that the proletariat would become ever poorer, an assumption which seemed reasonable enough in 1848. In *Capital*, Marx would present a more complex account of the contradictory factors at work.

The spectre of communism was haunting Europe in the 1840s because Europe was where capitalism was developing, and capitalism will always be haunted by communism. Capitalists have tried to deny or dismiss it as something conjured up by troublemakers, to exorcise it by whatever means they can find, but it can't be escaped, because it is capitalism that creates communism by continually recreating and developing the reasons for it to exist. Far from becoming out of date, communism becomes only more relevant the more capitalism develops.

Capitalism continually advances the technologies, organisation and knowledge that make possible a more democratic way of organising society. It's difficult to imagine what sort of economic setup might have been cobbled together – or fallen apart – if the proletariat had somehow managed to overthrow the bourgeoisie in 1848. Even in the 1920s, the Bolsheviks were well aware of the challenge they faced – one of the slogans that Lenin promoted at the time was, 'Communism is Soviet power plus the electrification of the whole country.' Today we not only have electrification of virtually the whole world but also global communication networks, increasingly efficient renewable energy, supercomputers, high-speed rail, artificial intelligence, robotics, satellites... Capitalism keeps presenting us with more resources that will make it easier to organise a better system.

Meanwhile, capitalism continues to base its legitimacy on the idea that it can provide equality and freedom, and constantly shows itself incapable of delivering on either. Even its most impressive attempt at greater fairness and sustainability, under Keynesianism, could not be sustained for long.

The prediction of the manifesto that has turned out to be most problematic is that capitalism creates its own gravediggers. It unquestionably creates a permanent majority who have an objective interest in burying it, but Marx's expectation that this majority would develop the consciousness and organisation to do so has been constantly frustrated. Trade unions have generally been focused on representing the interests of their members within capitalism, not on challenging it. And where communist or socialist parties have made real advances, they have always ended up failing in one way or another.

The spectre of communism will never stop haunting capitalism. The question is, will communism's concrete representatives in the working class ever develop the sort of consciousness and coordination required to be able to dance on capitalism's grave? The reasons for wanting to do so are clear enough. The reasons to believe it could be done are surely persuasive. All that's required is that the workers of the world unite!

Conclusion

Everything is changing. Everything that changes affects everything around it. There are, in fact, no separate 'things'. Human beings change themselves and each other and society, and they are shaped by the way society is changing. Nobody can know to what extent, or in what ways, it's possible for society to change, or how different human beings are capable of being.

There must be limits, but it's difficult to see how anyone could know what those limits are, or indeed, why anyone would want to stop testing them. Some people are pessimistic about how much our genetic past determines what we can become. They believe we're incapable of escaping characteristics like aggression, tribalism or greed. They can point to evidence that seems to confirm their opinion. But it's equally possible to point to evidence that seems to confound it.

No matter how many historical precedents or anthropological comparisons might be made, the evidence gathered could never be enough to say what kind of future we're capable of making, or what human beings might be like in that future. It's impossible to know to what extent living in a very different world would affect the human beings who were shaped by it.

No one has experienced the effect of growing up in a world where nobody has to go hungry or be homeless or lack any of the essentials of life, where everybody is helped to make the most of what they can be, and where the reaction to disagreement is not to set about deciding who gets to win and who loses out, but to look for a solution that can work for everyone – and failing that, to get as close as possible to everybody being able to live their life in the way they want, whilst allowing everyone else to do the same. No one has grown up in a world where every child learns in school about how humanity moved beyond the age of division, and where they're encouraged to explore how their own experience of life can be changed by the ways they think and feel about themselves and others and the world.

Nobody can know what people who were shaped by such a world would be like. But equally, nobody can know whether such a world could be created by people who have been shaped by the world in which we live today. Human beings are going to choose how the world changes. That is what the human part of the world does. But the human part of the world is divided amongst billions of people with different understandings of themselves and of each other, different views of what's possible or desirable. And the way the world is currently organised encourages them to focus on pursuing their own interests and to see doing so as having little to do with what's good for others – to see others as competitors for scarce resources or opportunities.

With their focus on how to make ends meet or how to increase their material wealth, people end up believing things that there's no reason to believe at all: that everyone is greedy, that nothing ever changes, that the poor will always be with us, that the way for a society to be prosperous and secure is to keep other people out and to spend billions on armies and armaments. Even if they can imagine a better world, people can see no way of contributing to bringing it about, because they experience their lives as isolated and disconnected.

The unfortunate reality for Marxists – as for Buddhists – is that, if we present the most positive account of what we believe is possible, few are likely to be interested and fewer still persuaded. Such accounts bear too little connection to people's actual lives and to what their experience tells them is possible. The most realistic way forward may be to try to convince people that they can improve their lives in ways far less significant than we believe is possible, in the hope that, when they do so, they will become more open to believing they can improve their lives, and the world, in more radical ways.

Apparently, annoyingly, we have to be realistic. Given all the ways that Marxist and Buddhist ideas relate to each other, even complement each other, it doesn't seem out of the question to me that a significant social movement could emerge that's influenced by both. You never know, do you? But, realistically, probably not. I doubt that many of those drawn to Marxism are likely to show interest in a religion, or practice, that's all about acceptance and letting go. And I'm not sure many who develop an interest in Buddhism are likely to see engaging with class conflict as a likely part of the path to awakening. But that's okay, because both Marxism and Buddhism make sense in their own terms, and in each case there are good reasons to believe their influence will grow.

Whilst the increase in the number of people explicitly describing themselves as Buddhist may be modest, Buddhist ideas are clearly gaining more influence. For all its limitations, the growing popularity of mindfulness is leading some who practise it to investigate what else Buddhism has to offer. And an increasing number of people who are looking for the kind of rewards that religions offer, but who can't take seriously the supernatural claims that religions seem to demand, are recognising that Buddhism may provide what they're looking for.

Capitalist society, however, is – to put it mildly – not a good place to be trying to follow the Buddhist path. It provides lots of the sort of stress and suffering that would lead people to try mindfulness. But by the same token, it constantly undermines the aim of letting go of desire and of the sense of self. The way of relating to the world that capitalism encourages, with its individualism and consumerism, takes what Buddhism would see as the most problematic aspects of being human, and does everything it can to encourage them.

The circumstances in which Buddhism would be most likely to flourish is surely in the sort of world Marxists would hope to create after capitalism. As we moved beyond a world characterised by inequality, injustice and material need, people would find that they still had a sense of something lacking, that life still seemed unsatisfactory, and they would look for new explanations and solutions. Unlike today, it would increasingly be the case that Buddhism would offer the more obviously relevant answers. And with less division, more cooperation, and a greater sense of everyone working together, it would surely be easier – or at least less difficult – to let go of the sense of an isolated self and to maintain an attitude of compassion and empathetic joy.

Buddhists have good reason to want to see an end to capitalism, both because it could create a world more suited to Buddhist practice, and because it would mean addressing the many causes of suffering that Buddhism does not address but which any good Buddhist would care about changing. But with the best will in the world, it's difficult to see how anyone can believe that Buddhism has the most suitable answers to overcoming the problems that capitalism causes. To do that, ideas like those of Marx are the most relevant. Fortunately, Marxism too has reason to be positive about the future.

The prospects for Marxism have undoubtedly improved over recent years. Admittedly, the developments have not generally been associated with Marxism in particular, but with a more diffuse understanding of socialism and of the wider left. But such advances always go hand in hand with the influence of Marxism.

The increasing relevance of the left, not surprisingly, has come about partly as a result of a deepening crisis of capitalism – and the inability of mainstream politicians to offer an adequate response. To see just how inadequate their response has been, you only have to compare the two biggest crashes in capitalist history.

The effects of the 1929 crash led to the development of Keynesianism – the biggest economic innovation in the history of capitalism. And Keynesian policies led to steady increases in workers' wages and made possible the creation of the welfare state. By contrast, after the 2008 crash, the most significant innovation was 'quantitative easing' to bail out the banks. There was some Keynesian-style public spending to prevent a full-scale depression, but in many countries this was followed by austerity policies that cut welfare systems to the bone and led to wages stagnating, or even falling.

The changes that Keynesianism brought about in the post-war period had convinced workers that their lives could continue improving within capitalism; neoliberalism convinced most to accept there was no alternative. Since 2008, increasing numbers of people are questioning both claims.

The political consequences of this have varied according to the circumstances in different countries. In Europe and other Western countries one development has become known as 'Pasokification'. The term comes from the Greek social democratic party PASOK, that saw its share of the vote in national elections fall from 43.9 per cent in 2009 to 4.7 per cent by 2015. But this was only the sharpest expression of a wider trend, as electorates became disillusioned with social democratic or centre-left parties that continued with neoliberal policies.

In some places this development was accompanied by the rise of nationalist and right-wing politics, but it also saw the appearance or growth of left-wing alternatives such as Syriza in Greece, Podemos in Spain and La France Insoumise in France.

Developments in the UK and the US were affected by electoral systems that made it difficult for any new party to gain votes. In the US, a revived left organised around Bernie Sanders' attempt to become the Democratic Party's candidate for president. In the UK the conflict between those who were enthused by the re-emergence of the left and those who were horrified by it took place in a concentrated, confusing and acrimonious form inside the Labour Party. Jeremy Corbyn went from being a backbench MP who many dismissed as a relic of the 'old left' to being elected party leader; and while the movement around him tried to shift the party and the country to the left, others did everything they could to prevent any such change from succeeding.

It's true that none of the advances the left has made delivered everything they seemed to promise. The advances were followed by significant setbacks. After decades of marginalisation, the left was not prepared for the opportunities it was presented with. But the reasons why those opportunities arose have not changed. Mainstream politicians have no answers to the challenges that society is facing, and no vision for how people's lives could be changed for the better.

Despite the setbacks, the left gained significantly from the period of its revival, in ways that mean it will be better prepared for the opportunities that capitalism will continue to provide. A new generation of people have become involved in developing new movements and ideas – and there have been plenty of new mistakes to learn from!

The increased number of people actively engaged with socialist politics is important, but in a sense, what is even more significant is the change in attitudes in wider society – the greater acceptance that alternatives can be taken seriously. All of which has reminded us of what, for a long time, it was easy to lose sight of – that socialism is not some outlandish concept, difficult to sell and complicated to explain; it's largely common sense that addresses people's real concerns and presents people with the prospect of a better future.

This is a reality that was well expressed by G.A. Cohen in the opening of his book *Why Not Socialism?* Before going on to discuss socialist values and whether socialist organisation is feasible, he offers a 'preliminary case' for socialism in the form of a description of people on a camping trip. He describes how people typically behave in such situations, concluding:

> It is commonly true on camping trips, and, for that matter, in many other nonmassive contexts, that people cooperate within a common concern that, so far as is possible, everybody has a roughly similar opportunity to flourish, and also to relax, on condition that she contributes, appropriately to her capacity, to the flourishing and relaxing of others. In these contexts most people, even most *anti*egalitarians, accept, indeed, take for granted, norms of equality and reciprocity. So deeply do most people take those norms for granted that no one on such trips questions them: to question them would contradict the spirit of the trip.[1]

In other words, the socialist way of relating to each other is what comes naturally to people when nothing in their circumstances is encouraging them to do otherwise. There's no way to prove this to somebody who can't see it, but I think most people would agree that it's true.

If this is the case, then we have to ask what prevents people from interacting with each other in this way when we're not dealing with a few people in a situation like a camping trip, but with a nation, or a world, of people working out how to live together. A complete answer would no doubt be complicated, but if we're looking for the most significant barrier to people relating to each other in this way, then it is surely capitalism.

There was plenty of conflict and division before capitalism, of course, but then there was also scarcity. We are now in a post-scarcity world. That may sound absurd, even insulting, from the point of view of many people even in the most economically successful nations, let alone in the rest of the world. But where people today think they see scarcity, what they're actually seeing is needless inequality and resources being wasted because they can't be used to make a profit.

We are living in a post-scarcity world in the sense that we have the knowledge and technology that could make it possible for everyone to have all the necessities of life, to have whatever support they need available whenever they need it, to have opportunities to develop their talents and abilities, and to have plenty of free time to do with as they wish.

Capitalism contributed to producing these possibilities, but it has now become the barrier to taking advantage of them for the good of humanity as a whole. Capitalism encourages the worst in people – selfishness, greed, and the kind of competition that leads to division and alienation. It celebrates the individual, but it encourages individuals to see themselves as separate from and in conflict with society. It prevents us from choosing to produce what we consciously decide is most worth producing and sharing it out in the way we think is fair.

Moving beyond capitalism would not magically make everything perfect. It's impossible to know what we can achieve and what future challenges we might face. But if we can develop the compassion and the solidarity that will be needed to move beyond the barriers, the divisions and the alienation, then we could reach a point where we can be confident that the world will continue to develop a deeper and more rewarding understanding of what it can make of itself.

NOTES

CHAPTER 1: NOT SUFFERING

1 https://www.dhammatalks.org/suttas/SN/SN6_1.html
2 The earliest Buddhist texts were written in Pali, but many were later written in Sanskrit. This can lead to confusion because many of the words are identifiably the same, but spelt differently, for example dhamma/dharma, sutta/sutra, kamma/karma. I won't be using such words often, but where I do, I'll generally opt for the Pali unless the Sanskrit version has clearly become better established.
3 Some commentators have argued that the truths follow the approach of a physician – identify the disease, diagnose the cause, work out a cure, prescribe a course of treatment. But given that the diagnosis offered in this case is something that most people would have their doubts about, I think 'counter-intuitive argument' is at least as reasonable a description.
4 Leigh Brasington *Right Concentration: A Practical Guide to the Jhanas* (Boston: Shambhala Publications, 2015), p. 4.

CHAPTER 2: PHILOSOPHICAL ECONOMICS

1 John Stuart Mill is mainly remembered as a liberal philosopher, but his 1848 book *Principles of Political Economy* formed an integral part of his understanding of capitalism and was a standard text on the subject until replaced by books such as Alfred Marshall's *Principles of Economics*.

2 Adam Smith *The Theory of Moral Sentiments* (London: Penguin Books, 2010), p. 3.

3 Friedrich Engels *Socialism: Utopian and Scientific* in Robert C. Tucker *The Marx-Engels Reader* (n.p.), p. 636.

4 Karl Marx *A Contribution to the Critique of Hegel's Philosophy of Right. Introduction* in Karl Marx *Early Writings* (London: Penguin Books, 1992), p. 243 (italics in the original).

5 Karl Marx *Letters from the Franco-German Yearbooks* in Karl Marx *Early Writings* (London: Penguin Books, 1992), p. 210.

6 Karl Marx *Economic and Philosophical Manuscripts* in Karl Marx *Early Writings* (London: Penguin Books, 1992), p. 324.

7 Ibid., p. 349.

8 Sidney Hook *From Hegel to Marx* (New York: Columbia University Press, 1994), p. 54.

9 Ibid., p. 55.

10 Adam Smith *The Wealth of Nations: Books I-III* (London: Penguin Books Ltd, 1999), p. 131.

CHAPTER 3: SELF SEARCHING

1 Walpola Rahula *What The Buddha Taught* (London: Oneworld Publications, 2014), p. 62.

2 Bertell Ollman *Alienation: Marx's Conception of Man in Capitalist Society* (New York: Cambridge University Press, 1976), p. 231.

3 Chris Niebauer *No Self, No Problem: How Neuropsychology is Catching Up to Buddhism* (San Antonio: Hierophant Publishing, 2019), p. 55.

4 Guy Newland *Introduction to Emptiness: As Taught in Tsong-Kha-Pa's Great Treatise on the Stages of the Path* (Ithaca, NY: Snow Lion Publications, 2008), p. 32.

CHAPTER 4: VISIBLE HANDS

1 Yuval Noah Harari *Sapiens: A Brief History of Humankind* (London: Vintage, 2011), p. 312.

2 Ibid., pp. 350, 352 and 353.

3 Adam Smith *The Wealth of Nations: Books I-III* (London: Penguin Books Ltd, 1999), p. 152.

4 https://www.marxists.org/reference/subject/economics/keynes/general-theory/ch24.htm

5 See for example, Grace Blakely *Stolen: How to Save the World from Financialisation* (London: Repeater Books, 2019), Guy Standing *The Corruption of Capitalism: Why Rentiers Thrive and Work Does Not Pay* (London: Biteback Publishing Ltd, 2016), Mariana Mazzucato *The Value of Everything: Making and Taking in the Global Economy* (Penguin Books, 2019).

6 Karl Marx *The Civil War in France* in Robert C. Tucker *The Marx-Engels Reader* (n.p.), p. 585.

7 Ibid., p. 580.

8 https://jacobin.com/2018/11/german-revolution-centennial-rosa-luxemburg-social-democrats

9 https://en.wikipedia.org/wiki/Hungarian_Soviet_Republic

10 https://en.wikipedia.org/wiki/Revolutions_of_1917-1923

11 Rosa Luxemburg *The Russian Revolution* in *Reform or Revolution and Other Writings* (New York: Dover Publications, 2006), p 215.

CHAPTER 5: SOMETHING GIVES

1 The Dalai Lama *Practicing Wisdom: The Perfection of Shantideva's Bodhisattva Way* (Somerville, MA: Wisdom Publications, 2005), p. 27.

2 Ibid., p. 93.

3 Rob Burbea *Seeing That Frees: Meditations on Emptiness and Dependent Arising* (West Ogwell: Hermes Amara Publications, 2014), p. 271.

4 Peter Harvey *An Introduction to Buddhism: Teachings, History and Practices* (Cambridge: Cambridge University Press, 2013), p. 369.

CHAPTER 6: CAPITALIST GROWTHS

1 Adam Smith *The Wealth of Nations: Books I-III* (London: Penguin Books, 1999), p. 118.

2 Ha-Joon Chang *Bad Samaritans: The Guilty Secrets of Rich Nations and the Threat to Global Prosperity* (London: Random House Business Books, 2008).

3 Ibid., p. 55.

4 Ibid., p. 31.

5 For an account of the political and economic developments in Russia see Naomi Klein *The Shock Doctrine: The Rise of Disaster Capitalism* (London: Penguin Books, 2008), Chapter 11.

6 For details of these developments see Isabella M. Weber *How China Escaped Shock Therapy: The Market Reform Debate* (London: Routledge, 2021).

7 Grace Blakeley *Stolen: How to Save the World from Financialisation* (London: Repeater Books, 2019), p. 89.

8 Leigh Phillips and Michal Rozworski *The People's Republic of Walmart: How the World's Biggest Corporations are Laying the Foundations for Socialism* (London: Verso, 2019), p. 3.

9 Mariana Mazzucato *The Entrepreneurial State: Debunking Public vs Private Sector Myths* (London: Penguin Books, 2018), p. 70.

10 David Schweickart, *After Capitalism* (Lanham, MD: Rowman & Littlefield Publishers, 2011), p. 26.

11 Ibid., p. 72.

12 Robin Hahnel, Eric Olin Wright *Alternatives to Capitalism: Proposals for a Democratic Economy* (New Left Project, 2014), p. 119. This book contains a debate between Hahnel, advocating for Participatory Economics, and Erik Olin Wright for a form of market socialism.

13 Ibid., p. 8.

14 Robin Hahnel *Of The People, By The People: The Case for a Participatory Economy* (Soapbox, 2012), p. 2.

CHAPTER 8: TO BE DETERMINED

1 Karl Marx *Preface to A Contribution to the Critique of Political Economy* in Karl Marx *Early Writings* (London: Penguin Books, 1992), p. 424.

2 Friedrich Engels *Letter To Joseph Bloch* in Robert C. Tucker *The Marx-Engels Reader* (n.p.), p. 689.

3 Karl Marx and Friedrich Engels *The Holy Family* quoted in Sidney Hook *From Hegel to Marx* (New York: Columbia University Press, 1994), p. 38.

4 Karl Marx *Capital: Volume I* (London: Penguin Books, 1976), p 283.

5 Gil Fronsdal *The Dhammapada: A New Translation of the Buddhist Classic* (Boulder: Shambala Publications, 2005), p. 1.

6   References to the jhanas often talk about the 'eight jhanas' but it's clear that 'jhanas five to eight' were originally a separate practice, sometimes practiced after the four jhanas but which later traditions added to them and renamed the 'immaterial jhanas'.

7   *Digha Nikaya* (2.83) – quoted in Leigh Brasington *Right Concentration: A Practical Guide to the Jhanas* (Boston: Shambhala Publications 2015), p. 68.

8   The Dalai Lama *Essence of the Heart Sutra* (Somerville, MA: Wisdom Publications, 2005), p. 30.

9   Rupert Gethin *The Foundations of Buddhism* (Oxford: Oxford University Press, 1998), p. 141.

10 Linda S. Blanchard *Dependent Arising In Context: the Buddha's core lesson in the context of his time, and ours* (Narada Publications, 2012).

CHAPTER 9: MORAL UNCERTAINTIES

1   Andrew Olendzki *Unlimiting Mind: The Radically Experiential Psychology of Buddhism* (Somerville, MA: Wisdom Publications, 2010), p. 95.

2   Kenan Malik *The Quest for a Moral Compass: A Global History of Ethics* (London: Atlantic Books Ltd, 2014), p. 223.

3   Alasdair MacIntyre *A Short History of Ethics: A History of Moral Philosophy from the Homeric Age to the 20th Century* (London: Routledge, 1998), p. 136.

4   Malik, p. 301.

5   Hegelian philosophy, which influenced Marx in many ways, sees conflict, or contradiction, as a necessary and inevitable part of change. Change happens through contradictions being resolved but giving rise to new contradictions at a higher level. This strikes me as overly systematic for a description of the messy real world (although, perhaps less so in an idealist world). But even if it were true, or true in some circumstances, it's perfectly compatible with the approach I'm suggesting, which merely aims to resolve whatever conflicts exist at the time, not necessarily assuming that all conflict or contradiction could disappear.

6   Karl Marx and Friedrich Engels *The Communist Manifesto* (London: Penguin Books, 2002), p. 230.

Chapter 10: Awakenings

1 There are numerous translations available online, for example here: https://web.stanford.edu/~funn/zazen_instructions/Fukanzazengi.pdf Or here: https://terebess.hu/zen/dogen/Fukanzazengi-6.pdf. The quotes I use below come from the translation by Norman Waddell and Abe Masao in John Daido Loori (ed.) *The Art of Just Sitting: Essential Writings on the Zen Practice of Shikantaza* (Somerville, MA: Wisdom Publications, 2004).

2 Koan study is often associated with the Rinzai school of Zen and shikantaza with the Soto school, although in fact Soto practice does include the use of koans.

3 Culadasa (John Yates, PhD), Matthew Immergut *The Mind Illuminated* (London: Hay House UK Ltd, 2017), location 399, Kindle Edition.

4 Ibid., location 385.

5 Ibid., location 490.

6 Ibid., location 213.

7 See, for example, Keren Arbel *Early Buddhist Meditation: The Four Jhanas as the Actualization of Insight* (London: Routledge, 2016), or Analayo *Early Buddhist Meditation Studies* (Barre, MA: Barre Center for Buddhist Studies, 2017).

8 Bhikkhu Bodhi *What does mindfulness really mean? A canonical perspective* in *Mindfulness: Diverse Perspectives on its Meaning, Origins and Applications*, ed. by J. Mark G. Williams and Jon Kabat-Zinn (London: Routledge, 2013), pp. 19-39 (p. 30).

9 This account is based on the interpretation of dependent arising given in Linda S. Blanchard *Dependent Arising In Context: the Buddha's core lesson in the context of his time, and ours* (Narada Publications, 2012).

10 Ronald E. Purser *McMindfulness: How Mindfulness Became the New Capitalist Spirituality* (London: Repeater Books, 2019), p. 131.

11 Ibid., p. 251.

12 Ibid., p. 183.

13 The Buddha initially didn't want to admit women to the sangha (perhaps seeing some relevance to the challenges of overcoming desire?), but after a discussion with his aunt and his assistant Ananda, he decided to admit them, albeit with a few extra rules.

CHAPTER 11: REVOLUTIONS

1 https://www.marxists.org/archive/marx/works/1872/09/08.htm

2 Karl Marx *The Eighteenth Brumaire of Louis Bonaparte* (Trans. Terrell Carver) in Mark Cowling, James Martin (Eds.) *Marx's 'Eighteenth Brumaire': (Post)Modern Interpretations* (London: Pluto Press, 2002), p. 19.

3 Ibid.

4 Ibid., p. 20.

5 Guy Standing *The Corruption of Capitalism: Why Rentiers Thrive and Work Does Not Pay* (London: Biteback Publishing Ltd, 2016), location 465, Kindle Edition.

6 Owen Jones gives an account of how things went wrong in *This Land: The Struggle for the Left* (London: Penguin Books, 2021) , although the book is not without its critics: https://jacobin.com/2020/10/jeremy-owen-jones-this-land-labour-review

7 Christine Berry and Joe Guinan *People Get Ready!: Preparing for a Corbyn Government* (London: OR Books, 2019), location 2625, Kindle Edition.

8 Vivian Gornick *The Romance of American Communism* (London: Verso, 2020), p. 130.

9 Rand's admirers include Alan Greenspan who spent nineteen years as chairman of the US Federal Reserve, and former UK Chancellor of the Exchequer Sajid Javid, whose attempts to woo his wife included reading Rand out loud to her! Other famous admirers include Steve Jobs, Peter Thiel, Elon Musk, and many others.

10 It's notable that most of Rand's heroes are introverts. The introduction to Hank Rearden and his family is pure 'group of extroverts incapable of connecting with or appreciating an introvert', which I imagine reflects Rand's own experience. Rand clearly accepted – and embraced – the view some extroverts hold, that excessive introversion is an expression of selfishness.

11 Erik Olin Wright *How to Be an Anticapitalist in the Twenty-First Century* (London: Verso, 2019), p. 9.

12 Ibid., p. 18.

13 Jeremy Gilbert *Twenty-First Century Socialism* (Cambridge: Polity Press, 2020), p. 46.

14 G.A. Cohen *Why Not Socialism?* (Princeton: Princeton University Press, 2009), p. 18.

15 Karl Marx and Friedrich Engels *The Communist Manifesto* (London: Penguin Books, 2002), p. 230.

CONCLUSION

1 G.A. Cohen *Why Not Socialism?* (Princeton: Princeton University Press, 2009), p. 4.

ACKNOWLEDGEMENTS

A number of people were kind enough to provide feedback on earlier versions of some chapters of the book. Thanks to Zoe Tribe, Jessica Johnson, Sean Johnson and Penni Garg. The professional editing skills of Susan Watt undoubtedly improved the final version even more. Needless to say, any errors or inadequacies that remain are entirely my own.

Anyone who has read the book will realise that the list of people whose contributions towards it deserve acknowledgement is virtually endless. Not only those who are mentioned in the book, but everyone who has contributed to the development and understanding of Marxist and Buddhist ideas. I hope what I've written might, in its small way, be a worthwhile addition to everything that made it possible.

After Capitalism (Schweickart), 120–21
After Virtue (MacIntyre), 162
alienation, 24–7, 37–8, 54–5, 78–9, 146
    in Buddhism, 54–5
    in Hegel, 24, 38
    in Marx, 24–7, 37–8, 54–5
anicca. See impermanence
anatta. See no-self
arhat, 185
Aristotle, 162–3
Atlas Shrugged (Rand), 207–8
austerity, 59, 125, 220
authoritarianism
    and communism, 69–71, 76
    in the workplace, 78–9
Ayacana Sutta, 6-9

Bad Samaritans (Chang), 103–4
Berry, Christine, 201–4
Blakeley, Grace, 111
Blair, Tony, 124
Blanchard, Linda, 143
Bodhi, Bhikkhu, 181
Bodhidharma, 83
bodhisattva, 40, 185
Bolsheviks, 74–6, 214

Brahmaviharas, 86
Brasington, Leigh, 14
Buddhism, different schools of, 40–1
Burbea, Rob, 87

Capital (Marx), 17, 29–35, 109–11, 139, 199, 214
capitalism
    advances created by, 35–6
    alternatives to, 116–23
    as commodity production, 29–35
    contradictions of, 60–65, 100–102, 107–12, 196–7
    democracy and, 67–8, 76–7
    developing nations and, 102–4
    emergence of, 18–20, 21–2
    See also finance
Chan Buddhism, 40. *See also* Zen Buddhism
Chang, Ha-Joon, 103–4
childcare, 61–2
China, 72, 102–7
Civil War in France, The (Marx), 70
Cohen, G.A., 211, 222
commodities
    as basis of capitalism, 29–35
    circulation of, 109–15
    See also use-value, exchange-value
commodity fetishism, 37
Communist International, 74
Communist Manifesto (Marx), 28, 213–5
communist nations
    in Eastern Europe, 71
    in former colonies, 71–2
    See also China, Soviet Union
compassion, 8, 40, 84–7, 93–5, 185
concentration. *See* meditation
cooperatives, 70, 80, 120–21
Corbyn, Jeremy, 125, 202, 221
Culadasa, 176–9

Culamalunkya Sutta, 144

Dalai Lama, 85, 142–3
democracy
  and Marxism, 70, 76, 209–10
  and capitalism, 67–8, 76–7
  in proposed alternatives to capitalism, 120–2
Dependent Arising in Context (Blanchard), 143
dependent origination, 41, 44, 48, 87, 142–3
Descartes, 42
desire (*tanha*)
  and the four noble truths, 10–12
  and caring about the future, 13, 94–5
  and impermanence, 41
  and 'living in the moment', 93
  and no-self, 43–4, 91–2, 95
dhamma, 7, 8
dictatorship of the proletariat, 69–70
division of labour, 21, 61, 101, 145
Dogen, Ehei, 170–73
dukkha. See suffering

Eighteenth Brumaire of Louis Bonaparte, The (Marx), 197–200
eightfold path, 9, 10, 12–14
empathetic joy, 86, 91, 94, 95
emptiness (*sunyata*), 40, 44–7, 52–3, 85, 95, 177
end of history, 2, 194
engaged Buddhism, 185–6
Entrepreneurial State, The (Mazzucato) 118–19
equality, 106, 111, 120, 158, 161, 196, 209–12
equanimity (*upekkha*) 86–7, 94, 177
Essence of Christianity, The (Feuerbach), 25
exchange-value, 34–9, 93, 127, 129
exploitation, 33, 39–40, 129, 186, 246

feudalism, 39, 41, 225–7
Feuerbach, Ludwig, 25, 26

finance
    financial controls, 106, 110
    financial crisis, 112–15, 124
    financial sector, 105, 110–15, 120, 124, 201, 203
First international, 28
forces of production, 138, 195
four noble truths, 9–12, 94. *See also* suffering, desire, eightfold path
France, 68, 75, 103, 125, 203, 221
French Revolution, 22, 23, 209
Fukanzazengi (Dogen), 170–72

Germany, 23, 68, 72–4, 103
Gethin, Rupert, 143
Gilbert, Jeremy, 210
Gornick, Vivian, 206
Guinan, Joe, 201–4

Hahnel, Robin, 122–3
Harari, Noah, 58
Harvey, Peter, 96
health service, 62–3
Hegel, G.W.F., 23–5, 27, 159–60
Hobbes, Thomas, 20, 157
Hook, Sidney, 27
How to Be an Anticapitalist in the Twenty-First Century (Wright), 209
Hume, David, 47

idealism, 23–8, 141, 144, 145
ideology, 77
immigration, 108–9
impermanence (*annica*), 39, 41–2, 44, 177
individualism, 157–63, 187–91, 209–10
inequality. *See* equality
insight meditation. *See* meditation
International Working Men's Association, 28
invisible hand of the market, 37, 68, 76, 105

Japan, 40, 102, 103, 189
jhanas, 141, 178–9
just sitting (*shikantaza*), 175. *See also* meditation

Kabat-Zinn, Jon, 180, 186
Kant, Immanuel, 158–9, 162
karma, 154–6, 174
Keynes, John Maynard, 64–5, 110
Keynesianism, 110, 111–12, 215, 220
koan study, 170, 175, 180
Kronstadt rebellion, 75

Labour Party, 4–5, 124, 151, 202, 203, 221
labour-power, 31–6, 78–9, 102, 108–9, 196, 199
landlords, 64–5, 120
Lenin, Vladimir, 74–76, 213, 214
liberal democracy, 68, 194
liberalism, 68, 205, 209–11
    and morality, 157–9, 161, 163
    See also individualism, neoliberalism
Libet, Benjamin, 136
'living in the moment', 92–3, 97, 185
loving-kindness (*metta*), 86–7, 93, 94, 95
Luxemburg, Rosa, 75

MacIntyre, Alistair, 160, 162–3
Mahayana Buddhism, 40, 44, 51, 86, 141, 185
Malik, Kenan, 159, 163
market socialism, 119–21, 123
materialism, 24–7, 139–41, 144, 146, 205. *See also* idealism
Mazzucato, Mariana, 118–19
McMindfulness (Purser), 186–8
meditation, 13–14, 55, 86, 169, 175–83
    concentration (*samatha*), 141–2, 177, 179
    insight (*vipassana*), 176–7, 179–80
    just sitting (*shikantaza*), 175
    See also mindfulness

metta. See loving-kindness
Mill, John Stuart, 20
mindfulness, 13, 142, 176, 219
  in traditional Buddhism. *See* vipassana
  critique in 'McMindfulness', 186–8
  Mindfulness-Based Stress Reduction (MBSR), 180–82
Mind Illuminated, The (Culadasa), 176–9
Mondragon, 120–21
morality
  Buddhist, 13–14, 154–6
  liberal, 20, 157–9, 161, 163
  Marx and, 160–62, 165
  religious, 153–4, 163
  See also Kant, utilitarianism, virtue ethics

national independence movements, 72
neoliberalism, 103–4, 109, 111–12, 113, 124, 187, 220–21
New Labour, 124
Newland, Guy, 48
Niebauer, Chris, 48–9
Nietzsche, 159, 161
no-self (*anatta*), 39, 44–56, 85, 94–8, 177–8
No Self, No Problem (Niebauer), 48–9

Olendzki, Andrew, 155
Ollman, Bertel, 46

parinirvana, 184
Paris Commune, 28, 70
Participatory Economics (Parecon), 122–3
People Get Ready! (Berry and Guinan), 201–4
People's Republic of Walmart, The (Phillips and Rozworski), 116–17
Phillips, Leigh, 116–17
Podemos, 221
precariat, 200–201
proletariat, 69, 72, 73, 199–200, 214
profit. *See* surplus-value

Purser, Ronald E., 186–8

Rahula, Walpola, 43
Rand, Ayn, 207–8
rebirth, 43, 174, 184–5
relations of production, 137–8, 195–6
religion, Marx's view of, 25–7
rentier capitalism, 64–5. *See also* finance
Romance of American Communism, The (Gornick), 206
Ruge, Arnold, 26
Russia. *See* Soviet Union

samatha, 141–2, 177, 179. *See also* meditation
Sanders, Bernie, 125, 203, 221
sangha, 3, 154, 189
Sapiens: A Brief History of Humanity (Harari), 58
Satipatthana Sutta, 142
scenarios relating to no-self and compassion, 87–93, 96
Second International, 73, 74
self
    comparison to solid objects, 52–4, 55
    comparison to the market, 54–5
    in neuropsychology, 48–9
    in social sciences, 50–1
    See also no-self
shikantaza, 175. *See also* meditation
shock therapy, 104–5
Schweickart, David, 120–21
skandhas, 42, 44, 145
Smith, Adam 20–23, 30, 37, 64, 99
social contract, 157–9, 161, 164
Social Democratic parties, 72–4, 124, 203, 204
    in Germany, 72–3
    in Russia, 73–4
social movements, 211–13
solidarity, 80, 122, 205, 209–10, 223
South Korea, 103

Soviet Union
    1917 Revolution, 72–5
    alienation in, 78
    authoritarianism and, 75–7
    democracy and, 77
    economy, 65–7
    ideology, 77–8
    influence on communist states, 71–2
    transition to capitalism, 104–5
stagflation, 111
Stalin, Joseph, 76, 206
Standing, Guy, 200–201
suffering (*dukkha*), 10–11, 15, 39, 92, 189
sunyata. See emptiness
surplus-value, 33–5, 109, 114
Syriza, 203, 221

tanha, 10. *See also* desire
tariffs, 20, 103, 106
Thatcher, Margaret, 111, 124, 125
Theory of Moral Sentiments, The (Smith), 20–22
Theravada Buddhism, 40, 41, 179, 180, 181
three marks of existence, 39, 41
Tibetan Buddhism, 41, 174. *See also* Mahayana Buddhism
trade unions, 17, 36, 72, 111, 200–201, 205, 215
twelve links. *See* dependent origination
Twenty-First Century Socialism (Gilbert) 210
two truths doctrine, 51–2

unions. *See* trade unions
United Kingdom, 22, 68, 111, 113, 124, 202, 221
United States, 71, 103, 111, 113, 203, 221
use-value, 29–31, 33–4, 60, 79, 108
utilitarianism, 157–9, 164, 166

value. *See* exchange-value, surplus-value, use-value
vipassana, 176–7, 179–80. *See also* meditation

virtue ethics, 162–3

Wealth of Nations, The (Smith), 20–3
Why Not Socialism? (Cohen), 211, 222
Wright, Erik Olin, 209, 210

Yogacara, 141
Young Hegelians, 23–7

Zen Buddhism, 40–41, 83–84, 98, 169–76, 183
    See also Mahayana Buddhism

www.ingramcontent.com/pod-product-compliance
Lightning Source LLC
Chambersburg PA
CBHW031120020426
42333CB00012B/166